The Destruction of Memory

The Destruction of Memory

Architecture at War

Robert Bevan

REAKTION BOOKS

Published by Reaktion Books Ltd
33 Great Sutton Street
London EC1V ODX, UK
www.reaktionbooks.co.uk

First published 2006

Printed and bound in Great Britain by CPI/Bath Press, Bath

British Library Cataloguing in Publication Data
Bevan, Robert
    The destruction of memory: architecture at war
    1. Buildings – War damage 2. War and society 3. Culture conflict
    4. Historic buildings
    I. Title
    303.6'6

ISBN–10: 1 86189 205 5

Contents

1 Introduction: The Enemies of Architecture and Memory

The implied objective of this line of thought is a nightmare world in which the Leader or some ruling clique controls not only the future but the past. If the Leader says of such and such an event, 'It never happened' – well, it never happened . . . This prospect frightens me much more than bombs – and after our experiences of the last few years, that is not a frivolous statement.

GEORGE ORWELL[1]

There never were any mosques in Zvornik.

BRANKO GRUJIC, SERBIAN MAYOR OF ZVORNIK (after its Muslim population had been expelled and its mosques destroyed[2])

There is both a horror and a fascination at something so apparently permanent as a building, something that one expects to outlast many a human span, meeting an untimely end. As an architecturally obsessed child I was often absorbed in film footage of the destruction wreaked on Europe's built heritage by the Second World War, or I could be found in the local branch library dragging volumes, half my height, about vanquished treasure houses over to the carpet tiles of the junior section. At the same time it felt wrong even to be considering the fate of inanimate art objects and architecture in the face of the contemporaneous footage demonstrating the perverse suffering inflicted on people in the Holocaust. The latter was by far the greater evil and infinitely more moving. Dwelling even for a moment on the shattered remains of museums and churches felt, at best, self-indulgent and, at worst, an indication of warped priorities, especially as the Holocaust had touched the lives of family friends terribly.

The levelling of buildings and cities has always been an inevitable part of conducting hostilities and has worsened as weaponry has become heavier and more destructive, from the slings and arrows of the past to the daisy-cutters of today. Continents rather than cities can be devastated. This damage may be the direct result of military manoeuvres to gain territory or root out a foe, or a desire to wipe out the enemy's capacity to fight. The division of the spoils also plays a part. But there has always been another war against architecture going on – the destruction of the cultural artefacts of an enemy people or nation as a means of dominating, terrorizing, dividing or eradicating it altogether. The aim here is not the rout of an opposing army – it is a tactic often conducted well away from any front line – but the pursuit of ethnic cleansing or genocide by other means, or the rewriting of history in the interests of a victor reinforcing his conquests. Here architecture takes on a totemic quality: a mosque, for example, is not simply a mosque; it represents to its enemies the presence of a community marked for erasure. A library or art gallery is a cache of historical memory, evidence that a given community's presence extends into the past and legitimizing it in the present and on into the future. In these circumstances structures and places with certain meanings are selected for oblivion with deliberate intent. This is not 'collateral damage'. This is the *active* and often systematic destruction of particular building types or architectural traditions that happens in conflicts where the erasure of the memories, history and identity attached to architecture and place – enforced forgetting – is the goal itself. These buildings are attacked not because they are in the path of a military objective: to their destroyers they *are* the objective.

Such was the purpose of the Nazi destruction of German synagogues on Kristallnacht in 1938: to deny a people its past as well as a future. More than this, Kristallnacht, as I argue in this book, can be seen as a proto-genocidal episode – an act of dehumanization and segregation and a further step down towards the limitless dark cellars of barbarism. The erasure of architecture is a crazed and dusty reflection of the fortunes of people at the hands of destroyers. During the 1990s the wars in the former Yugoslavia, with the torture, mass murders and concentration camps of Bosnia on the one hand and the razing of mosques, the burning of libraries and the sundering of bridges on the other, made me realize that my childhood guilt at considering the fate of material culture was misplaced. The link between erasing any physical reminder of a people and its collective memory and the killing of the people themselves is ineluctable. The continuing fragility of civilized society and decency is echoed in the fragility of its monuments. This cultural cleansing, with architecture as its medium, is a phenomenon that has been barely understood. It is the reason this book has been written. The research has been informed by visits to many places, from India to Bosnia, from the West Bank to Ireland. It has been compiled using my own interviews, reports filed by other journalists and the work of many specialist academics, historians, campaigning bodies and human rights groups around the world.

One casuality of Germany's Kristallnacht was the vast synagogue of 1911–13 at Essen designed by Edmund Körner. Its interior was largely destroyed by fire, but the structure survived and was used after the war as a design museum (which destroyed any remaining fittings) before becoming a Holocaust memorial in 1979. A recent attempt to begin Jewish services there once again has been resisted by politicians in the city, who have argued that this would upset the 'neutrality' of the memorial space.

Much has been written about the deliberate repression of minority cultures – their language, literature, art and customs – but little about the repression of their architecture. This book looks at how the experiences of people and architecture under fire have gone hand in hand over the last century, at how architecture has become a proxy by which other ideological, ethnic and nationalist battles are still being fought today. Numerologists could have a field day with this *matériel*: Kristallnacht began just before midnight on 9 November, the 9/11 of 1938. On the same date in 1989, the first sections of the Berlin Wall began to tumble. Four years later on 9/11, Stari Most, Mostar's historic bridge, was finally brought down into the Neretva

Mostar's Stari Most before the Bosnian war. The symbol and social hub of the once cosmopolitan city of Mostar, the bridge (1566) was designed by Mimar Hajruddin, a pupil of the great Ottoman architect Sinan. It is flanked by two 17th-century fortified towers.

Following concentrated shelling by Croat gunners, Mostar's bridge fell into the Neretva river on 9 November 1993. It was a catastrophic loss captured in unique footage by an amateur cameraman. The stone bridge has since been rebuilt in replica. For ordering its destruction, Croat General Slobodan Praljak has been indicted by the International Criminal Tribunal for the former Yugoslavia at The Hague.

river by Croat gunners. Then, of course, came 9/11 in New York – a different day, of course, given the date sequencing used in North America – but the numerals do seem to mark a day for destruction. This is not to make the case for some sort of cosmic agency at work – other dates could equally be matched up for their destructive significance. Such coincidences are possible because of the ubiquity of the deliberate and meaningful destruction of architecture and monuments.

I begin with an examination of the fate of buildings as part of genocide and ethnic cleansing and go on to examine the targeting of buildings in campaigns of terror and conquest, in the structures erected and demolished to keep peoples apart or force them together, and those levelled at the hands of revolutionary new orders that want to build Utopia on the ruins of the past. There is a bestial carousel quality to the past century's destructive activity: ethnic cleansing can be part of conquest; conquest can be ideological as well as territorial; territorial acquisitiveness can be genocidal and end up in partition. The coverage is thematic rather than geographical or chronological in order to bring connections to bear more readily. Such themes inevitably overlap; the fate of Jerusalem's buildings since the creation of Israel, for instance, could equally be looked at as an example of ethnic cleansing, partition or conquest (where it appears in this book). It aims to weave together some of these threads (it is too widespread an experience to hope for comprehensive coverage) to show the forces at work leading to the *targeted* destruction of architecture beyond that caused by purely military considerations. It looks at the political forces at work in order to make plain the politicized nature of what is happening when China demolishes Tibet's monasteries or Berlin struggles with its National Socialist and Stalinist past. Why did al-Qaeda decide that the World Trade Center was a suitable target and why did the Taliban defy world opinion and reduce the Bamiyan Buddhas to dust? Clausewitz's well-known dictum, 'War is not an independent phenomenon, but the continuation of politics by different means', is the thinking behind the architectural dismemberment under examination.

The violent destruction of buildings for other than pragmatic reasons also happens in peacetime, of course, and it is impossible to separate out fully the depredations of 'progress' – modernity and industrialization, with all their implicit ideological content – from conflicts between classes and other groups within societies that are all part of the continuous remaking of our environments; as cities evolve and change, so structures become redundant or more valuable uses for a site are found.[3] Demolition has often been deployed to break up concentrations of resistance among the populace; the Haussmannization of Paris is the most obvious case (although this too was in the wake of violent revolutionary upheavals). Benign or culpable neglect is the more common phenomenon. This may include the bastardization or demolition of a building that no longer has a community to serve it or where its builders lack the economic or political power to resist threatening 'regeneration' or 'improvement plans'.

It accompanies the decline in the power or presence of a community, ethnic or religious group, or class in a locale, or, conversely, can reflect hostility to a group's rise (every time a Bangladeshi family in London's East End gets petrol-soaked rags pushed through its letterbox, this is ethnic cleansing in miniature). That which is valued by a dominant culture or cultures in society is preserved and cared for: the rest can be mindlessly or purposefully destroyed, or just left to rot. These issues are touched upon where the legacy of conflict still determines a country's demolition and rebuilding decisions, or where a country is fragmenting as war approaches. The wars and revolutions of the twentieth and twenty-first centuries, however, where these processes are at their most explicit and brutal, and are pursued with a brutality that escalates with the conflict, are the focus of this book. The intentional collapse of buildings is intimately related to social collapse and upheavals.

It should be remembered, though, that there is nothing intrinsically political about the style of a city's buildings: classicism as an aesthetic, for instance, has served well as an urban model for fascism, Stalinism or liberal democracy in Berlin, Moscow and Washington, DC. Modernism, too, while excoriated by Hitler and long linked to the left, found a role in Mussolini's Italy. That is not to say that the design and production of architecture is free from ideological content; quite the opposite, it is saturated with it. But this content is not inherent in form but arises when those forms are placed in a societal and historical context. It is the ever-changing meanings brought to brick and stone, rather than some inbuilt quality of the materials or the way in which they are assembled, that need to be emphasized. Fundamentally it is the *reasons* for their presence and behind the desire to obliterate them that matter. Buildings are not political but are politicized by why and how they are built, regarded and destroyed.

András Riedlmayer, who has been a vigorous campaigner against the destruction of Bosnia's and Kosovo's cultural heritage, quotes historian Eric Hobsbawm in relation to the context for this ideology of destruction:

> History is the new material for nationalist, or ethnic, or fundament-
> alist ideologies, as poppies are the raw material for heroin addiction .
> . . If there is no suitable past it can always be invented. The past legi-
> timises. The past gives a more glorious background to a present that
> doesn't have much to show for itself.[4]

Such uses and abuses of the historical record to reconstruct or re-represent the past as evidenced by attacks on architecture are legion. Hobsbawm has also argued that the invention of new traditions is an essential part of creating continuity with the past, often in the interest of creating nationalist loyalties. Singing a national anthem, reinvigorating indigenous crafts or waving resurrected historic symbols and flags, he says, activate this invented continuity by dint of repetition.[5] Rather than relying on repetition, I would argue that the virtue of a built record to this method of ideological production lies in the apparent *permanence* of bricks and stone. Buildings and shared spaces can be a location in which different groups come together through shared experience; collective identities are forged and traditions invented. It is architecture's very impression of fixity that makes its manipulation such a persuasive tool: selective retention and destruction can reconfigure this historical record and the façade of fixed meanings brought to architecture can be shifted.

The loss felt by those whose architectural patrimony has been reduced to rubble is not simply dismay at the material cost involved or sorrow over the mutilation of the aesthetic worth with which the structures are regarded. Rather, as Hannah Arendt has argued: 'The reality and reliability of the human world rests primarily on the fact that we are surrounded by things more permanent than the activity by which they were produced.'[6] To lose all that is familiar – the destruction of one's environment – can mean a disorientating exile from the memories they have invoked. It is the threat of a loss to one's collective identity and the secure continuity of those identities (even if, in reality, identity is always shifting over time). The philosopher Henri Lefebvre noted this process: 'Monumental space offered each member of a society an image of that membership, an image of his or her social visage . . . It thus constituted a collective mirror more faithful than any personal one.'[7] This is a step onwards from Lacanian mirror theory; instead of the developing individual recognizing himself as a discrete entity, it is about tying that individual back into a wider community. It is about belonging.

External threats can rally even heterogeneous groups together in defence of a national cause and the architectural representations of statehood. By contrast, in wars between ethnic or religious groups, either within a country or across its borders, there is an atomization, a rallying not to the national flag but to their sub-national communities. Here personal identity – the individual self grounded within the collective self – is in danger. In these circumstances there is an intensification of allegiance to the group reflecting a desire for preservation. Ethnicity or religious identification, for instance, can become more important than identifying with a neighbourhood, city or nation-state. It is, in part, this fear of oblivion and defence against it that can make these conflicts so brutal and the destiny of architectural representations of group identity so vital. Nietzsche, identifying in monuments 'the stamp of the will to power', could easily have written the same regarding their demolition as their building. A particular barbarism is fostered in wars between such groups, even if their manifestations sometimes disguise essentially political, economic or territorial concerns, because the consequence of the intensification of identification with a community also results in its corollary – the definition of those outside the group as 'the other', whose 'otherness' is commensurately deepened by this intensification. All conflicts, whether clearly ethnic or economic and expansionist, invoke the notion of the other, whether the other's nationality, race, class, religion, ideology or values. It is the emphasis on the differences between those within and those outside the group that leads to the devaluation of outsiders and their material patrimony.[8] This dehumanization is an essential step towards making it acceptable to dismantle an enemy's heritage, to maltreat and eventually kill them; sometimes these actions are telescoped into one event, such as the burning alive of congregations in their places of worship. The importance of architecture in such conflicts is heightened, especially in the case of commemorative monuments or sacred buildings belonging to the other. Sometimes it is as if the very bricks and stones are guilty of being the other as well as being representative of the other's presence. Their very form can reflect an alien mode of thinking and being; a different cultural genesis – mosque, onion dome, star or steeple.

It is not just the grandest, oldest or most architectonic of monuments that are targeted. Housing, too, especially vernacular housing, can be monumental in the sense of acting as a stimulus to the memories that evoke group identity. The term monument is used here in its broadest sense. These chapters are looking at both 'intentional' and 'unintentional' monuments – those that are directly commemorative and the many more buildings that, by virtue of their history and the identification their builders and users have with them, have had meaning thrust upon them.[9] More figurative works, such as statues, are touched upon but direct iconoclasm has been debated at length elsewhere.[10] Similarly the consequences of war for other artworks, such as looting, have also been well rehearsed (although it is interesting to

Built in 1896 as Sarajevo's City Hall, the neo-Moorish National Library was shelled and burned out on the night of 25 August 1992 by Serbian forces besieging the city. The building was left in ruins, but it is the destruction of its contents, along with those of the nearby Oriental Institute shelled some months earlier, that are an incalculable cultural loss. The country's written history went up in flames. A plaque on the building reads 'Remember and Warn'.

note that in ethnic conflicts destruction and burning is far more common than seizure of property – the pecuniary advantages are subordinated to the desire to eradicate).[11] Instead, the arguments set out in the following pages look specifically at the complexities of architecture: buildings gather meaning to them by their everyday function, by their presence in the townscape and by their form. They can have meaning attached to them as structures or, sometimes, simply act as containers of meaning and history. Each role invokes memories. We are not talking a Proustian subtlety of scent, taste and texture here, although architecture can certainly have these evocative subtleties. But it remains true that the mere sight of a building – a former home, an old trysting spot, or a hated workplace – can be an instant memory-jerker. Equally, the sheer familiarity of a street, an unconscious sense of a particular degree of enclosure, its sunny side, a familiar turn, can create a rootedness in a place and an affiliation with the locale and its community.[12]

Both individual memories and collective memories are in play. Here, collective memory is considered as a bundle of individual memories that coalesce by means of exchanges between people and develop into a communal narrative about its architectural record. This is not a narrative independent of the generations of people who create and re-create the memories but it is independent of any individual within that group. In part, we recognize our place in the world by an interaction with the built environment and remembering these experiences and by being informed of the experiences of others: the creation of social identity located in time and place.

Adrian Forty, an academic who has written convincingly about forgetting, rejects the idea that architecture is capable of embodying memories. It is not the case, he suggests, that 'memories formed in the mind can be transferred to solid material objects'.[13] He goes on to question the thesis of the architect and theorist Aldo Rossi, who considered that 'The city itself is the collective memory of its people, and like memory it is associated with objects and places.'[14] The themes developed here, however, are definitely not an argument in support of the view that memory somehow magically attaches itself to buildings and places, imprinted like ghosts on their fabric. Nor is it suggested, as Rossi does in his writings, that there is somehow an ahistorical *genius loci* attached to sites that transcends the ages in an almost spiritual fashion – a city's own memory of its historical development embodied in its material. In this, Rossi comes close to Jung's notion of the collective unconscious – of inherent memories of archetypes. It glides towards a timeless mysticism and in employing the notion of collective memory I have shied away from this abstraction.

Memories clearly remain within people's heads, or are discussed and written down as history. The built environment is merely a prompt, a corporeal reminder of the events involved in its construction, use and destruction. The meanings and memories we bring to the stones are created by human agency and remain there. These memories are, of course, contested and they change over time. It is a process that is always unfolding and remains ever unfinished. In talking of collective memory I am building on the arguments of writers such as Joël Candau[15] and Paul Ricoeur,[16] rather than on Maurice Halbwachs's position that individual memories are fragments of an all-encompassing collective memory.[17] Candau's (and my) view is of a collective or common memory that emerges where individual memories interact within a framework provided by societal memory. It leads, to some extent, to an homogenization: a shared memory and, consequently, a shared attitude to representations of the past – including architecture.

However, a continuity of successive experiences, setting down layers of meaning, can, I suggest, result in an especially strong power of place – a psycho-geography, an 'awareness' of the past (rather than an architectural avatar of a petrified spirit) that is dynamic, handed down by people rather than recorded on the very stones, and is specific to a particular historic and political context. The worth of such places increases where efforts to destroy them remind communities of this value. If the touchstones of identity are no longer there to be touched, memories fragment and dislocate – their hostile destruction is an amnesia forced upon the group as a group and on its individual constituent members. Out of sight can become, literally, out of mind both for those whose patrimony has been destroyed and for the destroyers. The 'how' of the precise psychoanalytic mechanisms at work – whether things are truly forgotten or still present and repressed and therefore unavailable to conscious thought – is best left to physiologists and psychologists.

The French historian Pierre Nora has argued that such *lieux de mémoire* (realms of memory), be they places, rituals, symbols or texts, have become increasingly important to societies as the 'real', 'living' memories communicated face to face in peasant cultures (where the past is part of their everyday life) have vanished in the mass culture of modern, industrial societies where memories are, by contrast, both distanced from the individual and artificial, bureaucratized and institutionalized. History has accelerated and what 'needs' to be remembered is beyond the scope of any individual. The huge upsurge of interest in memory studies today is also, Nora suggests, a consequence of a democratization by which minority groups are using the past to reaffirm their identities. 'Modern memory is, above all, archival,' he states. 'It relies entirely on the materiality of the trace, the immediacy of the recording, the visibility of the image.'[18] Memory is simply what was called 'history' in the past; the two have merged.[19] It is an intriguing analysis. If it is accepted that in contemporary life the 'materiality of the trace' has become crucial to history and memory, this may, in part, go towards explaining why the targeting of architecture – a material reminder *sine qua non* – has become an ever more prevalent phenomenon. In such a climate, memory becomes especially vulnerable to attacks that aim to repress or obliterate its outward representations.

These archival memories may no longer be 'living', in Nora's terms, but they are no less real or valuable for that.

Memories, like history, however, will always be partial and problematic. Historian David Lowenthal has argued: 'No absolute historical truth lies waiting to be found; however assiduous and fair-minded the historian, he can no more relate the past "as it really was" than can our memories.'[20] There are few 'absolutes' in life or history, of course, but there is an assumption in this book that there is a duty to move *towards* absolute truth as far as that is possible; to give up on this task is to be swamped by relativism. The forces tending to the destruction of architecture are not necessarily always rational, though. There are contradictions, inconsistencies and a myriad of local subtleties to the meanings brought to buildings and the actions taken against them; these in themselves change over time. There is no unity of process and purpose but a cluster of interwoven vectors. And in conflicts there will always be a confusion of motives and responsibilities. But there are facts to be pursued.

Gathering these facts is important because the destiny of buildings in war is often evidence of crimes against humanity, including ethnic cleansing and genocide, and is slowly being recognized as such. The trials being held at the International Criminal Tribunal for the former Yugoslavia at The Hague are crucial in this respect. The levelling of architecture has real-world consequences for the future well-being of communities, especially those suffering repression: 'The struggle of man against power', wrote Milan Kundera, 'is the struggle of memory against forgetting.'[21]

Even in early recorded history, the destruction arising out of such contests to retain memory or assert forgetting is often present. Then these acts were usually linked to religion, even when embedded in a campaign of conquest. The destruction of Akhenaten's built record in Pharaonic Egypt or the capture of a rival king's temple in ancient India are two instances where the power of kingship and a deity were interrelated and these struggles were played out in the sacking and toppling of shrines. Herodotus is peppered with examples of temple destruction. When an army of the conquering Persian king Cambyses, a notorious despoiler of temples, vanished for ever in a desert dust-storm while on its way to destroy the oracle of Amun at Siwa, Herodotus suggests divine retribution for the loss (he was also swift to invoke the notion of the 'other' for non-Greek barbarians). Iconoclasm as a fight between faiths or between factions within a faith continues through Byzantium's Quarrel of the Images to the Reformation and beyond. Such religious iconoclasm with its internal doctrinal intricacies regarding the place of the image in faith (as opposed to the destruction of sacral architecture by a competing ethnic/faith group in a war or in a war against religion) is a subject in itself and is largely outside the scope of this book. This ancient pattern of destruction, however, also had a secular character. From the era of

A pre-Bosnian war photograph of the Serbian Baroque steeple of Mostar's Orthodox cathedral (*top right*), built in the late Ottoman period with a gift from Sultan Abdulaziz. The two minarets below (one looking like a church steeple) belong to a 17th-century mosque.

the city-state to the nation-state, the siege as well as the set-piece battle has been a regular feature of conflict. Cities themselves were the goal – the locus of power, the economy and religious identification. Their capture was, at once, a material prize, a chance to slaughter the enemy, civilian or soldier, and to injure its military capability by razing its fortifications. It was also a chance to strike a blow at a cultural or political rival. Rome's erasure of Carthage was an act of urbicide – the murder of a city. Carthage had already been demilitarized following its defeat in battle by a treaty of 201 BC, but the Romans still hankered after its total destruction. M. Porcius Cato called for *Carthaginem esse delendam* ('Carthage must be destroyed') at the end of all his political speeches. When Rome struck in 146 BC the Carthaginians were given the option of retreating ten miles from the city while it was being razed, but instead they fought to the end, only to see its temples, spectacular circular dock complex, its multi-storey apartment blocks and city walls brought down to rubble. The Romans systematically flattened its ruins; the site was cursed and, according to legend, sown with salt as a symbol of eternal sterility. Carthage, the economic powerhouse of its age, was to be erased from history. Its language, culture and religion did not survive except in the most tattered fragments. Jerusalem, too, temporarily vanished at Roman hands, and Rome itself almost ceased to exist following its sack by the Visigoths in AD 410 and the Ostrogoths in AD 455. The city fell into decay and rapidly depopulated, leaving it an empty shell. It seems rather unfair that it was to be the Goths, who sacked Rome but did not destroy its buildings, who went down in history as the enemies of culture. Rome's ancient pillars and arches vanished into cow pastures but remained, *in situ* if in pieces, until the marble blocks from its tumbled temples were quarried and ground to dust to make lime-mortar for the churches of the new Rome.

Christianity, though it has had its pragmatic moments, has always been rather given to destroying the religious architectural heritage of its rivals. Islam, by contrast, has generally, although by no means consistently, been more flexible in its treatment of the churches of unbelievers, converting them to mosques rather than demolishing them: a saying attributed to the Prophet is 'Let the man be a reprobate who sells a slave, injures a fruit-bearing tree, and makes lime from chiselled marble.' Mainstream Islamic law has also long professed to safeguard civilian property from military destruction, however shakily this has been carried out in practice. The war in Spain between the Christians and the Moors, however, led to repeated demolition or adaptation of each other's buildings as the mood took. Córdoba's cathedral

From the same viewpoint in June 2001. The minarets were damaged by JNA shelling in 1992 and by the Croat army in 1993–4. In June 1992 the Orthodox cathedral was blown up by Croat extremists.

started out as a Roman temple (demolished by the Christian Visigoths). A subsequent church on the site was replaced by a mosque following the Arab conquest of the early eighth century. Some seventy years later this was itself demolished to create the first stage of a massive new mosque. The Christians recaptured Córdoba in 1236 and consecrated the building as a cathedral. Some alterations were made, but it was not until the sixteenth century that a vast new cathedral, still known as the Mesquita (mosque), was inserted into the shell of the mosque and a bell-tower was built on the site of the minaret. It is said that the mosque's lamps were melted down to make new bells for the cathedral of Santiago de Compostela, 800 km to the north. This probably seemed only fair, since the lamps had themselves been made from Santiago's original bells: when the Moors had conquered the city in 997 they had dragged the bells to Cordoba and melted them down into lamps.

In the conquistadors' assault on the New World, however, the destruction was all one way – colonial greed for gold and territory was matched only by the Inquisition's greed for American souls. The years following Columbus's arrival in 1492 witnessed the world's largest ever cultural and human genocide. Huge numbers of the estimated population of 100 million living in North, South and Central America died in the following decades, killed by disease, slaughtered or starved in the chaos of conquest. Their civilizations died with them. The cultural and human losses are traced in Ronald Wright's unparalleled history *Stolen Continents*.[22] The Aztec capital, spread across the twin lake-bound cities of Tenochtitlán and Tlatelolco, which together formed one of the planet's biggest urban centres of the time, was razed to the ground. Its stone ziggurats, temples, palaces and houses were levelled and its canals filled in by the colonizers. All physical traces of Aztec culture were burned or looted and the people killed or forcibly converted to Christianity. Indigenous languages were banned and a new colonial city built on the site of Tenochtitlán. A church dedicated to St James was consecrated where Tlatelolco's great pyramid once stood. There was to be no backsliding and no reminders of the past. In 1790 when a massive Aztec idol and the famous Calendar Stone were accidentally uncovered in the central square of the Spanish incarnation of Mexico City, they were swiftly reburied to prevent evidence of their past greatness fermenting unrest among the Indians (as the Aztecs now were). The Mayans, the Inca and their cities suffered a similar fate. All the great American cities of the Pre-Columbian era vanished under the pressure of climate and political changes. It was not until the completion in 1863 of the dome of the Capitol building in Washington, DC, that the tallest Mayan pyramid, built 1,000 years previously, was equalled in height in the Americas. Little is left of these cultures, which once covered a large area of the globe (some three centuries before the arrival of the Europeans, for example, the Mississippian city of Cahokia, outside present-day St Louis, had equalled in size the Paris or London of its day). Even now, history text-books give scant attention to the sheer extent of these civilizations and their destruction. As late as 1979, historically important Woodlands-region archaeological sites of the Cherokee were still being drowned under the rising waters behind the dams of the Tennessee Valley Authority. The civilizations of the Pre-Columbian Americas, beyond the few temples that remain, have been largely forgotten.[23] Not until the Enlightenment did notions of the protection of cultural heritage properly arrive. Previously buildings and monuments were demolished, replaced or adapted when they had outlived their usefulness. The notion of a respect for cultural heritage, especially one that lay outside one's own tradition, was in large part an Enlightenment idea. But the Enlightenment also ushered in a new period of heightened destruction – the French Revolution – and new reasons for the demolition of monuments where their deliberate erasure took on an ideological flavour: this was an iconoclasm that was anti-clerical rather than intra-clerical. A rapidly urbanizing population and the emerging working and middle classes had the potent architectural representations of the old order in their sights. In the Revolution, rationality was to replace superstition and divine right with equality. Many churches and cathedrals were desecrated and closed or turned into Temples of Reason. Manor houses, castles and abbeys burned. The storming and demolition of the Bastille, like the earlier destruction of London's hated Newgate Prison during the Gordon Riots of 1780, was an attack on the embodiment of royal authority. The Bastille prison was targeted despite holding only seven prisoners, none of them remotely political. It was a symbol of state oppression rather than a significant site of the practical exercise of that power.

The critic Georges Bataille went further, suggesting that monuments do not just symbolize an enemy but *are* in themselves the enemy:

> It is obvious, actually, that monuments inspire socially acceptable behaviour, and often a very real fear. The storming of the Bastille is symbolic of this state of affairs: it is difficult to explain this impulse of the mob other than by the animosity the people hold against the monuments which are their true masters.[24]

The Bastille's stones were broken up and sold as souvenirs – secular relics almost – a commodification process repeated with the fragments of the Berlin Wall 200 years later.

In *The Destruction of Art*, Dario Gamboni's examination of figurative iconoclasm, Gamboni also notes the anthropomorphic quality that can be brought to attacks on buildings. The mansions of the rich in Lyon's Place de Bellecour were condemned to death during the French Revolution because the 'magnificence' of the Place Bellecour was 'an insult to the poverty of the people and the simplicity of republican morals'. The first blow against the façade was struck with a ceremonial silver hammer by the people's representative, who shouted: 'I condemn you to be demolished in the name of the law.'[25] Bell-towers were also threatened with demolition because 'their height above other buildings seems to contradict the principles of equality'.[26] Figurative statues by their representative nature have similarly been subject to rough treatment, beatings and beheadings right up to the fall of the Eastern Bloc and Saddam Hussein. In a suburb of Madrid during the Spanish Civil War, Republicans executed a statue of Jesus by firing squad. Architecture is never so obviously representational, but its destruction is equally used as a scapegoat for other less tangible targets.

At the same time, the French Revolution specifically provoked demands for the protection of cultural property. Rare voices in the past had sought to protect religious architecture, but it was not until the eighteenth century that such ideas began to be extended to secular cultural monuments. Emmerich de Vattel wrote in his 1758 *Le droit des gens*: 'for whatever cause a country be devastated, these buildings should be spared which are an honour to the human race and which do not add to the strength of the enemy, such as temples, tombs, public buildings and all edifices of remarkable beauty. What is gained by destroying them?'[27] During the French Revolution, Abbé Henri Grégoire, the radical Bishop of Blois, spoke out against the destruction of art and claimed coinage of the term 'vandalism' as an attack on civilized

During the French Revolution, churches and the houses of the rich were frequent targets for revolutionaries. Here, the mansions of Place Bellecour in Lyon are condemned to death as an insult to Republican morals. Bell-towers were also threatened with demolition because 'their height above other buildings seems to contradict the principles of equality'.

values expressed in art and architecture. The concept of *patrimoine* (heritage) also emerged out of the upheavals.

The damage caused by conflicts increased with the military inventions of the late nineteenth century and the early twentieth: heavy artillery, the gunboat, the tank and the Zeppelin. The Brussels Declaration of 1874 regarding the law and customs of war was the first international attempt to protect historic monuments from 'wilful damage'. It was never ratified but International Peace Conferences at The Hague in 1899 and 1907 used its concepts to establish the first international treaties to protect cultural property in times of war. The 1907 Hague Convention also agreed an emblem to be placed on buildings due protection. War from the air and the devastations of both World Wars, however, demonstrated the weakness of the 1907 Convention and the 1954 Hague Convention for the Protection of Cultural Property in the Event of Armed Conflict was designed to tighten up protection. This is the key piece of international legislation under consideration. Its preamble recognizes that:

> cultural property has suffered grave damage during recent armed conflicts, and that, by reason of the developments in the technique of warfare, it is in increasing danger of destruction . . . damage to cultural property belonging to any people whatsoever means damage to the cultural heritage of all mankind, since each people makes its contribution to the culture of the world.[28]

The measures contained in the 1954 Convention are complex but, in short, call on warring parties to avoid damaging cultural property, indeed actively to protect it. This obligation may be disregarded 'only in cases where military necessity imperatively requires such a waiver'. This has served as a generous loophole. In 1977 the Hague Convention's provisions were incorporated into the humanitarian laws of the Geneva Convention and the loophole narrowed somewhat. But still the fatally intertwined experience of genocide and cultural genocide has yet to find its proper place in international law.

A century of protection then, matched by a century of savagery and cultural devastation: the ethnic riots and demolition of mosques in contemporary India; Stalin's destruction of churches; Hitler's destruction of synagogues and the built heritage of the Slavic people; Guernica, Dresden, Cambodia, Bosnia. Wave after thunderous wave of an unparalleled cultural cataclysm. This book examines why, in the face of agreed protection and a growing acceptance of a collective world heritage, such destruction has, and is still, taking place. It dwells on the fate of architecture rather than the fate of the people to whom the buildings belong and who have given them meaning, but this does not mean that these people have been forgotten. It is their stories, told to me directly on my travels or recorded by other journalists and writers, that have reinforced for me the value people place on their architecture even in times of conflict – or, perhaps, especially then: a woman who recalls how, as a Muslim teenager in Mostar, everybody emerged after hiding from the shelling in basements for ten months to weep at the destruction of the old bridge; the Dubrovnik woman who remembers the aftermath of a fierce raid on her city as the saddest day of her life. It is a sadness also felt by Afghanis at the Taliban's obliteration of Bamiyan's Buddhas; by the children dragging me by the hand to see the bombed monuments of Nablus and by the survivors of the Holocaust who saw their families and their synagogues perish.

 'Who today speaks of the massacre of the Armenians?' Hitler was able to say of the Armenian genocide, accompanied as it had been by the systematic levelling of the Armenians' built heritage.[29] The architectural evidence of a people, and the crimes committed against it, had largely vanished. Protecting the architectural heritage of those targeted for domination or elimination helps ensure that such peoples can never be erased entirely from history despite the determined efforts of their persecutors and destroyers.

2 Cultural Cleansing: Who Remembers the Armenians?

> The first step in liquidating a people is to erase its memory. Destroy its books, its culture, its history. Then you have somebody write new books, manufacture a new culture, invent a new history. Before long the nation will begin to forget what it is and what it was.
>
> MILAN KUNDERA, *THE BOOK OF LAUGHTER AND FORGETTING*

It took the Croat gunners on Hum Hill some 60 shells, but eventually they brought down the sixteenth-century Ottoman bridge at Mostar. Its cat's-back arch collapsed into the waters of the Neretva river on 9 November 1993. Bridges can be almost too readily symbolic. In this case, however, the iconic status is in no way forced. The very name 'Mostar' means bridge-keeper, and the structure united the Ottoman old town on the east bank with the more heterodox west. For many, it represented the final physical sundering of what, before the war, had been perhaps the most cosmopolitan city in Bosnia-Herzegovina, even allowing for Sarajevo. Pre-war Mostarians were proud that the city had the highest rate of mixed (Croat, Serb or Muslim) marriages in the country – that is until these couples were forced out of West Mostar or violently separated. The Stari Most bridge, built by Mimar Hajruddin, a pupil of the great Ottoman architect Sinan, was both the symbol of the city and a living space where people came together. It was a meeting point, a courting rendezvous for generations, the platform for summer diving competitions. The attack on the bridge was an attack on the very concept of multi-ethnicity and the co-joined communities it had come to embody. Muslims who had been hiding in the old town basements for months to escape Croat shelling and snipers emerged into the light to see it with their own eyes and weep: 'I enjoyed my first kiss on that bridge,' said 70-year-old Borjanka Santic. 'I remember even now the stars and the moon shining down. I remember how I dropped stones into the clear water. Now that has all been wiped out.'[1]

Together with the shelling of Dubrovnik, attacks on the bread queues of Sarajevo and the discovery of the Omarska and Keraterm concentration camps, the collapse of Mostar's bridge remains an abiding image of the Bosnian war: 'Why do we feel more pain looking at the image of the destroyed bridge than the image of massacred people?' asked the Croatian writer Slavenka Drakulić at the time:

> Perhaps because we see our own mortality in the collapse of the bridge. We expect people to die; we count on our own lives to end. The destruction of a monument to civilisation is something else. The bridge in all its beauty and grace was built to outlive us; it was an attempt to grasp eternity. It transcends our individual destiny. A dead woman is one of us – but the bridge is all of us forever.[2]

Sarajevo's main mosque and Mostar's bridge were two of the thousands of Ottoman monuments destroyed or severely damaged in the Bosnian war, just as were many Croat Catholic and Serbian Orthodox buildings across Bosnia and Croatia, as front lines shifted, peace treaties were revised and people were expelled and murdered. It was the Ottoman heritage, caught between Croats and Serbs, that suffered most. Few buildings from the community's spectacular built heritage escaped scarring altogether. Religious and cultural buildings fared worst; libraries, museums, Islamic schools, tombs and fountains were the enemy.

Fifty-five years, to the day, before Mostar's bridge fell, the glass in the first of 75,000 Jewish shop windows all over Germany was shattered. Kristallnacht began at one minute to midnight of 9 November and continued in earnest for the next 24 hours. Along with the shops, 267 synagogues, more than a dozen other Jewish community buildings, countless Jewish homes and many other commercial premises were attacked during the early hours of 10 November 1938. At least 200 people were killed and tens of thousands more were rounded up into concentration camps.[3]

The story of the Final Solution has left an architectural as well as a human trail, leading from Kristallnacht to the creation of ghettos and their eventual liquidation. The broken glass of 'Crystal-night' arguably marked the beginning of the Holocaust, even if, as some scholars argue, the decision to attempt the extermination of European Jewry was not taken or fully articulated until later. In the following years destruction spread north to Denmark and south, though Bosnia, to Greece. In Sarajevo, the conquering Nazis turned the old Sephardic synagogue into a garage: one instance of a pattern of desecration and elimination. The Kristallnacht attacks presaged the destruction of a people, not merely harsh discrimination against them; it was a step-change. Sarajevo's synagogue was restored after the Second World War, only to be shelled by the Serbs during the year-long siege of the city that began in spring 1992. The Roman Catholic cathedral and the central Gazi Husrev Beg mosque were also hit during the siege as part of the Serbian offensive against the multi-cultural city. By the end of the Bosnian war, the region's Ottoman heritage was shattered. In terms of comprehensive destruction, it shares a place with the eradication of Turkish Armenian and European Jewish built heritage.

It was the Holocaust that led to the 1948 UN Convention for the Prevention and Punishment of the Crime of Genocide, which provides the codification of the crime of genocide into international law as a 'crime against humanity'. Article II of the Convention sets out the definition of genocide: 'Acts committed with intent to destroy, in whole or in part, a national, ethnical, racial or religious group.' The measures by which this could be judged were also set down: killing; causing serious bodily or mental harm; deliberately inflicting conditions of life calculated to bring about its physical destruction; measures to prevent births and, finally, transferring children of the target group to another group. These definitions related to the destruction of the corporeal – the living bodies of a group. How that group defines, identifies or understands itself – its collective culture – whether material or not, is not included as a measure by which to judge genocidal actions.

Ethnic cleansing, meanwhile, is a term that has been derided as a euphemism for mass murder. It was supposedly coined by Serbian extremists during their campaigns against Croats and Bosnian Muslims in the 1990s, but its etymological roots lie deep within historic anti-Semitism. It can be summarized as the elimination, by genocide or forced expulsion, of a group (as defined above) from a territory. It is a broad term and remains uncodified in international law, although it can include mass killings that fall short of officially defined genocide. Beyond the circles of art and architectural historians, however, the destruction of material culture, the burning of libraries, blowing up of places of worship and the erasure of monuments as part of the 'cleansing' process has been largely ignored. Overlooking these attacks on cultural patrimony and failing to understand their direct links to the cultural survival of a people risks setting aside some of the very attributes that give meaning to a group identity. More than this, where a group is under physical attack, the destiny of its representative architecture is an excellent indicator of whether genocidal intent is present or incipient.

Jewish built heritage has been suffering for centuries, from the destruction of the Temple in Jerusalem onwards through the Diaspora. In Europe, periods of tolerance have been followed by periods of attack and expulsion. A recent discovery that might throw some light on one of these has been the excavation of what some scholars believe is a late twelfth-century synagogue in

Guildford, Surrey. This appears to have been deliberately demolished and filled with rubble during the 1270s,[4] perhaps after Eleanor of Provence, widow of Henry III of England, ordered the expulsion in 1275 of all the Jews living in English towns under her control, including Guildford. Countless sites across Europe tell similar tales. The chilly tone for what was to come under the Nazis was set by Martin Luther in his 'Against Jews and their Lies' in 1543:

> First their synagogues or churches should be set on fire and whatever does not burn up should be covered or spread with dirt so that no one may ever be able to see a cinder or stone of it . . . their homes should likewise be broken down and destroyed . . . We must drive them out like mad dogs.[5]

The destiny of their enemies' cultural property was an intrinsic element of Nazi operations – whether through vandalism, theft or forced acquisition. The looting of countless paintings, altarpieces and even whole rooms (in the case of the Amber Room from the palace at Tsarskoye Selo) was matched by the ferocity of the destruction of items outside the Nazi approved canon – be it 'degenerate' art, burning down Magnus Hirschfeld's Berlin Institute for Sexual Science or the obliteration of entire Jewish neighbourhoods as part of the Führer's plans for rebuilding the Reich capital. Nazi ideology was obsessed with the 'ever-present' and 'verminous' Jews, whose supposed conspiracies, simultaneously and contradictorily both Bolshevik and Zionist, were everywhere. Unlike the experience of other religious or ethnic groups, the reality of their existence, their presence in the community and nation was never denied. The purpose of the 'Final Solution' to the 'Jewish question', as formalized at the Wannsee conference on 20 January 1942, was the intention to eradicate a race and all evidence of its culture, apart from representative examples of Judaica that would be housed in a museum in Prague – victory represented as archaeology: 'The Jews were not to be annihilated and then forgotten', wrote historian Elizabeth Domansky, 'but annihilated and then remembered forever . . . Eternal death was not to be oblivion, but the torture of being eternally remembered by the persecutors.'[6]

By 1938 around 300,000 Jews remained in Germany out of a population of roughly half a million just a few years before – the rest had fled. Even before Kristallnacht proper, Jewish businesses and religious buildings began to suffer. Architect Albert Schmidt's main synagogue in Munich, built in 1887 and large enough to hold 1,800 worshippers, was condemned on 7 June 1938 on the grounds of 'traffic technicalities', and demolition began the next day.[7] Nuremberg's synagogue was destroyed two months later, following the forced sale of the building and beginning with the toppling of the stone Star of David from the roof. The crane was operated by the Nuremberg gauleiter

Julius Streicher. Synagogues in Hesse and Magdeburg Anhalt (now Sachsen-Anhalt) were burnt out in September.[8]

But it was the murder of Ernst vom Rath, a diplomat at the German embassy in Paris, by the Jewish youth Herschel Grynszpan that was the trigger for the official campaign of violence on Kristallnacht. The destruction was well planned and orchestrated. Gestapo orders explicitly allowed the burning of synagogues (unless it endangered German lives or property) and the destruction (but not looting) of Jewish homes and businesses.[9] The Jews were to be excluded economically and then physically, but valuable Jewish assets were to be safeguarded for the benefit of the Fatherland and the petit-bourgeoisie, who were Hitler's staunchest supporters and stood most to gain. The mob had to be incited and controlled at the same time.

Architecturally, many German synagogues of the nineteenth century, as in the rest of Europe, reflected a new-found confidence following the closure of the Jewish ghettos. The final European ghetto was demolished in Rome in 1870 and replaced with a monumental temple crowned with a cupola.[10] Previously synagogues had been self-effacing, with decoration limited to the interiors. In Germany, they had been confined to outer districts of the city or hidden in courtyards. The new synagogues were often exotic and Eastern in their influences (such as those in Leipzig, Nuremberg and Kaiserslautern) or designed in a Romanesque Revival style that deliberately expressed an architectural attachment to Germany.[11] Whatever their style, their presence as landmarks in German cities was an affront to anti-Semites expressed in spatial terms. For the Nazis, this topography of emancipation had to be repressed symbolically and the ghetto physically resurrected. Houses, shops, at least one Jewish school and a hospital were attacked, but it was the representative synagogues that bore the brunt.

Although the official line was that the attacks were spontaneous uprisings by ordinary people (SA and SS men taking part were supposed to be out of uniform), the planning was in some cases meticulous. In Berlin, the attacks were delayed while police were put in place, road barriers erected and water, telephones and other services to target buildings cut off. Nine of the city's twelve synagogues were soon on fire; in one case, the caretaker and his family were said to have died inside.[12] The authorities had lists of Jewish properties and, in some cases, clear priorities as to where to hit first across Germany, Austria and the Sudetenland. In Cologne, synagogues were to begin burning at 4 a.m., city centre shops and houses by 6 a.m., with the suburbs to follow after 8 a.m. The spontaneous riot was scheduled to be over by one in the afternoon.[13] In Austria, dozens of synagogues and thousands of shops were attacked and many totally destroyed. Out of 21 synagogues in Vienna, only the central synagogue survived – and that held the identifying records of the Jewish community, which the Nazis were to use in their round-ups.[14] Sacred objects from synagogues across the Reich were either destroyed *in situ* or desecrated and destroyed after being thrown into the streets. Humiliation and terrorization were an important part of the process. Jewish men who had been rounded up in Baden-Baden were beaten in the synagogue, forced to walk over prayer shawls, made to recite paragraphs from *Mein Kampf* and to urinate on the walls before the synagogue was burned and they were sent off to Dachau.[15] An eyewitness, Alfons Heck, described the scene outside one synagogue:

> My neighbour Helmut and I were on our way home from school, walking past the synagogue, when a group of men led by Paul Wolff, a local carpenter and fervent member of the ss, marched in front of us singing. Suddenly they broke into a run and stormed the entrance of the building. Seconds later, the intricate lead crystal window above the door crashed into the street, and pieces of furniture came flying through doors and windows. A shouting sa man climbed to the roof, waving the rolls of the Torah. 'Wipe your asses with it, Jews,' he screamed, while he hurled them like bands of confetti on a carnival.[16]

Altogether, 191 synagogues burned – many to the ground – and another 76 were demolished during Kristallnacht. Hundreds more vanished in the years following. Among the most significant architectural losses – buildings

The Romanesque synagogue at Baden-Baden in Germany was built in 1898, some 40 years after Jews were officially allowed to reside in the resort town. It was one of hundreds destroyed by the ss during Kristallnacht. Around 80 Jewish men were rounded up and marched to the synagogue, where they were forced to read *Mein Kampf* out loud and walk over prayer shawls.

The Baden-Baden synagogue was then burned down and its congregation taken by train to Dachau concentration camp. The remains of the building were used for road fill and the site became a public park. The shops and homes of the small Jewish community were attacked.

that formed an important part of their respective cityscapes – were Gottfried Semper's 1840 Dresden synagogue, Edwin Oppler's vast, domed Hanover synagogue (1870) and nine of Berlin's twelve monumental synagogues. Munich's remaining synagogue was burned by the SA, who poured on petrol and prevented attempts to douse the flames as they reached the Jewish schoolhouse next door.[17] After Kristallnacht, Goebbels demanded that the Jews themselves pay for the damage and for the clearance of synagogue sites. The Aryanization of property was in full swing.

Despite all this destruction it was the built presence of a people, commercially and symbolically, not the people themselves, that was the primary target on Kristallnacht. But the attack on buildings was a rehearsal for an assault on people who had been progressively dehumanized and humiliated, a softening-up process for the killing to come. It was also an act of cultural genocide in its own right. It was part and parcel of making the Reich *Judenrein*. It created a people without a built cultural record. What remained were fragments of this record but, ultimately, not the people who created and cared for it – and to whom their representative buildings acted as evidence of their history, continuing identity and as containers of memory.

The economic, cultural and eventually physical estrangement of the Jews was not lost on extreme-right Serb nationalists, even prior to Kristallnacht. In his 1937 lecture 'The Exile of Arnauts', delivered to the Serbian Cultural Club, the historian Vasa Cubrilović noted that:

If Germany can exile tens of thousands of Jews, if Russia can resettle millions from one side of the continent to the other, then no world war will result because of some hundreds of thousands of Arnauts [a term for ethnic Albanians in Kosovo] . . . Only the mass eviction of the Arnauts from their triangle is efficacious. The first condition for mass eviction is the creation of advisable psychosis . . . Economic measures would include the non-ceding of land registration certificates . . . denial of licences for cafés, shops, crafts . . . It can be done by the maltreatment of their clergy, destruction of cemeteries, inhibition of polygamy . . . We must send Chetnik veterans into the Arnaut regions . . . We must instigate a wave of Montenegrins from the hills.

There is one weapon, efficaciously used [against Muslims] in Serbia after 1878: the secret torching of villages and the wharves of the Arnauts in towns . . . The exiled Arnauts will leave not only land but houses and equipment . . . The fight for land can only succeed if it is done brutally.[18]

It could have been Radovan Karadžić or Slobodan Milošević speaking more than half a century later.

Unlike Nazism's attitude to German Jewry, however, the Serb and, to some extent, Croat ethnic cleansers of 1990s Bosnia seemed more often than not to deny the presence of Muslims either contemporaneously or historically. History was not being made as much as revised. While certainly genocidal in its implementation, the ambitions of the players in the Bosnian war were primarily territorial and politically motivated in the wake of the break up of the former Yugoslavia. Genocide, the expulsion, rape and murder of Bosniaks (Bosnian Muslims) was, for the advancing Serbs and Croats, a way of securing an ethnically pure and historically, or mythologically, justified land. The destruction of Muslims as a race *per se* was not the overarching project but it was the chosen method. Far from being ever present, as the Jews were to the Nazis, the Muslims of Bosnia were denied a past as well as a present. For the Serbs, this was necessary to make concrete the fulfilment of nationalist ambitions. It was also an opportunity to redress long-standing nationalist wounds, such as the catastrophic defeat of the Serbs by the Turks at the Battle of Kosovo in 1389 – a turning point in Serbian history – and their sufferings at the hands of the Nazis and their Croat allies in the Second World War.

The complex history of this area of the Balkans – the meeting point of the Eastern and Western Roman empires, between the Ottoman and Austro-Hungarian empires, and of NATO and the Eastern Bloc – has led to a melding as much as a clash of cultures. The recent conflict in the former Yugoslavia has been seen (lazily) as simply the continuation of a centuries-old conflict re-emerging after the death of Tito, who instituted a careful system of checks and balances. Although there has certainly been conflict along this fault-line over many centuries, the physical evidence, the region's heterodox architectural heritage, was equally a material testimony to coexistence. It was Milošević who stirred this melting pot to boiling point in the interests of creating a Greater Serbia, mixing a potent brew from nationalist sentiment of the sort spouted by Cubrilović, fantastical reports of threats to Serbs, and historic Serbian myths dating back to the Ottoman conquest of the region. Serbs trace their ignominy back to their defeat and the slaughter of their nobility at the Battle of Kosovo. The Serbian Orthodox heartland was in enemy hands. By the end of 1463 Bosnia, too, had been conquered. Islamicization followed.

Ottoman rule was by no means totally benign but there was a level of tolerance to other faiths and ethnic groups. On the one hand, sultans gave land for Orthodox churches, but, on the other, permission was necessary to build a church and was not always granted – especially to the Catholic Church of the hostile Western powers. Some Franciscan monasteries were destroyed following the Ottoman conquest and some churches became mosques (such as those in Foča, Srebrenica and Zvornik in Bosnia).[19] Even as late as 1872 there was a dispute in Sarajevo over the building of the Serbian Orthodox cathedral, with the Ottoman authorities ruling that the structure could be no higher than the minaret of the nearby central mosque (Islam has long had a problem with infidel bells too). Legend has it that the Sultan said that the new cathedral could be no bigger than an ox-skin. In response, a wily old man sliced a skin into many yards of thin strips and used it to set out the building's footprint. While these disputes were relatively minor affairs within a broader, more tolerant picture, they, together with the identification of Muslims in general as an urbanized ruling elite above the Serb and Croat peasants, were used to legitimize the horror to come.

Cynically, and in the interests of justifying a Greater Serbia, the Serbs have used the fact that Bosnia's indigenous population was Islamicized in the 150 years following the Ottoman conquest as a rationale for arguing that Bosnia's Muslims are at root Serbs (or Croats) with no valid separate history. At the same time, and in total and illogical contradiction, Serbians insult Bosniaks as 'Turks', that is as outsiders with an alien culture. Both arguments have been used in an attempt to delegitimize Bosnian cultural identity and claims to nationhood, ignoring, with either argument, the last 500 years of history as well as Bosnia's distinctive pre-Ottoman identity. This gross misuse of history enjoyed popularity following resurgent Serb nationalism in the nineteenth century. It continued in many forms under Tito and throughout the life of the post-Second World War communist Yugoslavia that incorporated Bosnia. All religious groups and their buildings suffered in the Second World War. The Nazis and their Croat allies paid particular attention to destroying Jewish and Serb heritage. Bosnia's Muslims fought on all sides and their architectural record was damaged accordingly in attacks and reprisals.

During the Second World War, and then in the overtly Stalinist period that followed (before Tito's break with Moscow), many Catholic churches and monasteries were closed and some destroyed. Islamic law, elementary schools and the wearing of the veil were suppressed. Several hundred mosques were destroyed or severely damaged in the war and by 1950 almost two hundred remained disused. Some were converted into museums, others into warehouses or stables. Islamic graveyards were cleared for parks or built on. It was presumed that, under communism, Muslims would gradually begin to identify themselves as either Serb or Croat. It was only in the 1961 census that the authorities formally recognized Muslims as a distinct ethnic group within the country, while historic mosques continued to be demolished in small numbers, in the name of modernity and progress, as recently as the late 1990s. The Serbian Orthodox church, by contrast, was able to restore many of its sacral buildings by the mid-1950s.

In the years following Tito's death in 1980, Milošević, who was appointed Serbian party leader in 1986, began his campaign to create a Greater Serbia. He stoked all these historic Serbian grievances and prejudices, not least the lack of retribution for war crimes inflicted on the Serbs by the Nazis and their allies (these included a short-lived Bosnian Muslim ss division, the Handžar). The *Memorandum* issued in 1986 by the Serbian Academy of Science and Art encapsulated Serb fears and prejudices around the fragmentation of the former Yugoslavia and the declining control of the Serbs.[20] Then, in 1989, before the six-hundredth anniversary in June of the Battle of Kosovo, Yugoslavia saw the spectacle of the body of Prince Lazar, the Serb national hero who fell at the battle, being processed around the country. It was the warm up to Milošević's implicit call-to-arms speech at the battlefield site outside Priština, Kosovo's capital, and had a deeply ideological purpose: in the mind of extreme nationalist Serbs, 'Wherever Serb blood is spilt, and wherever Serbian bones are buried, this must be Serbian territory.'[21] The inconveniently visible architectural history of half a millennium of indigenous Muslim culture in Bosnia and Kosovo had to be removed, along with its resistant people, if the dream of a Greater Serbia was to be realized. Bosnia's Muslim-built heritage was about to be devastated and the built historic record of Croatia and Bosnian Croats severely damaged. The breakaway of Slovenia, closely followed by a declaration of independence by Croatia in 1991, was the signal for the invasion by the, now Serb-controlled, Yugoslav army (JNA). A third of Croatia was soon in Serb hands. As observed by the Western media, two assaults stood out at this stage of the war: the siege of the Baroque city of Vukovar in the more heavily Serb-populated Eastern Slavonia, and the shelling of Dubrovnik, the 'Pearl of the Adriatic'.

Vukovar was rebuilt as a Baroque town after being destroyed by the retreating Ottoman Turks in 1692. During the three-month siege in 1991, half a million missiles were launched by the Serbs, who eventually occupied the city. More than 1,700 people died and thousands more, in and around the city, were wounded or disappeared. The Serb campaign in Croatia, and the Vukovar siege in particular, prefigured the future conduct of the war in the rest of the former Yugoslavia. Ethnic cleansing was widespread, with Serbs clearing Croats from villages in the region and Croat reprisal cleansing following quickly – the brutality was shocking, with around 10,000 dying. Another feature that came to characterize the war as a whole was also evident here: the deliberate destruction of the enemy's cultural patrimony.

In warfare it can be notoriously difficult to determine what is destroyed as part of the destructive process of war itself, what has been ruined in a casual or criminally negligent fashion, and what has been identified as a cultural target; in Vukovar itself the answer remains largely unclear. Many monuments were destroyed, indeed most of the city centre, including the Franciscan friary, the Municipal Museum, the History Museum and New City Hall. The Baroque Eltz Palace, with its priceless collections of Croatian art and artefacts, was also badly hit, despite having a hospital in the basement and flying the chequered flag of the Hague Convention, which indicates that a site is culturally important and strictly off-limits to military activity on either side. The Serbs countered with video evidence of machine-gun nests perched on the castle. There is no doubt that the Serbs looted art treasures from Vukovar, ethnically cleansed it and changed its street names, and that Belgrade's political leadership suggested rebuilding the city in an Orthodox Byzantine style. More direct evidence of the destruction of ethnically totemic architecture, however, had to wait until later in the war.[22] But not for long – within a year hundreds of Catholic (Croatian) churches, monasteries and other historic monuments had been desecrated. Burned, bombed and dynamited, the destroyed buildings were often miles from any front line. The Croatian government claimed that 63 Catholic churches had been destroyed by June 1994 and another 500 monasteries and churches severely damaged. The Serbs claimed that 243 Orthodox religious buildings had been lost.[23]

The propaganda role of such statistics has to be reckoned with and the truth is sometimes hard to discern. Robert Fisk recounts a visit to the historic Croatian town of Karlovac, where the locals argue that the eighteenth-century Orthodox church of St Nicholas was shattered by accidental shelling from the Serbs themselves. Among the undergrowth, however, 'lies the steeple and its flattened dome – with a stout inch-thick steel hawser looped around the top, just below the cross'. The Serbs did indeed accidentally bomb the church, instead of the nearby Catholic church, leaving the bell-tower standing. But, according to Fisk, its comprehensive destruction was a deliberate act by Croats some time later; as was the dynamiting of the Orthodox archbishopric building on the other side of the square. Croats could be as determined ethnic cleansers as the Serbs.[24] The accuracy of the targeting, although at times erratic, as demonstrated by the fate of St Nicholas, could also be disturbingly to the point. According to Durda Lipovscak, an urban planner in Karlovac, he received a phone call from the Serbs across the front line telling him that the historic archives in the fortress town would be shelled the next morning at 9 a.m. The promise was kept to the minute.[25]

The port of Dubrovnik had no such clear warning. The astonishingly well-preserved walled Renaissance city is a World Heritage site of no military importance whatsoever. Neither is there any historic Serbian claim to the city, which, as Ragusa, was an independent republic for centuries before being incorporated into the Austro-Hungarian empire and later into Yugoslavia after the First World War. The ethnic cleansing of the city and its incorporation into a Greater Serbia does not appear to have been seen as a war aim. So why was it bombarded from land and sea? Pure vandalism, terrorism, envy? The fate of this city is considered in more detail in chapter Three.

The Serbian assault on Croatia was undoubtedly territorial in its desire to create a Greater Serbia (the excuse being the protection of the Serb minority in the region), but the extent to which the cleansing of Croatian cultural patrimony, which is itself not in doubt, was pre-planned and organized remains a moot point. When war broke out in Bosnia, however, following its declaration of independence in March 1992, the pattern of intent was inescapable and systematic. In Bosnia there was a clear escalation from simple territorial gain and the murderous expulsion of the local population to actual genocide and systematic cultural cleansing. Here, the pointed erasure of collective memory and history, as expressed in cultural patrimony, accompanied the degradation and erasure of a people as a people.

Today Sarajevo's former National and University Library building is a shell. It was housed in the Vijećnica, the former city hall, an eclectic, neo-Moorish edifice redolent with nineteenth-century Romanticism. Its great dome has been repaired, courtesy of the Austrian government, but elsewhere the carved brick is blistered and the inside filled with the debris of floors collapsing onto floors. Time has been taken, however, to erect a plaque on the boarded up exterior:

> On this place Serbian criminals on the night of 25–26 August 1992 set on fire the National and University Library of Bosnia-Herzegovina. Over 2 millions of [sic] books, periodicals and documents vanished in the flame:

Do not forget:
Remember and warn!

Dr Kemal Bakaršić, the then librarian of the National Museum in Sarajevo, described the destruction of the National Library:

> All over the city sheets of burning, fragile pages of grey ashes floated down like dirty black snow. Catching a page, you could feel its heat and for a moment read a fragment of text in a strange black and grey negative, until, as the heat dissipated, the page melted to dust in your hand.[26]

Sarajevo is a linear city strung along the valley of the Miljacka and creeping up the surrounding hills. The old Ottoman quarter is a grid of single-storey wooden shops, stone mosques, a covered market and a travellers' han. It was a scrap of a settlement at a river crossing before the Turks transformed it into a substantial city on the Balkan trade routes between the Bosphorus and Western Europe. Since then the city has been redeveloped and extended westwards, with first a pronounced Austro-Hungarian flavour and then Tito-era modernism as the valley widens towards the airport. Years after the Bosnian war, the journey from the airport back to the largely restored city centre still takes one past impromptu roadside cafés in the ruins of buildings and office blocks with floors collapsed like shredded felt. Graves are everywhere, including on the verge of the dual-carriageway, so close to the crash barriers you could almost reach out and touch them. It had long been a cosmopolitan city, sheltering Sephardic Jews expelled from Spain and making room in its heart for a Serbian Orthodox cathedral. Its architecture is the legacy of a mix of faiths and shifting empires; its citizens intensely proud of its combination of multi-ethnicity and modernity. It was this modernity, the 'non-otherness' of Sarajevo, that shocked Western television viewers who witnessed the city's descent into chaos during the 1,000-day Serbian siege. Here were a people and a city, recognizably European and cultured, unravelling into barbarism. Dubrovnik was similarly familiar to two decades of package tourists.

What is particularly striking about Sarajevo is the fate of the city's secular cultural buildings; it was not simply the more obvious sacral institutions that suffered. The shelling and burning of the National Library by Serbs dug into the surrounding hills incinerated an enormous Bosnian heritage. Only about 10 per cent of its up to three million items remained after at least 40 incendiaries hit the building. Among those volumes lost, as the columns of the 'Moorish' main reading room came crashing down, were thousands of books dating back to the fifteenth century. Sarajevans dodged snipers to form a human chain to rescue books from the library. One librarian was shot and killed in the process. Water to the city had been cut off by the Serbs earlier that day and the firemen's attempts to douse the blaze were further hampered by hoses split by machine-gun fire.[27]

Altogether more than 1,386 historic buildings in Sarajevo were destroyed or severely damaged in the war.[28] Few escaped intact. This is a very conservative estimate reflecting a low base of officially 'listed' historic monuments. Many more unlisted buildings were also wrecked. The venerable Ottoman quarter was among the areas severely damaged by shelling. Gazi Husrev Beg, the central mosque dating from 1530, received 85 direct hits from the Serbian big guns. Other damaged buildings included the Catholic cathedral, the synagogue, a madrasa, Ottoman baths and the historic covered market. Nearby, the Serb Orthodox cathedral was also hit by shell-fire and suffered slight damage (one can only assume by accident). Most of the city's historic mosques were damaged; minarets were a favourite target and were repeatedly bombarded until they were toppled or reduced to stumps. The historic synagogue was also damaged and the hillside Jewish cemetery desecrated by Serbs digging in to create gun emplacements. Sarajevans proudly claim, and with some justification, that no Serbian religious building was damaged in reprisal.

In May 1992, months before the National Library was gutted, the Oriental Institute was one of the first significant cultural casualties of the Serb offensive. In many ways this was an even greater loss than the National Library, particularly as far as Ottoman Bosnian history was concerned. It was arguably the richest collection of Ottoman documents in the entire Balkans. Illuminated volumes on science, theology, Sufi works, natural history, occultism, astrology and poetry were stored here. Centuries of Ottoman court rulings, decrees and tax records, including a shari'a law manuscript dating from 1023, were destroyed. The collection included rare works in Adzamijski, Bosnian Slavic written in an Arabic or Turkish script. These and other documents provided real evidence of a distinct historic Bosnian identity and culture, and of the Ottoman foundations of Sarajevo: a history that Serbian ideology and its reinvigorated mythology sought to deny. Now the remains of the unique collection do not even fill the shelves of a single metal cabinet. Just a few carefully wrapped wads of fine calligraphy on singed rounds of paper toast remain; about 0.05 per cent of the collection was saved.

Oriental Institute director Behija Zlatar claimed the attack was a clear attempt to

> destroy the collective memory of the people. It was planned. I lived close to the building and I talked to the fire brigade. It was a navigated rocket meant to destroy even metal cases. Several shells were fired in a line across the building at the same time. Then they shelled around

it to stop the fire brigade; the same thing happened at the National Library . . . The collection was important because it showed clearly that Sarajevo was not, as Karadžić said, a Serb city. Historiography from Belgrade was always trying to represent the history of Bosnia as a Serb land. There has been an attempt to forge Bosnian history and it is still going on.[29]

Kate Adie, the BBC's war correspondent in Bosnia, was also reported to have become embroiled in this cultural cleansing. Exasperated with the continued Serb shelling that appeared to be aimed at Sarajevo's Holiday Inn, Adie, one of many reporters staying there, stomped up the hill to the Serb positions to ask them what they thought they were doing. Apparently, they apologized; the real target, they explained, was the National Museum across the road from the hotel.[30]

The neo-classical quadrangle of the museum houses an eclectic collection of Roman archaeology, Ottoman folk art, natural history and Bosnia's unique heritage of carved tombstones. The collection reflected the multi-ethnic character of the country. It was shelled repeatedly, until, Sarajevans claim, a Serb general at his headquarters in Pale ordered the shelling to stop because the museum also contained Serb artefacts.[31] Either the general or Adie had some effect, since the damage to the museum has not been terminal. On my visit there were still empty display cases and rubble in the marble halls of the entrance wing, but elsewhere the displays of historic Bosnian domestic interiors, mouldering stuffed mammals and the geology section, with its jaunty Sputnik-era backdrops, were still in place. One of Sarajevo's most important treasures, the fourteenth-century illuminated Sarajevo Haggadah, was, however, rescued at the last minute from the museum's pitch-dark basement as, according to some (questionable) accounts, it rapidly filled with water from pipes burst by the shelling. The Jewish codex was brought to the city by Jews expelled from Spain in 1492 and has become a talisman for Sarajevan tolerance, especially since being hidden during the Second World War to keep it safe from the Nazi occupiers.

It is difficult to verify with certainty the degree of planning in the campaign against historic and cultural monuments. Belgrade is unlikely to open its archives to an investigation of what is, after all, a war crime, but Bosnians are certain of this, and the evidence appears to support them in the form of devastated cultural monuments across the country. According to heritage experts in Sarajevo, the planning started even before open hostilities began, with the removal to Serbia of icons, paintings and other items of Serb heritage from collections and churches.[32] The thoroughness of the destruction also suggests premeditation, with smaller archives and not just the large historic collections in Sarajevo and Mostar being targeted. The Institute for the Protection of Cultural, Historical and Natural Heritage of Bosnia &

Herzegovina on the outskirts of Sarajevo was one of many other cultural sites that were razed. What happened to those records of the country's historic environment remaining within (some had already been removed by the Institute for safe keeping twelve days before) is still unknown. Even during the course of the war, however, the university in the Serb stronghold of Banja Luka was establishing new faculties with material that, it is claimed, had been looted from Sarajevo's institutions.[33]

Ferhad Mulabegović, the post-war director of the burned Institute, argues that the gathering of information made the selection of cultural targets straightforward:

> Maps were made in the Geo-Political Institute in Belgrade – there were no secrets from them; all statistical information on people, culture and heritage were kept in Belgrade because in the former Yugoslavia each institute sent information to Belgrade. They knew exactly where they could find each object in each [Bosnian] building and they certainly did remove pieces of art from Orthodox churches and monasteries to Belgrade.[34]

The Bosnian federal culture minister, Dr Sabrina Husedžinović, agrees:

> They had the co-ordinates of each and every building – it didn't happen by chance. You don't have to look down the sights [of artillery]; you know the figures and press the button.

Such claims of pinpoint military accuracy are suspect in any conflict but, again, the evidence on the ground tends to supports the thrust of the contention.[35] Dr Husedžinović, an eyewitness to the systematic demolition of some of Banja Luka's sixteen mosques, all of which were destroyed in the war, is one of many who point to the specificity of damage to historic buildings compared with relatively light damage to surrounding structures, and to the strafing of an area to prevent incendiary shells being extinguished. The latter was also a feature of Hitler's Baedeker raids on historic British cities. The minister, now based in Sarajevo, had lived for many years in Banja Luka restoring its historic mosques. After she was expelled she sneaked back to take photographs of the damage: 'I lived through that [destruction] as if someone had attacked my own life,' she recalls, tears welling. 'If you've spent 24 years of your own life working on a mosque you know every detail and love them like your own family member.'

Accuracy in shelling can never be total, however, and misses may have saved more than one building from complete destruction. The fate of architecture in Serb- and Croat-occupied areas was far worse; demolition by dynamite proved far more effective than shelling from a distance. The majority of

The Bosnian town of Banja Luka, now in the Republika Srpska enclave, once had 16 mosques dating from the 15th and 16th centuries. In the Bosnian war, all were destroyed by Serb extremists and the Muslim population expelled. The Ferhadija mosque complex (1579) included three historic mausoleums, a fountain and a graveyard. The complex and a nearby clock-tower were blown up in May 1993 and the remains later bulldozed and used as land-fill.

The empty site of the Ferhadija mosque in central Banja Luka. Attempts to lay a new foundation stone in May 2001 met with violent riots by stone-throwing Serb nationalists. One of the elderly Bosniaks gathering for the ceremony later died of head injuries. A pig was let loose on the site to defile it. Plans for its reconstruction had been prepared by the School of Architecture in Sarajevo. Other mosques in Banja Luka have been successfully rebuilt but the Ferhadija's prominent location makes it particularly contentious.

these dynamited and torched buildings can never be repaired, even if the rubble hasn't been bulldozed away, as it has been in numerous cases.

If the complexity of determining the planning of cultural destruction within a city such as Sarajevo precludes *absolute* certainty about the nature of these attacks, set within the context of the wider destruction across Bosnia, Croatia and subsequently in Kosovo there can be no doubt as to the systematic tactics being employed. Ethnic cleansing was accompanied by a policy of cultural cleansing to render it permanent and irreversible. It was directed at collective memory, shared history and attachment to place and the built environment. It was designed to eradicate the historical presence as well as the contemporary lives of the target community. Destroying graveyards and monuments is a way of carrying out ethnic cleansing retroactively.

A 1995 report into the fate of Bosnia's Islamic, Catholic, Serb Orthodox and secular architectural heritage calculated that 3,226 buildings officially listed on the national historic register (again representing major monuments and only a fraction of the historic environment) had been destroyed or severely damaged. Of these 1,115 were identifiably Islamic (this figure later rose to 1,415 buildings), 309 identifiably Catholic, and up to 36 were Orthodox structures (Serb sources put the figure at more like 65–70).[36] In 24 towns across the country up to 90 monuments were affected in each location. In some places the figures are far higher, for instance, Mostar's 429 losses, Banja Luka's 219, Stolac's 167 and 222 in Trebinje. The report is regarded as being reasonably accurate, despite some known errors and a lack of direct access to sites in Republika Srpska.[37]

The level of destruction in the Bosnian war far exceeded the country's architectural heritage losses in the Second World War. This was not just damage in and around front lines or simply haphazard vandalism. The cultural cleansing could be swift and comprehensive, as at the very beginning of the war when the historic Muslim town of Foča was seized by the Serbs. Its inhabitants were subject to mass murder, mass rape and expulsion. This, however, did not take the ethnic cleansing far enough: the town's rich heritage of Ottoman buildings was flattened. Among the buildings destroyed were the venerable Imperial mosque (1500) and the Islamic community archive, both burnt down by Serb nationalists in April 1992. The same month saw mortars pound the 1546 Musuluk mosque. The list of architectural casualties in and around Foča goes on, more than twenty mosques in all, and its extent bears witness to the single-mindedness of the destruction of the area's mosques: Dev Suleiman-Bey (1633/4), Defter Memishah-Bey (late sixteenth century), Kadi Osman-efendi (1593/4) Mumin-Bey Mesdzid (sixteenth century) Sheikh Pirija Mezdzid (sixteenth century), Mustapha-Pasha (sixteenth century), Mehmed Pasha Kukavica (1751), Emin Turhan Bey in Ustikolina (1448/9, the oldest mosque in the country), the old mosque of

Jelec (fifteenth century) and the Naksibendiy Tekky (monastery).[38] There were no hostilities between rival forces in or around Foča during the 1992–5 war, since the area was firmly within Serbian-occupied territory. The destruction was a policy of erasure. Similar litanies could be recited for towns across Bosnia. In Bijeljina, for instance, six mosques were destroyed on the night of 13 May 1993 as part of an ethnic cleansing campaign carried out by the Serbs.[39]

Atrocities including the rape, torture, humiliation and murder of Bosnia's Muslims by Serb (and Croat) forces and of Croats by Serb forces (and to a small degree by Muslims) were repeatedly associated with the destruction of religious buildings in a manner reminiscent of the Jewish Holocaust. In August 2004 the bodies of many missing Foča Muslims were found buried at a depth of 7 m, hidden below the rubble of one of the town's, and indeed Bosnia's, former glories, the Ottoman Aladža Džamija, the 'multi-coloured mosque', which was bulldozed in 1992, trucked away from the city centre and dumped in the nearby Cehotina river.[40] The co-burial of the stones and bodies of Bosnia's Islamic community has also been reported elsewhere, for example in Brčko and in Novoseoci, a village near Sarajevo where Serb nationalist forces took away 45 Muslim villagers on 22 September 1992. In 2000, 41 bodies were exhumed from a nearby mass grave beneath the transported rubble of the village mosque. Other mosque sites were built on or became rubbish dumps, bus stands and car parks.[41] Such destruction was not just directed at significant centres of Muslim population. Hardly anybody lived permanently in Počitelj, near Mostar; the historic Muslim village had been an artists' colony and tourism highlight rather than home to a large Muslim community. Here too Muslims were expelled or killed, but it was the architecture that was, overwhelmingly, the target. In September 1993 the Croatian warlord Mate Boban ordered the settlement's destruction. Its mosque, the Ottoman houses, the former theological school, and the baths were all wrecked – some dynamited into oblivion. Croats subsequently attempted to justify their actions by arguing that the remains of a Catholic church existed below the mosque. It was an argument used elsewhere (including Banja Luka and Foča).[42]

If, less than a decade after the end of the war, rebuilt Sarajevo could at first glance appear simply as a shabby, economically depressed town on its uppers, the train ride down to Mostar, curving between the sublimely beautiful lakes and wooded mountains, gives ample evidence of a particular kind of conflict. On quotidian suburban housing estates and in villages along the way, pristine homes stand side by side with the blackened, roofless shells of the house next door. People have turned on their neighbours. As the train pulls into Mostar's unlovely Tito-era station in the Muslim east of the city, evidence of the destruction intensifies. There appear to be more ruins than intact buildings. Shiny steel silos lie, after being shelled, twisted and rusting

The Aladža ('multi-coloured') mosque (1551) in the once majority-Muslim town of Foča was one of the glories of Bosnian Ottoman architecture. It was designed by the Turkish architect Ramadan Agha and built by Christian master-masons from Dubrovnik. In 1992 Serbian militia ethnically cleansed the town, raping, murdering and expelling its Muslim inhabitants; they destroyed about 20 historic mosques in and around Foča, renaming the town 'Srbinje'.

on their sides like giant squeezed toothpaste tubes. On this visit, five years after Dayton, house after house and whole streets are in ruins, while burnt-out cars sink into the dust. The siege of the Muslim east of the city by Croat West Mostar was devastating.

In nearby Stolac, an old Bosnian town once considered for listing as a UNESCO World Heritage site, historic Ottoman-style residential complexes with their characteristic oriels, courtyards and fountains, as well as more prominent institutional and sacral architecture, were obliterated by the occupying Croat militias. Large tranches of the historic town centre were destroyed along with four mosques, including the 1519 Emperor's mosque and the Podgradska mosque, a rare surviving example of a mosque with an arcaded bazaar built into the ground floor. The old Islamic market, Tepa Square, was razed, cleared and used as a bus station. Around 8,000 Muslims, who once made up some 40 per cent of the population, were expelled – some to concentration camps. The Muslim graveyard survived until the Dayton Accord fixed the ethnic cantons and the status quo, then it too vanished. The Croats have since developed an urban design and rebuilding strategy that pays little regard to its multi-cultural losses.[43] Stolac, once charming, is now a sullen, ragged place of little beauty. The town comes to a dead stop when you drive in. On the road down to Dubrovnik you can see why with your own eyes: the countryside around has been trashed by a fringe of household debris, washing machines, bricks, prams, window frames – the domestic fall-out from the destruction, evidence of the horrors perpetuated on some residents by others.

In August 2004 the bulldozed remains of the Aladza mosque were found dumped in the nearby Cehotina river along with the bodies of many Muslims missing from the town since the war. The remnants were identified by the mosque's distinctive stone columns. The co-burial of victims of ethnic cleansing and their sacred buildings occurred elsewhere in Bosnia.

How many died in the wars in the former Yugoslavia, who died, and how many buildings were destroyed are still matters of dispute. Figures from reputable international sources suggest that anything between 140,000 and 250,000 Bosnians were killed. Between 20,000 and 40,000 people are still missing. More than 3,000 Islamic buildings (mosques, shrines, religious endowment buildings (*vakuf*), dervish lodges and religious schools) were destroyed or damaged.[44] What is clear is that Bosnian Muslims and their architectural patrimony were, despite significant Catholic Croat and Serbian Orthodox deaths and cultural destruction, by far the greatest victims of the conflict, caught as they were once again between hard-line Serbs and Croats, both bent on territorial gain.

As a witness to the International Criminal Tribunal for the Former Yugoslavia (ITCY), Harvard academic András Riedlmayer,[45] tabled as evidence a map that plotted the damaged, destroyed and intact mosques across Bosnia. Draw a line between the outer edges of the groups of red dots representing destroyed mosques and you get an outline of Serb-held areas such as the Republika Srpksa. Within those boundaries almost every mosque has been destroyed – three-quarters of all Bosnia's pre-war mosques. It is an area contiguous with those areas most ruthlessly ethnically cleansed by the Serbs.[46] The destruction is supporting evidence for a campaign of genocidal ethnic cleansing. The notorious Serbian police chief in Serb-occupied Prijedor, who was shot resisting arrest for trial at the ITCY, was proud of his work, which is reported to have included deciding who was sent to the Omarska concentration camp. He told one reporter: 'With their mosques, you must not just break the minarets. You've got to shake up the foundations because that means they cannot build another. Do that, and they'll want to go. They'll just leave by themselves.'[47]

The rationale as part of ethnic cleansing is clear: remove the Muslims themselves and destroy identifiably Muslim secular and religious buildings; bulldoze the remains and clear graveyards; seize identity papers and burn cadastral records. With women raped to give them 'Serb' or 'Croat' children,

The beautiful Ottoman town of Stolac in Bosnia-Herzegovina was being considered for World Heritage status before the ethnic cleansing of the Bosnian war, which saw much of its historic fabric torn down by Croat extremists. The town had four mosques built between the 16th and 18th centuries, including the 1736 Cuprija mosque and many vernacular houses, a market and baths.

The site of the Cuprija mosque. Stolac's mosques and other Ottoman-era buildings were destroyed by a Croat army unit in the summer of 1993 and their contents looted. The Orthodox Church of the Holy Assumption of Christ was destroyed the previous year. Several village mosques around the town were also levelled. In the face of much opposition, at least one mosque has been rebuilt since the end of the war.

the intent was to remove all reasons for an expelled community to return; or even to eradicate evidence of their ever having been there to begin with. Zvornik was once a town of a dozen mosques and a 60 per cent Muslim population, but after its cultural and ethnic cleansing Branko Grujic, the mayor of the, by now, Serb town, declared: 'There never were any mosques in Zvornik.'[48] Plans were then put forward to build a massive new Serbian Orthodox cathedral on the site of one of the mosques. History was being rewritten; a new future and a new past were being invented in the service of a Greater Serbia and a Greater Croatia.

Many Muslims and Croats in Bosnia ended up dead or in concentration camps during the Bosnian War, but many more survived in areas outside Serb control. What would have been their fate had Serb and Croat nationalists succeeded in overrunning the whole country? Would they all have been expelled or murdered? Events within the Republika Srpska suggest so. German expansionism under Hitler created precisely this dilemma for the Nazis. They had succeeded in economically and culturally isolating the Jews, pushing them into internal exile and excluding them from shared spaces. In Germany, Jewish segregation had begun to break down significantly by the nineteenth century, with many Jews flourishing within a wider German society as practising Jews or by being assimilated while maintaining a secular

Jewish identity. But from 1 April 1933, beginning with the boycott of Jewish business, segregation was gradually reintroduced with the aim of creating and controlling an alien 'other'. As a result of Kristallnacht the Jews in Germany and Austria had been finally rendered invisible, in so far as the architectural record of their collective presence as a group was concerned (and at the same time their individual visibility was ensured with the yellow star). Many thousands of German Jews had left Germany if, perversely, they were allowed to. But, with the defeat of Poland and the expansion of the Reich eastwards, Hitler was left with more Jews than when he started.

The 3.1 million Jews of Poland, the largest community in the Diaspora, had a richly expressive thousand-year-old cultural tradition. It was a lively, visible community, both in cities and the countryside shtetls. Jewish Poland had its own institutions, unions, parliament and literary and architectural masterpieces, the most exuberant expression being its synagogues. This architectural patrimony ranged from humble religious buildings, almost indistinguishable from housing (which saved a few stone and wood structures from their otherwise fate), to massive, confident Neoclassical and Baroque stone structures. The Jewish architectural historian David Dawidowicz points out that, unlike much of Western Europe, where Jewish sacral architecture flowered only with the end of the compulsory ghetto and emancipatory legislation of the nineteenth century, Poland had a Jewish cultural tradition that was relatively free and had avoided, in large part, wide-scale pogroms and expulsions. The built heritage of Polish Jews was almost as old as that of Poland itself.[49] The Nazi response was two-fold and murderous: the removal of Jews from public space as an intensification of otherness, and then their removal altogether – the Final Solution. The physical destruction of existing Jewish spaces and the creation of ghettos were integral to this.

Segregation and the maintenance of Semitic otherness has long been a feature of anti-Semitism; the ghetto takes its name from an early walled enclosure – the Jewish Ghetto of Venice, established in 1516. In *Flesh and Stone*, Richard Sennett describes the 'anxieties of difference' built into the fabric of the Venetian Republic.[50] The creation of the walled enclave in the former foundry areas (the meaning of ghetto) and specific laws regarding the segregation and control of the Jewish population were one outcome. After production was moved to the Arsenale, the old foundry islands became keeps for Jews – to keep the alien 'other' in, rather than to exclude Venetians in general. The three linked Venetian ghettos, created in stages over a century, were surrounded by walls and canal moats, accessible only by a few bridges and gateways that were sealed each night. Other external exits were closed up and outward-facing balconies removed. The Jews were effectively walled up at night.

The fear and imagery of disease and pollution via physical contact played a large part in Venetian ideology, as it did in the Nazis' justification for the creation of the Polish ghettos. In Venice, a contract with a Jew was agreed with a bow not a handshake. The walls did not protect the overcrowded Jews when a real plague came along and they were locked in day and night. Nor did the walls protect them from the pogrom – it made their mass slaughter all the easier: 'The segregated space of the Ghetto', says Sennett, 'represents a compromise between the economic need of Jews and these aversions to them, between practical necessity and physical fear.'[51] Under Nazism, Kristallnacht and the mass destruction of Jewish property in German-controlled Poland paved the way to the new ghettos. Weeks after Kristall-nacht, a leader article in the ss newspaper *Das Schwarze Korps* stated: 'The Jews must be driven from our residential districts, and segregated where they will be among themselves, having as little contact with Germans as possible . . . The result would be the actual and final end of Jewry in Germany, its absolute annihilation.'[52]

The segregation of the Jewish population had begun to gather momentum following the 1935 Nuremberg Laws. Physical exclusion was later built on to economic exclusion. Under post-Kristallnacht decrees issued by Göring, parks, theatres, hospitals, shops, whole streets and areas of cities were made out of bounds to Jews. Jews were to be excluded from public, shared spaces as well as public life. At a meeting to discuss the aftermath of Kristallnacht and the Nuremberg Laws, Goering said: 'You will not be able to avoid the creation of ghettos on a very large scale in all the cities.' Heydrich demurred for the present, but Poland provided the opportunity to make the ghetto a material fact.[53]

The reintroduction of the ghetto can be seen as part of a 'softening-up' process – seeing how far the Nazis could go before full-scale extermination. It intensified the otherness and the dehumanization of those on the inside of the ghetto wall. It also provided a ready intermediate solution to the issue of where to put the two million Jews of German-occupied Poland and the million other Jews in the Reich at this point, during the process of Aryan-izing selected conquered territories. In one of the Nazi's first acts following the defeat of the Poles, Heydrich issued secret instructions (21 September 1939) to the *Einsatzgruppen* regarding the concentration of Jews into the city from the countryside. The decision was made to 'dissolve' Jewish communities of fewer than 500 souls. Later that year it was spelled out that the Jews were to be placed in ghettos to 'ensure a better chance of controlling them and later of removing them'. It also ensured that they died of starvation and disease in large numbers.[54]

The first Nazi ghetto in Poland was created in April 1940 in Łódź and housed a quarter of the population of the 600,000-strong city. As a textile centre the Łódź ghetto was of great economic value to the Nazis and so it was permitted to survive until 1944. The corollary of creating these Jewish concentrations was the brutal cleansing of the Jewish population elsewhere in Poland and, later, under Operation Barbarossa, in the Baltic states and the western Soviet Union. The deadly rounding-up and destruction of Jews by the emboldened Nazis sometimes involved massacres of local populations *in situ* – Jewish inhabitants of towns and villages were gathered, often in front of the town synagogue, tortured, humiliated and murdered, and the building burned.[55] The elision of the two acts into one was not uncommon. In the city of Białystok several hundred Jews were brought to the city's principal synagogue (the largest in Poland), driven inside, and then the building was burned down. Anybody trying to escape the blaze was shot. More Jews were burned in their synagogue at Lipsk. The actions mirrored medieval pogroms in England and Germany, where Jews were burned alive inside their synagogues. The person and their property had become one in ideological terms. Similar atrocities occurred across Eastern Europe. In numerous towns and villages the Nazis' first act upon occupation was to raze the synagogue, other Jewish sacral and institutional buildings or even whole Jewish quarters. There was no single Kristallnacht of destruction but the physical results were the same. During September 1939, for instance, all the synagogues of Bielsko, Bydgoszcz, Piotrków, Włocławek and Zgierz were destroyed by fire or dynamite. In some communities Jews themselves were then charged with burning down their own buildings and fined. Muslims in Bosnia were later to be similarly accused. Dozens more acts of architectural destruction followed inexorably: Gniewoszów, Przemyśl, Łódź, Sosnowiec, Będzin. Jewish holy days or Nazi celebrations were often picked as suitable times for the attacks. Even after the ravages of the First World War, many thousands of Polish synagogues, stiebls, libraries, schools and study houses had remained. At the end of the Second World War, only around 200 synagogues remained in Poland (in various degrees of dereliction) and still fewer in Ukraine and Belarus.[56] One of the greatest cultural losses was the heritage of sixteenth- and seventeenth-century decorative wooden synagogues. This astounding architectural tradition, a sort of Jewish-Slavic Baroque indigenous to Poland and its environs, produced buildings notable for their complex, multi-layered roofs rising in tiers and domes. They were decorated with balconies and arches and were richly carved. Many incorporated concave or convex timber exterior and interior forms. Of the hundred or so that survived until the Second World War, only three minor and rather plain examples remain (at Szumowo, Wisniowa and Punsk). Wonders of timber architecture, such as the synagogues at Jurborg, Lithuania, and Narowla in Belarus, went up in smoke.[57] All these buildings were recorded, including many measured drawings, in a 1923 survey of historic synagogues by the Institute of Polish Architecture.[58] Much of this documentation was lost when the Nazis destroyed the Institute building in 1944. Other buildings that were not immediately 'killed' were 'humiliated'. According to Samuel Gruber, a leading campaigner for the protection of surviving Jewish heritage:

When spared, synagogue buildings were deliberately and publicly degraded. They were used as public latrines (Ciechanów), prisons (Kalisz), stables (Gniewoszów, Maków), factories and even brothels. In Częstochowa, for example, a synagogue was used as a police headquarters where young girls were sexually molested and tortured. Jews were often forced to desecrate synagogues and to destroy their furnishings, publicly burn Torah scrolls and to dance around them, singing, 'We rejoice this shit is burning.'[59]

The 'blitz-pogroms' that marked the early period of German occupation were later to be followed by mass-killings inside and outside ghettos and transportation for European Jewry to extermination camps, either directly or via the ghettos. A 403-hectare ghetto, the largest in Poland, was established in north central Warsaw to protect the German army and populations from 'the immune bacillus carriers of the plague – the Jew'.[60] Between 470,000 and 590,000 Jews were crowded into the area, six or seven to a room, and 62,000 Poles expelled to make way for them. The walls of existing buildings were employed in the enclosure. Doorways out were closed up and streets blocked with 3-m high walls topped with 1 m of barbed wire along the 16 km perimeter. At first, fears about disruption to industry and business meant that economic links were envisaged between the ghetto and the outside, but as the noose tightened its 22 gates were reduced to 15.

The superb wood-built synagogue in the village of Wolpa, now in Belarus, built *c.* 1643, was destroyed in 1941. Such carved wooden structures were emblematic of a 1,000-year-long Jewish cultural history in Eastern Europe that was snuffed out by the Nazis. The wooden buildings often incorporated complex Baroque geometric forms and delicate carving. Less than a handful of such synagogue survive today. The Jews of Wolpa, half the population, were killed immediately or first expelled. Around 900 died.

Gombin in Poland had a similarly beautiful wooden synagogue dating from 1710. Like Wolpa, it was a registered historic monument. The carved interior, partly lined in engraved brass sheets, included a chandelier surmounted by a Polish eagle and a gold-embroidered ark covering made from the saddle that once belonged to a Tartar general. In September 1939 the occupying Nazis set fire to the building in front of the brutalized Jews who had been gathered in the marketplace. They then razed the entire Jewish quarter. According to reports, some Jews were pushed into the flames by the Germans but managed to escape.

Hundreds died every day from cold, starvation and disease. By this stage, the Nazis had so successfully spatially separated the Jews that their 'subhuman' otherness became a tourist attraction. Coach parties of German soldiers visited. Whips were brandished to provoke the 'wild animals'.[61] Alfred Rosenberg reported on a visit for the Reich's press department: 'If there are any people left who still somehow have sympathy with the Jews then they ought to be recommended to have a look at such as ghetto. Seeing this race en masse which is decaying, decomposing, and rotten to the core will banish any sentimental humanitarianism.'[62] Gradually the ghettos were liquidated, with their inhabitants killed there and then or transported to the death camps. Where there was resistance, the ghettos were physically destroyed. In Warsaw, the entire ghetto was reduced to rubble following the uprising by the systematic blowing up or burning of the buildings block by block. Around 50–60,000 Jewish resisters were killed, thousands of these dying in burning buildings. The man in charge, Brigadeführer Jürgen Stroop, symbolically marked the end of the liquidation by dynamiting Warsaw's Great Synagogue on Tlomackie Street. A thousand-year-old civilization, its people, its books, theatre, art and buildings had been almost entirely eradicated. There are few physical reminders left of this great tradition and few Jews living among them to remember.

The Holocaust was not the first genocide of the twentieth century: that dishonour goes to the Turks and Kurds in present-day Turkey for the slaughter of up to 1.5 million Armenian men, women and children in a campaign that began in earnest in 1915. As under the Nazis and 1990s Serbian extremists, this was accompanied by thorough cultural cleansing. It was an attempt to destroy a people that Turkish governments deny and cover up to this day. The continued neglect and destruction of Armenian monuments in Turkey can be seen as part of this stance. Although Turkey reluctantly admits that around 300,000 Armenians died during the period, it attributes the deaths to starvation or exposure arising out of the chaos of the First World War. The reality is harsher: torture, pogroms, mutilation, rape and sexual slavery were part of the Armenian experience as the Young Turks murdered many Armenian men across the country and sent the remaining population of ancient Armenian towns and villages on forced death-marches. Primitive gas chambers using fires lit at the mouths of caves have also been reported. Those who survived ended up in Syria or behind the Russian lines in Russian-controlled Armenia.[63] Continued denial of the atrocities by Turkey is assisted, on the one hand, by those in the West wanting to keep Turkey, a NATO member and EU supplicant, on side, and on the other by Turkey's ongoing erasure of the Armenian architectural record.

Armenians were the first Christian nation, accepting the new creed at the beginning of the fourth century AD. They inhabited the uplands between the Black and Caspian seas for more than 2,500 years. At times independent, the culturally and linguistically distinct Armenians were eventually absorbed into the Ottoman Empire, but their cultural patrimony under the Ottoman system of government remained largely intact for hundreds of years. As non-Muslims they were second-class citizens, but also formed an important trading and business class especially, like the Jews, in areas forbidden to Muslims, such as banking. However, the decline of the empire in the nineteenth century led to increasing oppression of minorities within the empire and growing nationalist feeling within its constituent parts. Between 1894 and 1896 pogroms under the leadership of Sultan Abdul-Hamid II led to the massacre of up to 200,000 Armenians across eastern Turkey – the Armenian heartland – and the exile and forced conversion of thousands more. Turkish troops led the killings and were followed by plundering Kurdish gangs and the subsequent destruction of towns and villages.

Further massacres followed in 1909, a year after the Young Turks (Ittihadists) seized power in a military coup. In some ways the junta has been seen as progressive, more secular and modern in its vision for a future Turkish state emerging out of the fragmentation of the Ottoman world. But unlike the multi-ethnicity that characterized the Ottoman Empire, however problematically, the new regime's increasingly chauvinistic 'Turkism' quickly evolved into a desire to establish an exclusively Turkish nation state within Asia Minor. In the wake of the Balkan wars and the Russian threat to the East, the Armenians were also regarded as an internal threat, a view intensifying with the outbreak of the First World War. The redrawing of borders and mass resettlements creating ethnic nation-states was the emerging pattern across the region.

After a period of beatings and deaths, the genocide began on 23 April 1915 with the rounding up and murder of thousands of Armenian community leaders. Systematic mass murder followed throughout Turkey. Men and women were often separated and the men murdered immediately or sent to death camps, such as those at Ras-Ul-Ain and Deir-el-Zor. Those who survived the sadistic deportations were forced into permanent exile. Armenian churches, monuments, quarters and towns were destroyed in the process. Some Armenians were burned alive in their places of worship. One survivor from the town of Marash later told his tale to a US oral-history archive:

> Some two thousand Armenians had gathered, whom the Turks surrounded and poured gasoline all around and set them on fire. I, myself, was in another church that they were trying to set on fire and my father was thinking that this was the end of the family. He just gathered us around and pulled the movable pews around us as if he were trying to protect us and said something I will never forget: 'Don't be afraid, my children, because soon we will all be in heaven together.' And, fortunately, someone discovered some secret tunnels that the French had dug from that church to another vantage point and we escaped that way.[64]

In the genocide whole cities lost their Armenian populations, including the historic Armenian city of Van. More than 50,000 Armenians were killed and the city itself was almost entirely flattened (apart from two mosques) and the new Kurdish city of Van rebuilt nearby. Armenian property not destroyed during the massacres was transferred to the ownership of the Turkish state in September 1915.

In the late nineteenth century and the years that followed the First World War, Greeks and Turks also died in their thousands in forced population exchanges. Monuments and towns were razed. The entire northern part of the ancient and once beautiful coastal city of Smyrna (now Izmir), which included the Greek and Armenian quarters, was burned in September 1922: every remaining mosque in Athens that had not been destroyed in previous anti-Muslim attacks was later demolished. The Armenian genocide and the destruction accompanying the mutual expulsions were a devastating cultural as well as human loss. The early Christian tradition of Armenia had produced a unique architecture characterized by worked tufa stone rising in

Following the Treaty of Sèvres (1920) and the retreat of Greek forces in Anatolia, Turkish troops reoccupied the ancient city of Smyrna (now Izmir) in September 1922. Fires were set and engulfed the Greek and Armenian quarters of the city. Thousands of Greek and Armenian refugees died in the city or drowned in the sea (the numbers are disputed) in attempt to escape the fire and the Turkish assault. Foreign troop-ships looked on but refused to intervene.

domes and spires. The essential verticality of forms and the use of pointed arches, ribbed vaults and clustered piers prefigured the ecclesiastic architecture of European Gothic. Medieval Armenian kingdoms built on their tradition, creating spectacular churches and monasteries. Its craftsmen exported their stone-working skills to other religious and ethnic groups throughout the region.

A survey, not in itself comprehensive, prepared in 1914 by the Armenian Patriarchate of Constantinople listed 2,549 religious sites under its control, including more than 200 monasteries and 1,600 churches.[65] Many were destroyed in the process of the genocide but many more have since been vandalized, flattened or converted to mosques or barns. In contrast to Kristallnacht, where the destruction of architecture offered a warning of worse to come, the Turks have continued to remove, stone by stone, the evidence of millennia of Armenian architectural and art history *following* the mass murder and exile of the Armenian people. It was only in the 1960s that Armenian and other architectural scholars began the politically and physically dangerous task of recording and rescuing what remains of 1,800 years of Armenian ecclesiastical heritage. A 1974 survey identified 913 remaining churches and monastic sites in Turkey in various conditions. At half of these sites the buildings had vanished utterly. Of the remainder, 252 were ruined. Just 197 survived in anything like a usable state.[66]

In the late 1980s and early '90s the travel writer William Dalrymple found evidence of the continuing destruction of Armenian historic sites. Although many sites had fallen into decay through not so benign neglect, earthquakes or peasants searching for Armenian gold supposedly hidden beneath churches, there are clear instances of deliberate destruction.[67] He argues that the destruction accelerated in the 1970s and '80s in response to the emergence of a terrorist group, the Armenian Secret Army for the Liberation of Armenia, which had carried out attacks against the Turkish establishment. Censorship increased. In one 1986 incident, the editor of the Turkish edition of the *Encyclopaedia Britannica* was arrested and charged regarding a footnote that made mention of the historic Armenian kingdom of Cilicia. The book was banned.[68] Ten years earlier, French historian J. M. Thierry was sentenced, in his absence, to three months' hard labour after being arrested for drawing a plan of an Armenian church near Van. He escaped before being sentenced. Thierry also reported that the government had sought to demolish an Armenian church in Osk Vank in 1985 but the villagers resisted, valuing it for various utilitarian uses – a granary and a stable among them.[69] Although Dalrymple notes the difficulties of finding unequivocally clear evidence of deliberate destruction after the fact, a number of telling examples have been discovered. A collection of five important churches at Khitzkonk (now Beş Kilise), near Kars, had been officially off-limits to visitors since the genocide until the 1960s. Only the cupola of the eleventh-century St Sergius chapel remained by the time of Dalrymple's visit; its four walls had been blown out (no earthquake could cause such damage). The remaining churches had all but vanished. Locals said the buildings had been dynamited by the army.[70] Other shattered religious sites include Surb Karapet, partially destroyed in the 1915 massacres and then reduced to rubble by military target practice in the 1960s.

Elsewhere some remains cling on, including the tenth-century chapel frescos at Varak Vank, now a barn. The ninth-century basilica at Dergimen Koyu, near Erzinja, is a warehouse with a huge hole smashed in the side to allow vehicles entry. The Armenian cathedral at Edessa (now Urfa), converted into a fire station in 1915, was converted again to a mosque as recently as 1994 with the remains of its ecclesiastical fittings destroyed in the process. The town is, traditionally, the first outside the Holy Land to have accepted Christianity. There are no churches in use today. By contrast, ancient Armenian churches in Iran and Georgia have been restored using state funds. The Georgian restorations came with independence from the Soviet Union, long after Stalin destroyed more than 80 churches in the state. In areas hostile to the post-Soviet Union state of Armenia, monuments have not been so lucky. The Azeri campaign against the Armenian enclave of Nagorno Karabakh, which began in 1988, was accompanied by cultural cleansing that destroyed the Egheazar monastery and 21 other churches. Among the remains of one Armenian town in the enclave, half a millennium of history was reactivated. Jugha was first flattened in 1605 and its inhabitants deported to Persia (forced exile had long been a feature of Ottoman punishment). Its cemetery, although much damaged, remained and featured thousands of khachkars (medieval stone crosses) until 1998, when it was reported that Azeris had bulldozed a third of the monuments, trucking away the rubble before UNESCO intervention stopped the destruction.[71]

Greek heritage in Turkey has also continued to suffer. In 1955, in an echo of Kristallnacht, thousands of Greek shop windows in Istanbul were smashed during an anti-Greek riot, More than 1,000 houses, 26 schools and 73 Greek Orthodox churches were attacked and many destroyed, including the two main Greek cemeteries and the Greek Orthodox Tomb of the Patriarchs in the city.[72] The riot was fuelled by inter-communal violence in Cyprus and faked photographs in the Turkish newspapers of a Greek bomb attack destroying Kemal Atatürk's birthplace in the city of Thessaloniki. (It had been only very slightly damaged by a blast outside the Turkish consulate next door.)[73] Even in contemporary Istanbul, historic Armenian churches and graveyards continue to be neglected and vandalized. In recent years there have been reports of surviving khachkars being smashed and their rubble removed.

In 1987 the European Parliament called on Turkey to 'improve the conditions of protection of architectural monuments' and stated that Turkish

The Armenian monastery of Khitzkonk (Five Churches) was constructed between the 7th and 11th centuries above a river gorge about 40 km southwest of the important Armenian town of Ani in Turkey. It was abandoned after the Mongol invasions of the 13th century and resettled in the 19th. It is typical of the fine stone craftsmanship of Armenian church architecture, which prefigured the Gothic architecture of Western Europe.

denial of the Armenian genocide was an 'insurmountable obstacle' to Turkish membership of the EU.[74] Little action has resulted and the question of Turkish membership of the EU looks likely to be settled without this 'insurmountable obstacle' being addressed by either party. The World Monuments Fund has also attempted to take on the issue with limited success. Only the celebrated Armenian church on the island of Aght'amar in Lake Van looks set to be restored (after international pressure and with Armenian, not Turkish, money). As George Hintlian, the curator of the Armenian Museum in Jerusalem, says: 'The churches are all we have left. Soon there will be virtually no evidence that Armenians were ever in Turkey. We will have become an historical myth.'[75]

If the writing of history is the privilege of the victor, so is the successful rewriting of it. In Turkey the desire has been to deny the past, to continue to cover its tracks. The continued demolitions and deliberate neglect of Armenian monuments demonstrates a state that remains ill at ease with itself and its minority groups. Guilty reminders must be removed. The repression of the Kurds and the remaining Armenians and Greeks within Turkey is still with us and Kurdish heritage too is disregarded or drowned in enormous dam projects. Destruction here is both a denial of a victor's deeds and a mark of the incomplete nature of that victory. The architectural legacy of Ottoman multiculturalism was a witness to the security and strength of the Pax Ottomanica. The careful and partial promotion by the Turks of only favoured elements of that heritage is, by contrast, evidence of modern Turkey's insecurity and weakness.

If the situation in Turkey is an on-going cultural cleansing, after the fact, Kristallnacht was its opposite – a proto-genocidal act. And, as the Holocaust progressed, the gap between destroying the artefact and that artefact's creators narrowed and eventually coincided with the contemporaneous murder of Jews and burning of synagogues in Polish towns and villages. This was not simply the destruction of memory but the denial of a living future for the Jews. Nazi anti-Semitism and cultural genocide was as confident as it was ruthless. The Serbian campaign against monuments in the Bosnian war saw a simultaneous desire to rewrite the past and destroy the living and material culture of its enemies. The destruction of libraries, graves, mosques, vernacular houses, churches and archives went hand in hand with the creation of a mythological Serbian past in service to a new Greater Serbia. The thoroughness and ferocity of the eradication of representative architecture in the former Yugoslavia was integral to the process of ethnic cleansing and accompanied it at every stage. These crimes against architecture were not necessary as part of a Bosnian civil war and the fate of these

The same site today. Only the ruin of the Church of Surb Sargis (St Sergius) remains. The monastery was abandoned after the Armenian genocide and subsequently destroyed by Turkish forces at some time in the 1960s as part of a long-standing campaign of hostility against the remains of Armenian culture in Turkey. The inside of its dome (dating from 1025) bears the scars of explosives set at its four corners. Its robust structure and careful detailing is thought to have saved it from total destruction.

monuments is an indicator of the real character of the conflict: not a civil war, but a genocidal territorial grab.

It is the imperative to eradicate not just individuals but to eliminate a group and its collective memory and identity that makes widespread destruction a recurring tactic whenever wars against minorities are fought, whether driven by Nazi racial ideology, Turkish state building or Serbian expansionism. Who remembers the Armenians? Their narrative is now as fragmentary as their monuments; the material evidence of their experience is disappearing. Memories are still being erased.

3 Terror: Morale, Messages and Propaganda

I told you so. You *damned* fools.

H. G. WELLS, FROM THE PREFACE TO THE 1941 EDITION OF *THE WAR IN THE AIR* (1908)

'In the light of recent events in the United States we would like to draw your attention that [*sic*] this film does contain images of the Manhattan skyline which may cause offence.' How can a *skyline* cause offence? This peculiar note displayed in the box office of a London cinema showing Spielberg's newly released *AI: Artificial Intelligence* is indicative of just how imprinted the New York skyline is on the Western imagination. It has courted disaster in so many films over the years (in *AI* it is drowned) that when 11 September stamped a new image on the world's mind it had a paradoxically unreal quality. Life and artifice had fused into a confusing whole with the images of the World Trade Center towers crashing to the ground again and again on TV screens all over the planet. It is doubtful if images of that day would have quite the same impact if the Twin Towers had stood firm, even with a huge loss of life.

There is something about skyscrapers, from the Tower of Babel to *The Towering Inferno*, that suggests man's over-reaching hubris. In tragedy, *até* – destruction – is the response to such follies. Hence Hollywood's repeated recourse to images of the destruction of towers. They are dramatic dynamite.

For many years, the Empire State Building had served the role admirably: King Kong, for example, is buzzed by planes at its summit (the 1976 remake substituted the World Trade Center). Disaster movies have torched, zapped, flooded and exploded the Manhattan skyline ever since. And when the planet is under attack, we know this because Big Ben and the Eiffel Tower are razed too. These structures have become symbolic of a whole nation-state. In the case of *Planet of the Apes*, the half-buried Statue of Liberty stands in for the destruction of the entire planet: 'You maniacs! You blew it up!' howls Charlton Heston. *AI*, released in the UK just weeks after 11 September, may, however, have been too raw a reminder to pass without a warning to cinema-goers, even if the Towers themselves remain intact in the flooded city.

Attacks on buildings and cities can have a symbolic power all of their own, in fact as well as fiction, which is why strikes against them have been favoured by terrorists or in conflicts even when their levelling gives no direct military advantage. Victory is rarely expected from the act itself. From the area bombing of German cities in the Second World War to 11 September 2001, terror has been the aim, whether conducted under the name of 'war' or not. Fear is the key: the weapon used to sow terror among the population in order to lower morale and speed defeat, or simply to send a message that people should be afraid of the bombers. Terror as a means of control. Although it may be the apparent randomness that is an important compo-nent in creating fear (dislocation, shock, disorientation, and the loss or dis-tortion of a familiar and apparently fixed or solid built environment), at other times the symbolism of the target is highly important. Terrorism, it has been said, is an act of violent propaganda. Who the audience is for its message varies. Area bombing, by its lack of targeting, sends more diffuse signals when compared to the singling out of a particular structure. Its scattered effect aims at delivering a mood – demoralization – rather than an articulate message. The more general the target, the less precise the communication.

The carefully selected targeting of the World Trade Center on 11 September 2001 sent a clear and specific message to the Islamic world as much as to the US. Al-Qaeda knew exactly why they had chosen the WTC, the Pentagon and, possibly, Camp David (with the fourth downed jet). American commenta-tors and world leaders claimed the actions were an attack on 'freedom', 'democracy' or even 'civilization' by 'barbarians', an appellation also used by both Allies and Axis powers in the Second World War to describe the other's bombers. The terrorists, however, were clear that they were aiming at sym-bols of US military, economic and political hegemony (the US establishment probably sees no difference between this and concepts such as freedom and democracy). The assault of 11 September was an attempt to humble a super-power, puncturing its invulnerability, and either to sting it into withdrawing its far-reaching grasp or, a more likely outcome, pull it into catastrophic retaliatory conflicts that would further delegitimize its global engagement in the eyes of the Islamic world and beyond.

In a video broadcast by the al-Jazeera TV station on 7 October 2001, Osama bin Laden, part of the small, extremist Salafiyya Islamic movement, explained his actions: 'Hypocrisy stood behind the leader of global idolatry –

9/11 – the second plane hits. Terrorism always conveys a message, often embodied in the choice of architectural target. To al-Qaeda, the twin towers of the World Trade Center in New York represented, in part, Western idolatry and, in part, the economic hegemony of the United States in the world and particularly in the Middle East. The anti-American and anti-modern message was also a call to action for Islamic militants.

behind the Hubal of the age . . . Namely, America and its supporters.' (The Hubal was a stone idol worshipped by pagan Arabs at the Ka'ba in Mecca before Muhammad's followers conquered the city and destroyed the statue.)

Michael Scott Doran at Princeton University argues that the meaning of this statement would be obvious to Muslims.[1] Americans, bin Laden is arguing, are the consummate idol worshippers of our age, polluting the world with their cultural, political and economic power, to the extent that they have stationed their military in the holy territory of Saudi Arabia itself. 'Extremist Salafis', Scott Doran says, 'regard modern western civilization as a font of evil, spreading idolatry around the globe in the form of secularism.' The US is perceived as taking the lead in the 'Zionist Crusader Alliance' bent on subjugating Muslims. The message has since been reinforced by other activists with al-Qaeda links: 'The Crusaders and the Jews only understand the language of murder, bloodshed and of burning towers,' said terror leader Ayman al-Zawahri in a recording aired on al-Jazeera TV in May 2003, in which he urged Muslims to attack Western embassies and companies.[2] Later investigations into the 11 September plot suggested al-Qaeda had originally wanted to include an even greater range of targets within their sights that day. Downed jets were to have been aimed at five East Coast and five West Coast buildings, including the Los Angeles Central Library and the Sears Tower in Chicago, as well as bridges and Hollywood studios.[3]

There has been some speculation as to whether Osama bin Laden, a trained civil engineer, knew the twin towers would fall: that he was aware of the particular vulnerabilities inherent in their structure. There is no evidence to support this theory and the causes of the catastrophic failure of the buildings required an extensive post-mortem by experts equipped with detailed information on its construction unavailable to the plotters. What is clear is that Islam, and Salafist extremism especially, has long concerned itself with icons, idolatry, sacred spaces and geometry, repeatedly calling on Muslims to 'liberate the al-Aqsa Mosque and the Holy Mosque [in Mecca]', for instance.[4] Saudi Arabia will not allow churches or synagogues to be built in its sacred land and the relative height of church spires to Islamic domes was, historically, a recurrent cause for wariness in the relatively liberal Ottoman Empire.[5] Intelligence reports in the months and years following 11 September identified a number of other 'symbolic' targets being eyed by terrorists. These included the Eiffel Tower (the target of another 1994 plane smash plot), the Golden Gate Bridge, Disneyland, the Vatican, Melbourne's Rialto Towers and the towers of Canary Wharf in London's Docklands.[6] The Statue of Liberty and Mount Rushmore have both had their surfaces minutely scanned so that they can be rebuilt if they fall victim to bombers. Other architectural icons, such as the Sydney Opera House and London's St Paul's Cathedral, have had their security tightened even without a specific threat. Unsuccessful plots to crash jets into the White House, the arch-secularist

Kemal Atatürk's mausoleum in Ankara and the city of Tel Aviv, all in the decade preceding 11 September, have also apparently been uncovered in post-11 September investigations. And, of course, in February 1993 the Islamic terrorist Ramzi Ahmed Yousef detonated a massive bomb in the basement car park of the World Trade Center in an attempt, he said, to 'topple one tower into another'. The bomb ripped through five, mainly sub-terranean, floors, killed six and injured over a thousand people but, on that occasion, the Towers stood.[7] There is no doubt that there is a strong aware-ness among both attackers and defenders of the power of the built form.

It remains unclear whether the choice of targets on 11 September had its genesis in the al-Qaeda camps of Afghanistan (as seems likely and as al-Qaeda leaders claim) or with the operatives of the Hamburg cell who hijacked the planes (as German investigations have suggested).[8] One Hamburg hijacker, Mohammed Atta, however, was deeply interested in the expression of power-relations within the built environment. Atta trained as an architect and developed a strong interest in Islamic architectural heritage. He was horrified, for instance, at the way Western skyscrapers and modernist development intruded upon and overshadowed the old quarters of Aleppo, Syria, which he had studied for his doctorate, and at Egyptian government plans to regenerate an historic neighbourhood of Cairo as an 'Islamic Disneyland' for Western tourists. Islamic terrorists in general have been highly conscious of the notion of Islamicized space and its pollution by Westerners.[9] Mohammed Atta would have been in no doubt about the powerful messages sent by the destruction of architectural icons. Such spectacular acts also had the merit of ensuring a massive audience for the hijackers' *shahid* – martyrdom – to be witnessed by the faithful and inspire them to radical action.

In *The Secret Agent* (1907), Joseph Conrad's Mr Vladimir argues that terror-ism (his 'philosophy of bomb throwing') should be directed at the beliefs that underpin a society's understanding of its own prosperity.[10] In the case of *The Secret Agent*, science is the spirit identified and the target is the Royal Observatory at Greenwich (fictionalizing a real attempt on the building some years before). What better target for al-Qaeda than the World Trade Center – the primary signifier of economic power in the primary city of global capital? The death of the Twin Towers was an image of the mighty fallen in a way that the damaged Pentagon could never be, despite the latter's direct role in offensive operations and despite it being the world's largest building by floor area. It is hard to imagine the levelling of any low-rise building, unless it were a magnificent and resonant historic monument, having the same impact. It was H. G. Wells, that Cassandra of human destruction, who is said to have looked at Manhattan in awe and remarked: 'What a ruin it will make', before going on to conjure up the city's bombardment from airships in his 1908 *The War in the Air*.[11] And the ruin of the WTC was, indeed, more fantastical than the buildings were when intact.

The immediate response world-wide was astonishing; borders and airports closed, stock markets fell and office workers in towers on the other side of the Atlantic were evacuated. Commentators were immediately predicting the end of the skyscraper as a building type and the emptying out of agglomerated financial districts. Within months there were apparent copycat attacks: Luigi Fasulo committed suicide by flying a plane into Milan's Pirelli tower, the symbol of Milan's post-war commercial success. Shortly after, a fifteen-year-old killed himself flying into the 28th floor of the Bank of America Plaza in Tampa, Florida. These were relatively minor incidents in themselves, the resonance of which was magnified by the 11 September precedent. The fascination with towers continues, of course, as plans for the rebuilding of the World Trade Center clearly illustrate. For early Modernists, such as Hugh Ferriss, Mies van der Rohe and Le Corbusier, the skyscraper was an architectural representation of the future and of confidence in that future; there is no sign of architects or their clients now changing their views. The events of 11 September may have caused the Schwarzenegger vehicle *Collateral Damage* to be shelved (it revolved around terrorists blowing up a Los Angeles skyscraper) but the construction of towers and their fictional and, very probably, their actual destruction will continue.

The belief that the destruction of physical fabric – as distinct from human lives – has the capacity to demoralize is immensely strong, even in the face of considerable evidence of 'stiffened resolve' among those on the receiving end. This is obvious to those involved. On the first anniversary of the 11 September attacks, President George W. Bush said: 'The terrorists chose this target hoping to demoralize our country but they did not succeed.' He told an audience in the Pentagon (reinstated after a pointedly swift £322 million rebuilding): 'Within hours, in this building, the planning began for a military response . . . Within one year this great building has been made whole again . . . This place is a symbol of our country's might and resolve.'[12]

Perhaps people's understanding of the very logic of the intended demoralization process is exactly what helps dissipate the element of bewilderment and powerlessness that generates fear. So, given the repeated failure of terrorist bombings of non-military or infrastructure buildings (in terms of engendering demoralization leading to defeatism), only its propaganda virtues remain. The morale argument may serve to hide baser motivations: punishment and revenge. Motivations, though, are as diverse as the methods and targets: nationalist, religious, political, ideological and territorial terrorisms are all widespread. A look at US State Department reports on terrorism lists a huge range of terrorist groups and architectural targets across the world. In 1994, for instance, attacks aimed at buildings included: a Shining Path explosion at the Peruvian-Japanese cultural centre in Lima; a bomb outside the Goethe Institute in Athens (claimed by the Revolutionary People's Struggle); and two attacks by the Kurdistan Workers' Party on Istanbul's historic bazaars (an economic attack on the tourism economy, perhaps).[13]

Sometimes the attacks appear, on the face of it, inexplicable. A series of car bombs outside Italian cultural sites in 1993 damaged the Uffizi in Florence, the Teatro Parioli, the basilica of San Giovanni in Laterano and the church of San Giorgio al Velabro in Rome, and the Villa Reale and the nearby Padiglione d'Arte Contemporanea in Milan. Works by Rubens, Velázquez and Fra Bartolommeo were among dozens seriously damaged or destroyed in the Uffizi blast. No note was left and no responsibility claimed by any group. The Mafia, specifically the Cosa Nostra, have since been fingered as the suspects (they were under heavy government pressure at the time), although their more usual targets were individuals or directly governmental.[14] Cultural historian Khachig Tololyan echoes Conrad in suggesting: 'We need to understand the way in which different societies maintain their vision of their collective selves, and so produce different terrorisms.'[15] With this in mind, the cultural targets in Italy would have had enormous collective resonance and a guarantee of outrage among Italians, whose national identity draws heavily on the country's artistic heritage. The Mafia's intention, hotly disputed at a series of trials, was not to win the public over to a cause but, by intimidating the state, to enable themselves to operate more freely. One informant in the investigation recalled being asked by a Mafia associate, 'What would you think if one morning you woke up and you did not find the tower of Pisa?' He answered, 'If something like that happened it would be the death of a city.' The associate argued that 'choosing a single person as a target had limited meaning compared with the effect on different targets such as works of art'.[16] The ecclesiastical targets in Rome were thought to be a warning issued in response to Pope John Paul II's speech in Sicily earlier the same year urging the populace to distance themselves from the Mafia's activities.

Attacks on the buildings – embassies especially – of an oppressor by the oppressed have, in addition to the soft targets offered by transport systems, become the *lingua franca* of nationalist and regionalist terror groups. For example, despite its more recent reputation for concentrating on military and economic targets, the Irish Republican Army has a long history of attacking cultural targets relating to British state power, especially in the period before the establishment of the Free State. During the fight for independence in the years leading up to 1921 and in the civil war that followed many of the country houses of the Anglo-Irish ascendancy were burnt out by the IRA. Figures vary, but up to 200 (roughly 10 per cent) of Ireland's 'big houses' were destroyed at this time.[17] The families of most of their owners had arrived in Ireland in the service of the Crown in the fifteenth and

The ruins of Leemont House, Coachford, Co. Cork. In 1921 the house was burned out by the IRA and its owner, Mrs Mary Lindsay, shot. A strong Loyalist, she had informed the British forces about a Republican operation resulting in the capture and execution of IRA men. The IRA attacked a number of the colonial 'big houses' belonging to the Anglo-Irish aristocracy, but this attack and similar ones on buildings by both sides in the struggle were revenge targets.

sixteenth centuries and the grand houses were representative of an alien Protestant ruling class (however 'native' their inhabitants may have gone), which had overseen the pauperization of much of Ireland's Catholic majority. Landowners who were nominated to the new Irish Senate were especially vulnerable to having their houses razed. The attacks were aimed at a ruling class and its collective self-identity as expressed architecturally in their grand estates.

The end of the 'big house' era, memorably portrayed in the novels of Elizabeth Bowen, is now seen in somewhat elegiac terms and the historic architectural legacy of the houses is heavily promoted by the Irish Tourist Board, but for many Irish people, and for many years, they were hated 'monuments of landlordism and oppression'.[18] It was popularly thought that these stately piles were larger than their English counterparts, reflecting a more intense exploitation of Irish workers and peasants. The reality is that these homes were generally smaller and cheaper, but their place as symbols of the colonizers was important and the houses grew in the imagination. The houses themselves were often imperial in character, reflecting the Neoclassical and Palladian taste of their colonial owners. Even in the late nineteenth century, the Tudor and Gothic Revival houses then fashionable on the British mainland were a rarity in Ireland, which stuck to its version of the plantation style.[19] This is not to argue, however, that the IRA were discerning architectural critics.

Although many of the country houses were eventually rebuilt, the campaign had the desired effect of persuading many of the aristocracy to sell their land and move out of Ireland altogether. A series of land acts that seriously eroded their income was not an encouragement to stay, either. Fewer than 30 of the titled families, out of 1,200 at the beginning of the twentieth century, now remain in their ancestral homes: a class-cleansing, if you like. The decline in the country house was, until recently, mirrored in the steady peacetime erosion of Georgian Dublin. Its colonial heritage was not treasured in the independent Republic. This disregard for Georgian architecture was not unique to Ireland (it was only in late 1960s that the style began to be substantially rehabilitated in Britain) but its severity was marked and, perhaps, reflected a continuing antipathy to the imported style: 'I was glad to see them go, they stand for everything I hate,' said one Irish Culture Minister, Desmond Guinness.[20] Recent wealth and growing national self-confidence in the Republic has led to greater plurality and a re-evaluation of Ireland's architectural heritage.

Irish nationalism can also probably claim the doubtful distinction of having the longest history of urban terrorist bombing. The Irish Republican Brotherhood caused a catastrophic explosion when they bombed London's Clerkenwell Prison in 1867 in an attempt to free two of their leaders. They miscalculated the blast spectacularly, using two tonnes of explosive to blow a hole in the prison wall. Fifteen passers-by died and several houses nearby were wrecked and had to be demolished. It also lost them widespread sympathy for their cause among London's masses. Despite some concessions on Ireland from Prime Minister Gladstone, they were not deterred from bombing symbols of British power in a campaign between 1883 and 1885. The Tower of London, the House of Commons, the Carlton Club, London Bridge and Scotland Yard were among the places damaged by Fenian bombs. An unexploded device was also found at the foot of Nelson's Column. Nelson's Pillar, Dublin's columnar cousin to Trafalgar Square's resident, was less fortunate. 'Operation Humpty Dumpty' toppled the Admiral in a 1966 explosion laid by IRA dissidents who resented the presence of a British military hero in their capital half a century after the 1916 Easter Rising.

The Four Courts in Dublin was, though, the most catastrophic victim in architectural and historic terms. The grand Neoclassical building by James Gandon on the Liffey was destroyed in 1922 after a booby-trapped mine exploded. It was laid by besieged IRA members who had rejected the treaty creating the Free State and were holed up inside. It exploded after they surrendered to Michael Collins's Free State forces that were using British artillery to pound the monumental structure. The strong room of the Public Record Office in the same building, containing centuries-worth of priceless documents, was utterly destroyed. The blast triggered the Irish Civil War. The controversy over responsibility continues to this day. Some argue it was

In a plot codenamed 'Operation Humpty Dumpty', in March 1966 former IRA men blew up Nelson's Pillar in Dublin's O'Connell Street, the 40 m high granite cousin to the Column in London's Trafalgar Square. Erected in 1808, it preceded London's version by some years. The Doric column designed by Francis Johnson had a platform offering panoramic views over the city. The presence of a monument to British militarism was seen as an affront to Republican sensibilities, and its toppling a commemoration of the Easter Rising of 50 years earlier.

the shelling of the 'insurgents' within the building that set off the mine. Others suggest it was calculated cultural murder by the anti-treaty IRA. Irish academic Tom Garvin argues that 'effectively it constituted an attempt to murder the nation as a collective entity with a collective memory' by an authoritarian and anti-intellectual IRA.[21]

The IRA's bombing campaign on the UK mainland has, since the 1960s, concentrated its more devastating attacks against infrastructure and symbols of UK economic might: the City of London and the financial buildings in London's Docklands. Bombs in the shopping areas of Manchester and in Warrington could be seen as economic targets too, but pure terror appears to be the main aim. Casualties among innocent civilians proved no deterrent. But since the Republic's independence, cultural targets have been largely conspicuous by their absence (the bombing of Nelson's Pillar and Belfast's Grand Opera House notwithstanding). The IRA has been anxious to maintain its legitimacy as a military outfit with a political and territorial agenda, rather than be seen as a sectarian group engaged in cultural or ethno-religious conflict. The horrendous sectarian murders that have taken place (on both sides) during The Troubles severely undermine this stance, but a desire to avoid such labelling has dictated that the destruction of buildings has followed a different pattern over the past three decades. The consequent struggle over housing is discussed in detail in Chapter Five. A curious exception to this pattern of excluding representative architecture from the IRA's targets was the fire-bombing of Belfast's Linen Hall Library in 1993. The library holds important historical records of both the Republican and the Unionist movements, and the bomb was left in the Republican section. As with the Four Courts, the IRA sought to distance itself from the explosion, claiming that it was an accident caused by a passing bomber dumping his cache as he escaped. A wariness regarding explicit cultural or religious targeting remains.

Although clearly cultural targets, the destruction of Anglo-Irish country houses also has to be placed in the context of property destruction 'reprisals' that convulsed Ireland during the War of Independence. Frustrated at the

An explosion destroyed Dublin's Four Courts on Inns Quay, Dublin, in April 1922. The complex (1786–1802) designed by James Gandon was occupied by anti-Treaty soldiers at the beginning of the Irish Civil War. It was shelled by government troops, and a mine laid in the building exploded, destroying the national archives. The Courts were rebuilt in 1932.

IRA's ability to launch attacks on the police and then vanish back into its communities, the notoriously thuggish 'Black and Tans' and auxiliaries of the British army forces were unleashed on the population. Houses, pubs, shops and whole town centres, as well as nascent local industries such as creameries, were wrecked by the troops in 'official' and 'unofficial' reprisal attacks. Many buildings were burned to the ground and others dynamited. In reply the IRA made attacks on government buildings, and the houses of the pro-British establishment or collaborators suffered in return.[22]

The killing of two policemen in Clifden, County Galway, in March 1921 led to sixteen houses in the town being burned down. A year earlier, Cork's shopping streets were damaged after Black and Tans poured petrol into buildings and set them alight. Auxiliaries then cut the hoses of the fire brigade tackling the blaze.[23] It was a policy of punitive demolition in response to resistance that has had its counterparts of varying severity across the world and the centuries: the Nazi destruction of Lidice in Czechoslovakia and of Oradour-sur-Glane in France are among the more infamous examples. The fall of the Twin Towers can also be seen as the 'mother of all reprisals' by a terrorist group.

In terms of the sheer scale of devastation, it is state terror and state reprisals that have consistently outgunned those who attempt to usurp a state or claim a part of it for their own. Countless cultures have suffered as a result. Saddam Hussein's destruction of the Marsh Arabs' 5,000-year-old culture in the wake of the first Gulf War began with attacks on the unique latticed, reed-built villages of the Shi'ite community and then extended them to the ruination of an entire eco-system. Less than 10 per cent of the marshes, once the size of Wales, has escaped the destructive drainage programme. The Marsh Arabs' involvement in the uprising against the Iraqi regime following the war has cost them their civilization. Similarly, in the north of Iraq, many thousands of Kurdish towns and villages in Iraqi Kurdistan were destroyed and the rural population subjected to genocidal attacks as part of Saddam Hussein's Anfal campaign to suppress Kurdish nationalism and culture. Up to 180,000 Kurds died and hundreds of thousands more were forcibly resettled in Iraqi-controlled towns while their village homes were bulldozed. Again, the British were here first; one of history's first aerial bombardments against civilians was conducted against Iraqi villagers resisting British colonial rule in 1924. It was here also that 'Bomber' Harris (see below) was 'blooded'. 'They know', he reported, 'that within 45 minutes a full-sized village can be practically wiped out and a third of its inhabitants killed or injured by four or five machines that offer them no real target, no opportunity for glory as warriors.'[24] Across the border in Syria, President Hafez al-Assad more recently conducted an equally murderous campaign against the rebel city of Hama. In revenge for a bombing campaign on government buildings by the Sunni Muslim Brotherhood in 1980–81, Assad crushed the city in early 1982. War reporter Robert Fisk saw the beginnings of the devastation from outside its historic city walls, missiles crashing into its heart, cracking open the silver and blue domes of mosques. Between 10,000 and 20,000 people were murdered and many were tortured. The deaths in themselves were not enough for Assad. When Fisk returned a year later, the Old City had vanished: 'The walls, the narrow streets, the Beit Azem Museum – had simply disappeared, the ancient ruins flattened and turned into a massive car park.'[25] Attacks such as these have a duality of purpose. The more abstract rationales of retribution and inculcating fear are often coupled with concrete goals of eradication. Here terror merges with ethnic cleansing and genocide.

Ideologically driven demolitions can also be elided with the desire to impose terror or retribution. Stalin's campaign against what remained of Ukraine's architectural heritage, after the destruction of Jewish patrimony and the retreating Germans' scorched-earth policy, fulfilled a number of functions. It was revenge for collaboration by Ukrainian nationalists and also fulfilled his desire for Russification and secularization (see chapter Four). Ukrainian Catholic churches (a bastion of nationalism) were either destroyed or transferred to the more compliant Russian Orthodox congregations. Stalin's rule was certainly one of terror and the boundaries between war, terror, terrorism and violence will always remain murky.

The propaganda message of all these state-sponsored acts of destruction is the same – attempts at resistance will not just result in the murder of individuals, but also the destruction of their homes, their cities and even whole civilizations. The area bombing of German cities by RAF Bomber Command that followed the horrors of the Blitz on British cities in the Second World War still stands out for its savagery and the extent of the destruction it caused. It was a massive attempt to break down German resistance by bombing the country into submission. There had been aerial attacks on civilian centres in the First World War, but it was the Luftwaffe that was responsible for introducing carpet bombing of towns and cities early in the 1939–45 conflict, including devastating attacks on Warsaw and Rotterdam. This aerial storm was foreshadowed in 1937 by the bombing of the Basque capital, Guernica, by German forces during the Spanish Civil War. The cradle of Basque culture was obliterated. It has become symbolic both for the horror of the totality of its destruction from the air and the loss of material culture entailed. After Guernica, attacking civilian centres rapidly became a legitimate tactic for both the Allies and the Nazis, despite the thrust of international prohibitions.

The scale of destruction steadily rose during the course of the Second World War. At first it was mostly directed at military and industrial targets, but its use became steadily more indiscriminate and, on occasion, had a

strong whiff of retaliatory action. The obliteration of the medieval centre of
Coventry and its cathedral in November 1940, for instance, was met by
Churchill ordering the bombing of Mannheim in return. In the following
April, a British raid on Berlin, which destroyed the State Opera House and
damaged the Prussian State Library,[26] was answered a week later by a raid
on central London that resulted in damage to many monuments, including
St Paul's Cathedral, Westminster Abbey, the Houses of Parliament, the
British Museum, the National Gallery and the Tate. Coventry was a prime
industrial target, however, and cannot be seen as a deliberate instance of targeting an enemy's built heritage, no matter how important its architectural
record. Indeed, with the exception of the Baedeker raids discussed below,
neither side in the aerial bombing war admitted to or specifically formulated
such a tactic. Individual cultural targets were not singled out for attacks, but
their safety and their importance was, at the very least, disregarded under
Bomber Command's policy of carpet bombing city centres as a whole: cities
made up of tens of thousands of buildings – cultural, public, private and
industrial, historic and modern – were to be reduced to rubble. It was a campaign against architecture *en masse*. More than this, the British did at times
specifically seek out German towns and cites that had historic cores and so
were particularly susceptible to high explosives and incendiaries. This tendency towards extreme disregard for culture gathered pace towards the end

It was the RAF area-bombing raid on the port of Lübeck that sparked Hitler's fury and the
retaliatory Baedeker blitz. Lübeck's historic core comprised venerable timber buildings, and it
burned furiously in the raid of 28 March 1942. 'Bomber' Harris described the city as 'more like a
fire-lighter than a human habitation'. Around 80 per cent of the old town was destroyed. It was
targeted ahead of industrial works on the outskirts. The raid marked the beginning of the
destructive area-bombing campaign over Germany that wrecked virtually every significant city
in the country.

of the war, but was intimated at an early stage with the bombing of the historic German port of Lübeck at the end of March 1942. The raid marked the start of the RAF area-bombing campaign proper and revealed its later character. Lübeck, the medieval capital of the Hanseatic League, did have some minor industrial and munitions works on its edge but was not considered a potential target by the Germans, so its air defences were minimal. However, Sir Arthur 'Bomber' Harris, who had just been appointed head of Bomber Command, wanted his crews 'blooded' as he had been in Iraq. Lübeck was the chosen quarry. It also, as Harris's town-planning advisers noted, had a dense, combustible core of historic Gothic churches, warehouses and timber merchants' houses. It was, said Harris, 'more like a fire-lighter than a human habitation'.[27] Incendiaries and high explosives dropped by aircraft razed large parts of the Altstadt, which, rather than the peripheral industrial sites, formed the bull's-eye of the target. 312 people died. The raid was light in comparison with what was to come. Lübeck was not chosen because of its architecture and cultural monuments – apart from their merits as fuel. Rather, the town's great historic importance and civilian character was set aside in the interest of destruction for destruction's sake and as a test run for the systematic carpet bombing of Germany's urban centres that culminated in the horrors of 'Operation Gomorrah' (the razing of central Hamburg) and Dresden.

Hitler was furious with the Lübeck raid, an anger compounded by the RAF's bombing of historic Rostock shortly afterwards. 'British barbarians: historic monuments in Rostock bombarded' ran the headline in the *Völkischer Beobachter*.[28] His response to the attacks was to order a series of raids on British historic civilian centres that became known as the Baedeker raids (after the German tourist guidebooks). Goebbels ordered the leafleting of the chosen towns prior to their bombardment with images of destroyed Lübeck and Rostock. Exeter was the first to be hit (23–5 April), followed by Bath (25–6 April), then over the next few days Norwich and York and, some weeks later, Canterbury. Notwithstanding Bath's substantial Georgian swags, all were medieval cities at heart, with cathedrals, ancient churches, guildhalls, castles and plenty of flammable historic buildings in their compact cores for the incendiaries to fire and for blast bombs to split open. The largest fire in Exeter extended at one point for 23 acres across the city centre, destroying the High Street, public buildings and houses. German aircraft machine-gunners opened fire in an effort to hamper fire-fighting. The cathedral close escaped the worst, although not for want of trying: a German bomber circled low over the cathedral before dispatching a bomb that crashed down through its roof, causing enormous damage, shattering glass and choir screens and destroying the thirteenth-century Chapel of St Thomas and St James. Forty acres of the city were destroyed in total.

The pattern was similar in the other target towns. Bath suffered particularly badly, with architectural losses including damage to the Royal Crescent,

Ruins in the Lower Market area of the historic cathedral city of Exeter. Around 40 acres of the city were destroyed by German bombers in the Baedeker air raids of 1942 that targeted English historic cities in revenge for attacks by the RAF on their German equivalents. A combination of high explosives and incendiaries was used to shatter and burn the buildings. The medieval cathedral was damaged but escaped destruction.

the Circus and the Assembly Rooms. York's grand medieval Guildhall was gutted; churches and sites across the city were wrecked. A similar level of damage was seen in Norwich.[29] Thousands of citizens left the target towns each night to sleep more safely in open countryside – more than 10 per cent of Bath's population and a third of Norwich's, according to one report.[30] A Ministry of Home Security official described what he saw in Bath:

> The general impression we obtained was that it had more or less ceased to function as a town in the normal sense. The majority of the people one talks to show signs of having been under severe strain. They seemed faintly nervous and agitated . . . the streets are always full of people walking to and fro although the shops are not properly open and there is nothing in particular for them to do.[31]

This description, and the nightly treks to countryside safety, certainly suggest some level of fear and demoralization, and the attacks on Germany to come were to be much worse. There is no evidence though, from either side of the North Sea, that this demoralization led to defeatism or in anyway affected the outcome of the war despite the devastation caused.

York's 1455 Guildhall was one of the casualties of the April 1942 Baedeker raid on the historic city. It received a direct hit and was burned out. York Minster escaped, but St Martin's Church, the elegant railway station and thousands of houses were damaged or destroyed. The Guildhall was partially reconstructed after the Second World War.

Between the raids on Norwich and Canterbury, Bomber Harris launched his 'Thousand Bomber' raid on Cologne, causing wounds that made the injuries to England's cathedral cities seem like scratches. Cologne's spectacular ecclesiastical heritage, dating back to the tenth century, suffered the first of many mighty blows. Six hundred acres of the city were devastated, putting Exeter's suffering rather in the shade. The German revenge raid on Canterbury came soon after, in scale hardly comparable to Cologne as an eye-for-an-eye target, but convenient for the 80 bombers that the Luftwaffe could assemble. Thousands of incendiaries and high explosives rained down, razing much of the eastern core of Canterbury and threatening the cathedral itself. The tit-for-tat continued with an RAF raid on Bremen, resulting in an immediate response raid on Norwich. Around one thousand incendiaries fell within the cathedral precincts, which seemed to be a particular focus of the bombers, but fire-watchers ensured that the damage was contained. It has been suggested by commentators on both sides that the survival of cathedrals amid seas of devastation reflects a policy of avoidance of targets that would recoup bad publicity. There is no evidence for such a policy. Their survival rate, given the difficulty of accurate targeting from high altitudes, can be put down to both luck and the relative noncombustibility of their massive stone structures.

If anything, the opposite is true. This sequence of raids on historic cities was the start of an open season for the indiscriminate bombing of cultural and civilian centres. Monuments were fair game. Not that this was readily admitted; without valid military targets (and cities and civilians are not legal military targets) both sides were committing war crimes. After Lübeck the British Secretary of State Sir Archibald Sinclair denied in the House of Commons that there had been a change in bombing policy. The German Foreign Office, however, let the Nazi agenda slip out. At a press conference on 27 April 1942, Baron Gustav Braun von Stumm stated: 'Now the Luftwaffe will go for every building that is marked with three stars in the Baedeker.'[32] Goebbels swiftly distanced himself from the remark, which was the origin of a persistent myth that Hitler himself coined the term, guidebook in hand. Instead, rather feeble industrial targets were given as the official reason for the subsequent Baedeker raids. But Goebbels, in his diaries, did not just set aside cultural concerns; privately he sought to target historic monuments, even if official Nazi propaganda suggested otherwise. 'Like the English, we must attack centres of culture', he wrote. 'Such centres should be attacked two or three times in succession and levelled to the ground; then the English probably will no longer find pleasure in trying to frighten us by their terror attacks.'[33] At the same time, propaganda on both sides made much of the damage to their own nation's heritage. 'Many of our most cherished historical buildings were destroyed', ran a British broadcast to Germany justifying the 'Thousand Bomber' raid on Cologne. 'We are bombing Germany, city by city, and even more terribly, in order to make it impossible for you to go on with the war.'[34]

At first the Nazi regime defiantly sought to repair damaged monuments, but as raids intensified both British and German governments devoted more time to laying out hopeful plans for phoenix-like post-war construction of the towns, which would emerge even more beautiful and forward-looking than before. Both sides sought to emphasize the cultural damage inflicted by the other and then concentrate on their own accuracy in hitting solely industrial and military targets. German attempts to play down the extent of damage inflicted by the British earlier in the war were replaced by appeals to stoicism: 'The heart contracts when one stands before the ruins of a venerable monument of culture or history. But everyone in the areas menaced from the air knows that we would lose much if we gave the English the satisfaction of making us bow before their terrorism.'[35] In England, Coventry became the 'Martyred City' and a symbol of the damage to English culture (and, later, of its post-war rebirth).

While, Baedeker raids aside, there is limited evidence to suggest that monuments and historic cities were targeted for their cultural content *per se*, or for the effect on morale of the obliteration of architectural heritage specifically, the loss of these monuments was a consequence of the wider aim of achieving civilian demoralization through carpet-bombing, a methodology pursued by both sides. According to historian Nicola Lambourne, whose book *War Damage in Western Europe* looks closely at the propaganda messages and morale assumptions behind the British and US bombing campaigns, this Allied policy was made explicit in the Casablanca Directive of January 1943. Germany's architectural heritage was not to be spared, no matter how important. As Lambourne points out, lack of concern amounts to a policy in itself.[36]

British assumptions about the effect of the destruction of buildings on morale were in part based on a March 1942 study of the response to the bombing of residential areas in Birmingham and Hull. This used a highly questionable methodology and led to equally questionable assumptions being made. The memorandum advising Churchill on the matter used this evidence to calculate how many people could be made homeless in the principal 58 German towns and cities on the RAF target list – one-third of the German population, it was estimated: 'Having one's home demolished is most damaging to morale . . . there seems little doubt that this would break the spirit of the people.'[37] This statement is revealing of an approach to prosecuting the war that did not seek to avoid damage to housing, but rather to encourage it. Figures for German citizens who were 'de-housed' were included in the British bomb-damage assessments.[38] That there was lowered morale on both sides can hardly be doubted, given the threat to and actual death of loved ones, and the reduction of one's life possessions to rubble; the famous

Blitz spirit, for instance, has been overplayed and mythologized, concealing a great deal of understandable depression and dissatisfaction. Yet the British Cabinet should have been able to see what was happening right under its nose: the image of St Paul's Cathedral, its dome riding high above the smoke of the burning City of London, became emblematic of a spirit of resistance. The *Daily Mail* published Herbert Mason's famous photograph of St Paul's with the caption: 'War's greatest picture'. The dome also features in a 1941 propaganda film with Churchill intoning 'We shall never surrender' over footage of the dome. 'What did St Paul's represent?' asks Angus Calder in *The Myth of the Blitz*, 'English creative genius of course, since the great architect Wren had designed it. Christianity still more obviously, triumphant over neo-paganism. Also, London's metropolitan role – within Britain, within the British Empire.'[39] The image of St Paul's surrounded by fire defines our image of the Blitz to this day, indeed the photograph appeared in newspapers again in the wake of the July 2005 bombings on the London Underground explicity re-awakening the notion of the Blitz spirit. Germans presumably reacted to losses and survivals of their own cherished landmarks in a similar fashion. The precise effect on civilian morale of the loss of a treasured and familiar architectural environment was not researched by Second World War strategists, but there is little evidence that this would have led to an increased level of defeatism, any more than lowered morale from the general depredations would. More recently, Mostar's besieged Muslims may have left the safety of their cellars to mourn the loss of their beloved bridge in the Bosnian war, but it did not shift the front line with Catholic West Mostar an inch.

Nor did the area-bombing campaign have any discernible effect on war-time production, which actually rose. Coventry, Cologne and other cities rebuilt their industrial capacity rapidly. All this notwithstanding whether the plants had even been hit in the first place – even with improved targeting later in the war Bomber Command planes could still be more than 5 km off target. It also assumes that the plants were even aimed at. In his diaries, Bomber Harris later admitted: 'The destruction of factories, which was nevertheless on an enormous scale, could be regarded as a bonus. The aiming points were usually right in the centre of the town.'[40] Harris was keen to hit something, whether it was home, monument or hospital. He repeatedly avoided concentrating on Germany's oil supplies, as he was urged.

The Second World War continued to be prosecuted in this manner even when the British government began to have reservations. The sequence of reprisal Baedeker and RAF raids were just a prelude to the concerted Allied bombing that gave little quarter to culture and reached new levels of ferocity, comprehensively wiping out the centres of the major German cities. At the end of 1943 it was, at long last, suggested that some German cities should be proscribed from attack because they 'possess buildings or works of art of

The *Daily Mail* published Herbert Mason's shot of St Paul's Cathedral surrounded by the smoking, blitzed City of London in December 1940, describing it as 'War's Greatest Picture'. The image represented the defiant survival of imperial, Christian London. The picture was published once again in a British tabloid following terrorist bombings on the London Underground in July 2005.

exceptional historic or aesthetic value. This would appeal to an important section of public opinion which is concerned about the destruction of such monuments in the bomber offensive.'[41] The proposal was dismissed. The distinguished military thinker Major-General J.F.C. Fuller wrote an article for the *Evening Standard*, arguing against the bombing campaign: 'The worst devastations of the Goths, Vandals, Huns, Seljuks and Mongols pale into insignificance when compared to the material and moral damage now wrought.' It was never published.[42] British raids levelled dozens more German towns and cities: 'England's Assassination Attempt on European Culture' is how one German newspaper reported a further raid on Cologne in June 1943 that damaged the cathedral.[43] By this point, 200,000 tonnes of bombs had been dropped on German cities and around 26,000 acres of urban Germany had been razed.

In late July and early August the 'Operation Gomorrah' raids against Hamburg (pointedly named, as Lambourne also notes) devastated the city; more than 40,000 died and around 22 sq km were razed. One million citizens were forced out of their homes: '40,385 houses, 275,000 flats, 580 factories, 2,632 shops, 277 schools, 24 hospitals, 58 churches, 83 banks, 12 bridges, 76 public buildings and a zoo had been obliterated.'[44] People were turned to ash, or their bodies swelled up and exploded in temperatures that passed 1,000°C. Tarmac roads melted, trapping human torches as they attempted to escape. Thousands choked to death as air was sucked into the firestorm at 240 km/h.

Heavy raids on Berlin left huge areas of that city flattened too. The historic buildings, galleries, museums and government buildings along and around Unter den Linden, at the imperial heart of the capital, were destroyed or severely damaged. In *Bomber Command*, Max Hastings notes a report by Allied Air Staff Intelligence that imagined how a British newspaper might have reported damage of a similar scale on London:

> Government buildings have suffered severely. The Treasury is largely destroyed and the Foreign Office partially gutted. Scotland Yard is a soot-blackened ruin and so is the Ministry of Transport. The Cabinet Offices at No. 10 Downing Street are roofless, and fire has destroyed half of No. 11. Many other well-known landmarks in central London have disappeared. The British Museum Library and University buildings have been damaged. The Albert Hall and Drury Lane Theatre are smouldering wrecks. Big office blocks like Shell-Mex House and Bush House have been burnt out. The Ritz Hotel is no more, and fire has damaged part of the Savoy. The Café Royal is gutted from roof to basement . . . Railway stations everywhere are besieged by crowds of evacuees, but many of them are so badly damaged that few trains, or none at all, are able to leave . . . It is difficult to imagine devastation on such a scale in a modern capital.[45]

It is hard not to read a note of glee in this fantasy report, a morbid fascination at the scale of destruction that man can wreak on history. The grief for the disappearance of the venerable and monumental, if it had been visited on London, would have been deep, but at this stage of the war the Luftwaffe was incapable of launching such devastating strikes. Berlin was visited by the bombers and it is hard to accept that the damage was incidental to the targeting of military or industrial sites, most of which remained working until nearly the war's end. There is *Schadenfreude* here at Berlin's physical ruin. A triumphant and vindictive vandalism.

More raids were to come both in Europe and in Japan, where US air raids caused devastating firestorms that engulfed Tokyo and other urban centres, killing hundreds of thousands of people. Around 80 per cent of all bomb tonnage hitting Germany was dropped in 1945. In Germany, Dresden was the major casualty of these later attacks. The city was a cultural centre of world importance. It had very few military or industrial targets to speak of, despite a briefing note to the contrary prepared by Bomber Command before the raid, which described it as 'an industrial city of first-class importance'.[46] The 'Florence on the Elbe' suffered Hamburg's fate on 13 February 1945. The Baroque city with its palaces, churches and museums was in ruins.

Its Protestant cathedral, the Frauenkirche, remained standing briefly before crumbling into rubble, the result of its stones being baked in the firestorm unleashed by the raids. The rationale for the attack on Dresden remains unclear. Two reasons given were that it was 'the largest un-bombed built-up area the enemy has got', and that the attack was seen as a way of sowing confusion behind the retreating German front line in the face of the Russian advance.[47] Neither is a convincing reason for levelling a cultural treasure house packed with refugees; flame-throwers had to be used to scour its cellars of body parts. The railway yards, a legitimate infrastructure target, mostly remained intact. Estimates of the number who died have been used for political purposes ever since, beginning with Goebbels, who immediately inflated the figures – as does the German far right today. Recently, historian Frederick Taylor, who contends that the city's military and industrial impor- tance to the Nazis has been downplayed, has put a more realistic estimate at between 25,000 and 40,000 lives.[48] Destruction of this intensity and scale had never been seen before the Second World War. This was now urbicide, the murder of a city and its citizens in a continuing campaign of terror. The road to Hamburg, Dresden and, ultimately, Hiroshima followed this blighted logic. The widespread destruction of the man-made environment gives the *appearance* of winning a war even without any evidence to support this view.

With Bomber Command's first- and second-tier targets now in ruins (20 cities had been 'virtually destroyed', including Hanover, Munich and Cologne, and almost as many 'seriously damaged', including Berlin, Frankfurt, Nuremberg and Bremen), the RAF and USAAF were in danger of blasting rubble into rubble with repeat raids, so towards the end of the war a third tier of target towns was pounded, and in the month after Dresden, the Allies dropped more bombs over Germany than they had in the whole of 1942.[49] Like Lübeck, these later targets were often chosen for their combustibility, that is, they had historic cores. By this point damage to architectural heritage was not incidental but inherent to the strategy – even if unacknowledged or recognized as such. A BBC *Timewatch* documentary in 2001 used newly unearthed documents from the Public Record Office to show that the RAF had chosen 'burnable' towns with 'structural features' that were 'suitable or otherwise for fire attack'; these features included dense narrow streets and old buildings with combustible materials.[50] Among the casualties was the perfectly preserved Baroque cathedral town of Würzburg in Bavaria. One thousand tonnes of bombs were dropped in seventeen minutes on the night of 16–17 March. As with other later raids, a high percentage of this tonnage was incendiaries. More than 82 per cent of its historic buildings were destroyed. The city had no industrial or military targets to speak of.[51]

Less than two weeks later the area bombing campaign ended. Outrage over Dresden appeared to bring Churchill to his senses: 'The moment has come', he wrote, 'when the question of bombing German cities simply for the sake of increasing terror, though under other pretexts, should be reviewed. Otherwise we shall come into control of an utterly ruined land . . . the destruction of Dresden remains a serious query against the conduct of Allied bombing.'[52] In destroying Dresden, a city of delicacy, music and architecture, porcelain and art, the Allies had launched an assault on their own cultural selves. The gains won by causing terror, if any existed, were outweighed by the loss to the British sense of self as a cultivated people steeped in a European art tradition. 'Dresden was a city which an important section of educated Englishmen had heard of, read about, visited', wrote Hastings. 'Urgent questions were asked by important people about the reasons for destroying the city.'[53] The bombers were sending the wrong message.

Damage to an ethnic or national group's patrimony by an enemy has its own propaganda value, as both sides in the Second World War were aware. In recent conflicts, further appeals have been made to international opinion in order to paint the foe as barbarians, vandals or Hun (the language is centuries old), and their cause and methods as uncivilized. The complainant can then claim victim status and appeal for support against the aggressor. The destruction in the former Yugoslavia took this war of words over architecture to new levels, with various sides preparing reports mid-war and issuing press releases and statements on the web about the cultural destruction of their own built heritage by the other side. A report prepared for the Council of Europe in January 1994, *War Damage to the Cultural Heritage in Croatia and Bosnia-Herzegovina*,[54] is unusually lucid in its awareness of such agendas. It examines the cultural cleansing of the on-going war, drawing on a number of reports prepared by Bosnian, Croatian and Serbian sources, including national heritage institutes and the Serbian Orthodox Church. Some confusion regarding the extent of damage is inevitable, given the difficulties of fieldwork in a war zone, but beyond this the often partisan accounts of destruction had to be examined carefully for exaggeration, omissions and outright lies. The Council of Europe document notes the 'propagandistic purposes' of the Serbian and Croat documents, which, in addition to setting out the very real and widespread damage to their own patrimonies, attempt to shift blame for cultural outrages or are a repost to charges of cultural cleansing laid against themselves. A report by the Serbian Ministry of Culture describes the fate of Serbian Orthodox religious architecture in Croatia (the 'products of Serbian genius'). The opening words make its agenda clear:

> The present annihilation of cultural landmarks, Serbian Orthodox churches, in the territory of the Republic of Croatia is a continuation of the vandalism that lasted from 1941 to 1945 in the independent State of Croatia. Its basic goal was then and remains today the

destruction and assimilation of the Serbian people in the north-western region of Yugoslavia.[55]

Only the report by the Sarajevo-based Institute for the Protection of Cultural, Historical and Natural Heritage of Bosnia-Herzegovina mentions the destruction to the architectural legacy of all sides – Bosnian, Croat and Serbian.[56] It reflects the continuing Sarajevan commitment to multi-ethnicity; their cultural self-identity as Bosnians depended on preserving this cosmopolitanism, as expressed in the country's architectural pluralism.

A similar propaganda war developed when the conflict expanded into Kosovo, with both sides, Serbs and Kosovars, making sweeping claims regarding the extent of deliberate damage and cultural cleansing. The Serbian government and the Serbian Orthodox Church maintain websites that go further in charging NATO air attacks with causing enormous destruction to the churches and monasteries of their religious heartland. This damage was widely reported in the media internationally. Careful post-war research by Harvard University academics Andrew Herscher and András Riedlmayer nailed many of the lies, while making an objective assessment of the very real and extensive damage to mosques, churches, archives and vernacular buildings made by forces on the ground.[57] Two Ottoman bridges supposedly destroyed by NATO, for example, were in fact intact. Major damage to the Roman Catholic church of St Anthony in Gjakova, reportedly bombed by NATO, was actually committed by Serbian soldiers. The Memorial Museum of the League of Prizren was not destroyed by a 'NATO missile' but by Serbian police in March 1999 using rifle-propelled grenades.[58] Although the priceless Serbian Orthodox heritage of Kosovo was damaged during the Kosovo conflict and after (and Serbia itself did indeed lose some buildings to NATO raids), it is the Muslim heritage, as in Bosnia, that was devastated by the war. A third of Kosovo's historic mosques were destroyed or damaged, as were 90 per cent of the traditional *kulla* (stone tower-houses), as part of the Serbian campaign of ethnic cleansing that followed the pattern set in Bosnia, and made worse by the efficiency lessons learned there. The destruction of Kosovo's non-Serb architectural heritage was a planned and methodical element of ethnic cleansing.[59]

The shelling of Dubrovnik in 1991 was an instance where any benefit to the attackers resulting from the terror caused and cultural destruction wreaked was certainly outweighed by the international reaction to the siege. The attack on the city by the Serbian-controlled JNA and Montenegrin reservists provoked disgust world-wide. Dubrovnik has been celebrated for centuries for its beauty, its qualities recognized by its UNESCO World Heritage site designation. It had no military significance; nor did the Serbs have any credible historical claim to it (although they did suggest at one point in the war that its future, in a Serbian context, was akin to a city-state like Monaco). Suggestions that Serbia coveted Dubrovnik for its access to the sea are not entirely convincing, although I was told by one local architect, Marija Koyakovitch, that before the war she had been working in the city's 800-year-old archives at the same time as Serbian researchers looking for evidence that Ragusa was once part of Serbia.[60] In short, the bombardment by artillery from the escarpment above the city and from gunboats cruising beyond its mighty walls remains largely inexplicable, except in terms of a desire to terrorize and vandalize. The UN, the EU and the Western media responded vigorously to the shelling, recognizing it immediately as an attack on the world's collective architectural patrimony and calling for an end to the shelling: 'Like the Barbarian Hordes Advancing on Rome, the Federal Forces Have Abandoned All Restraint', thundered the front-page of London's *Daily Telegraph*.[61] This was a rare recent instance, along with the destruction of the Bamiyan Buddhas by the Taliban, of a cultural threat having such resonance. But then a Western audience would have been familiar with Dubrovnik's Renaissance perfection. The relatively low-key response to the destruction of Balkan Islamic heritage can be put down to a deep-seated cultural myopia, or even hostility, towards Islamic culture. The shelling of Dubrovnik was an enormous mistake for Serb propagandists.

Croatia's cultural defenders did rather better in the propaganda war because, while damage to Islamic monuments across Bosnia and Kosovo has been catastrophic, Dubrovnik itself escaped relatively unscathed. This was largely due to the failure of the besieging forces to occupy the city, whereas almost every monument and whole settlements in Dubrovnik's architecturally splendid hinterland were comprehensively burnt out or blown to pieces at close quarters by occupying Serb forces. From the outcry, the outsider was under the impression that the Old City was utterly in ruins. This, however, was not the case. Many of its tiled roofs were blasted apart, nine splendid historic town houses were burnt out, and many important buildings suffered shell damage to bell-towers, cloisters and the like, but no key monument was either entirely destroyed or severely and irreversibly damaged.

It was still terrible. During one continuous eight-day bombardment Marija Koyakovitch was sheltering in a garage in the suburb of Lapad, with steel sheets and filing cabinets pushed in front of the windows: 'I got seasick sitting on the floor, which was trembling from the shelling,' she says. There were 40,000 people in the city at the time, many refugees from the surrounding gutted villages. 'Of course, the priority is life – people not monuments', continues Koyakovitch, 'but when St Blaise Cathedral was shelled, tears came without my will.' The situation worsened with a heavy barrage on 6 December 1991. 'It was minus seven degrees, which was very unusual. In the evening, the radio called on inhabitants to fight the fire with bucket chains from the sea. It was the hardest battle of the war and we were worried about a fire-storm and losing the town.'

The shelling of Dubrovnik in late 1991 by the Serb-led JNA and Montenegrin reservists caused international outrage. The damage within the Croatian walled city was relatively light compared to the comprehensive destruction of monuments taking place in its architecturally rich hinterland and in nearby Mostar and Stolac. The city's familiarity to Western tourists and art historians, however, made its bombardment an instant *cause célèbre*.

'They particularly targeted monuments,' argues Koyakovitch. 'The Franciscan monastery got 56 hits and the houses nearby were hardly damaged. All the church belfries and the dome of the cathedral were shelled. We were crying, it was like your heart was wounded. It was the saddest day of my life.'[62]

While the world should be grateful that the Serb offensive was not worse and that the old city remained unoccupied, the threat to Dubrovnik and other reports of the damage suffered (more exaggerated than Koyakovitch's precise recollection) were accepted without question and without the often somewhat cautious damage assessment that Bosnian and Kosovar heritage has endured. In one report to the UN Security Council it was argued that the Serb shelling was knowingly concentrated on the part of the historic core of the city that was most vulnerable to collapse as a consequence of the 1979 earthquake.[63] There is no evidence to support this claim and it was not queried.

It is hard not to detect a degree of indifference to the architectural record outside the Western canon in comparison to an instinctive defence of that within.

Croatian writers describing the shelling of Dubrovnik certainly invoke the historic schism between East and West running through the Balkans. In *Dubrovnik at War*, a collection of writings published at the time, a number of authors looking for an explanation for the assault attribute the Serbian and

Montenegrin attack to the machinations of an envious and ignorant Orient:[64]

> The root of their hatred lies in the desperation, envy and bitterness which they feel towards shape, purity and beauty which is not theirs . . . A dirty man cannot tolerate cleanliness. (Božidar Violić)

> We knew that only wisdom and caution would enable us to confront Byzantine perfidy in order that the Western tradition of European civilization could be preserved. (Hrvoje Kačić)

> The ruthless and primitive Serbian army, asiatically [*sic*] cruel, communist, indoctrinated, wildly fanatical in their Orthodoxy and displaying Levantine duplicity . . . In contrast to the obscure Balkan market towns and brigands' holes, Dubrovnik was an ideal city. (Igor Zidić)[65]

Levantine? Byzantine? The Croats speak of the Slavic Serbs in terms the Serbs reserve for Bosnian Muslims and Kosovars. The denigration of the East lurking in many areas of Western thought comes to the fore when one's heritage is being bombarded and the others inexplicable behaviour needs explaining. There is certainly an element of urbicide in the attack on Dubrovnik – an atavistic, anti-urban, anti-cosmopolitanism, especially among the irregular troops from the countryside – but none of this is justification for the racism directed towards the 'Asiatic' peoples eastwards.

Parallels to such racist and xenophobic propaganda may be found in the arguments over barbarity and civilized standards in the air war of the Second World War discussed above and the disputes over German damage to French monuments (Reims Cathedral especially) in the First World War. As the art historian Dario Gamboni writes in his excellent study of iconoclasm in the fine and applied arts: 'During the First World War the ethno-historical connotations of the concept of "vandalism" were exploited to the full and German aggression was defined by the French as an attempt on the part of the "Teutonic barbarian" to annihilate "Latin civilization".'[66]

It is as if there is a deeply embedded cultural memory of a threat to Western European cities and civic values from hordes from the East. Wrapped up in this is an implicit hierarchy of cultural value illustrated by the fate of architecture worth targeting or worth protecting in conflict. It can be seen in the fate of architectural monuments in the Balkans and it could be seen in the attitude of the warring parties in the Second World War. Germany and England blitzed each other and the Allies caused terrible damage in their reconquest of northern France (which each nation has politely glossed over). When it came to clashes in Italy, however, much more care was taken. Allied veneration of Italian culture, especially the architectural heritage of the Renaissance and Baroque periods that was brought north by the Grand Tourists, ensured that the destruction of architecture in Italy was light in comparison to other battle fronts. Carpet-bombing was not a tactic here. There were significant architectural casualties in the historic centres of Pisa, Vicenza, Verona and Milan, and cultural vandalism by retreating German troops around Naples. But the razing of Montecassino and the accidental bombing of the Eremitani Church and its Mantegnas in Padua were made infamous by their exceptional nature. Fascist Italy may have declared the Allied campaign 'The War against Art' but, for the most part, the country's architectural treasures survived the war.[67] Rome was declared an open city and Venice completely bypassed by both sides in the conflict. Florence, too, escaped with not much more lost than some bridges. This strategy of protection was no accident – Eisenhower issued an order to all commanders in the field:

> Today we are fighting in a country which has contributed a great deal to our cultural inheritance, a country rich in monuments which by their creation helped, and now in their old age illustrate, the growth of the civilisation which is ours. We are bound to respect those monuments as far as war allows.[68]

Khachig Tololyan's concept of the cultural self could not be illustrated more clearly. What is valued is cherished, even sometimes by an enemy state if there is a conscious, shared cultural self. Conversely, sometimes it is this very understanding of the importance of, say, Dubrovnik or Canterbury to a nation's cultural self that has made these cities such choice targets to their enemies. It is, after all, why the World Trade Center made such a perfect target. Now, despite having possessed only a modicum of intrinsic architectural value, the Twin Towers have joined Dresden and Mostar Bridge as an icon of civilization's achievements laid low.

Dubrovnik's outraged writers may have had a point, though, when it comes to envy as being a motor of destruction; like a spurned lover shredding their partner's wardrobe, what one cannot possess can at least be destroyed. Envy and revenge are among the most deadly of motivations and very nearly led to the wholesale flattening of Paris in August 1944. When German forces were forced to retreat, Hitler ordered that the city must not fall into enemy hands: 'Or, if it does, he must find there is nothing but a field of ruins.'[69] The Führer had visited the city briefly in 1940 and for a few hours toured its monuments, including his favourite building, Garnier's Opera House. He had mused on the destruction of Paris even then, despite his appreciation of its beauty, but decided that the grandiose remodelling of Berlin would, anyway, put Paris in the shade. When he could no longer possess it as part of the Greater Germany's cultural treasures, he ordered it defended to the last man despite the inevitable cost to its heritage. When that proved unfeasible, he ordered the destruction of its monuments and the razing of whole quarters.

Among the buildings to be mined with explosives were the Eiffel Tower (the 'symbol of Paris', acknowledged Hitler), the Arc de Triomphe, Notre Dame, the Palais de Luxembourg, Les Invalides, the historic Seine bridges and twenty acres of monuments and streets around the Place de la Concorde. Even the Opera House was not to escape Hitler's pique. The rest was to be bombed by the Luftwaffe and v2 rockets. It was only the disobedience of his commander in Paris, Dietrich von Choltitz, that saved the city. He was an unlikely saviour, having presided over the destruction of Rotterdam and other cities: 'Since Sebastopol', he once said, 'it has been my fate to cover the retreat of our armies and to destroy the cities behind them.' This time, however, he grasped the enormity of the deed: 'We have the whole world watching us here, not just a handful of generals.'[70] Hitler was not one to care much about bad press. The obliteration of Paris would (in addition to being an unprecedented act of vengeance against architecture) have served as an enormous demonstration of ruthlessness, in much the same way as Bomber Harris and Churchill viewed Operation Gomorrah and the 'Thousand Bomber' raid on Cologne. The consequences of acts of destruction for the propaganda war, however, have to be carefully measured, as Churchill discovered in the wake of Dresden.

With tv and communication technology now relaying the conduct of a war around the world almost as it happens, images of conflicts can be defining – and not always in the interests of the aggressor. Vietnam is still summed up by Nick Ut's photograph of a naked, napalmed Vietnamese child running screaming down a road, and Bosnia by, among other incidents, the fall of Mostar Bridge. The messages sent by violent acts now affect not only the combatants on both sides but world opinion – and the right points need to be made. The attack on Baghdad in the second Gulf war began with George W. Bush's 'shock and awe' curtain-raiser, which as well as having the practical aim of bombing military installations and Saddam Hussein's palaces and ministries (the latter more useful as symbols of his power than being operationally significant) appeared designed to terrify Iraqis and leave them, and indeed the rest of the world, with the message that American military power is to be trembled at. Area bombing, while it still occurs, is no longer considered an acceptable means of waging war. Civilian body counts can undermine the legitimacy of a cause: hence the stress in Iraq on 'precision', 'surgical strikes', 'smart' bombs and avoiding 'collateral damage', even though the metaphorical language aims to obfuscate rather than illuminate. With its shaky Coalition, a hostile Arab world at hand and, crucially, the need to win the hearts and minds of Iraqis, the US invasion of Iraq has been accompanied by a need to be seen to be limiting attacks to purely military objectives – the invaders as liberators rather than conquerors.

The reality, still unfolding at the time of writing, is more complex but it is amply clear that the US has singularly failed to keep the Iraqis or world opinion on message. This is despite some determined efforts. One of the first acts of Baghdad's occupying forces was an irresistible piece of iconoclasm, the toppling of a large bronze statue of Saddam Hussein in Paradise Square on 9 April 2003. Closely cropped TV pictures gave the impression of a huge crowd of jubilant Iraqis engaged in an act of spontaneous pedestal-cleansing, assisted by US soldiers who helped put a noose around Saddam's neck and then pull the statue to the ground, where cheering Iraqi onlookers beat it with their shoes. A US marine attempted to hood the statue with a triumphal Stars and Stripes before it was hastily replaced with an Iraqi flag. There is no doubting the desire of most Iraqis to be free of Saddam Hussein, but in reality the events, even if initiated by Iraqis, were carefully choreographed; the vast square had been cordoned off by the US military for the exercise and there were at most 150 people in the square (including Marines and reporters) rather than the several hundred reported by outfits such as Fox News.[71] The scene prodded at the memory of media images of the fall of the Berlin Wall and the stone Lenins of the Eastern Bloc. US mechanized

The toppling of the Statue of Saddam Hussein in Paradise Square, Baghdad, on 9 April 2003 was a carefully orchestrated media event carried out with the assistance of the 3rd Battalion of the US army's 4th Marines. It echoed the tearing down of statues across Eastern Europe after 1989 with the fall of its Stalinist regimes, and had enormous propaganda value.

units continued to topple more statues and bulldoze giant portraits of the dictator across the country.

Toppling effigies of dubious aesthetic value and recent origin is one thing, but the destruction of Iraqi built heritage is a different matter; the country's ancient cities, historic mosques, museums, libraries and other monuments have all been put at enormous risk by the invasion. Iraq has a built record of human activity going back 8,000 years, scattered across thousands of archaeological sites in Mesopotamia. These are architectural treasures of global significance, the oft-quoted 'cradle of civilization'. As in Italy during the Second World War, there was obviously some regard to this collective cultural heritage of the Western and Arab world in the formulation of US invasion plans. But it was not enough. During preparations for the 2003 war on Iraq, US military planners identified 150 important archaeological sites to be avoided. US archaeologists responded with a list of 4,000 vital locations – a degree of 'duty of protection' that the Pentagon rejected despite international law demanding it.[72] The chaos after the fall of Baghdad saw the priceless collections of the National Library and Archives and the library of Korans at the Ministry of Religious Endowment go up in flames and the Museum of Archaeology ransacked. The US forces did not seek to prevent the destruction here and elsewhere, despite being implored to do so.[73] Instead of protecting these sites, one of the few buildings in Baghdad the US chose to guard was the Oil Ministry.

Saddam Hussein may have been highly selective and ideologically driven in his much vaunted protection of Iraq's ancient history, and looting occurred under his rule, but since his fall archaeological sites throughout the country have been damaged and looted at an alarming rate and many important provincial museums have also been robbed.[74] The US military presence is itself causing damage. Helicopter movements at a US base at the site of ancient Babylon have caused the collapse of a wall of the Temple of Nabu and the roof of the Temple of Ninmah, according to Zainab Bahrani, professor of Ancient Near Eastern art history and archaeology at Columbia University, who visited the site.[75] A more recent report by John Curtis of the British Museum has revealed further damage at Babylon, both deliberate and unthinking, including attempts to prise decorative bricks from the Ishtar Gate and the use of thousands of tonnes of archaeological material to fill sandbags and mesh crates.[76] Coalition forces have now handed back control of the site to the Iraqi authorities, but this has not ended the recklessness with which the country's cultural heritage has been handled. In late 2004, for example, US army snipers were positioned at the top of the great spiral minaret of the ninth-century al-Mutawakkil mosque at Samarra', drawing fire from insurgents who had previously occupied the tower, according to US military sources. This is a gross violation of international law regarding the military use of historic sites committed by both sides in the conflict.[77]

America's awareness of Iraq's contribution to its cultural self has not been comparable to Eisenhower's strong sense of the centrality of Italy's art treasures to Western culture. Instead it appears to have been diluted by several millennia of distance from the Mesopotamian past and a contemporary ignorance and disdain for the overlaying cultural achievements of the Islamic world.

Only in Najaf have the US forces been notably circumspect about protecting or avoiding further damage to the country's material culture. Despite the pressing demand to rout the rebellious Mahdi Army holed up within the turquoise-tiled walls of the Imam Ali shrine in the summer of 2004, the effect on Iraqi and wider Arab public opinion if US troops attacked and damaged Shi'a Islam's holiest shrine was not to be countenanced. A stand-off ensued that echoes the Israeli army's reluctance to attack Palestinian militants who sought sanctuary in Bethlehem's Church of the Nativity. Both sides knew that unacceptably sacrilegious messages would be sent out of Najaf if the Imam Ali shrine's sacred architecture were defiled. Responsibility for even very minor damage to its golden domes and tiled walls during the siege was passed from attacker to defender and vice versa.[78] The iconic status of the shrine protected it, but the wider Old City did not enjoy the same immunity despite its holy status. Mosques, khans, markets, catacombs and other historic buildings, including tombs and monuments in its important cemetery, were wrecked in the battle.[79]

It is hard to overestimate the importance of Iraq's heritage to the world, and it is incredible that the US forces have caused such damage across the country, through their own actions and, more so, by their inaction. To paraphrase Osama bin Laden, hypocrisy is indeed the Hubal of the age. This is the real message to be taken from both the Mahdi Army's provocative and sacrilegious occupation of the Imam Ali shrine and the US military record with regard to cultural protection in Iraq.

4 Conquest and Revolution

And on the pedestal these words appear:
'My name is Ozymandias, king of kings:
Look on my works, ye Mighty, and despair!'
Nothing beside remains . . .

PERCY BYSSHE SHELLEY, 'OZYMANDIAS'

When the German blitzkrieg that began on 1 September 1939 rolled over Poland and met the Soviet army advancing from the East, the jaws of Nazism and Stalinism snapped shut and tore the country to pieces. It was here in occupied Poland that the racist ideology and territorial ambitions of the Nazis came together in an obscene and brutal experiment. Almost one in five Poles died – half of them Jews – and its territory became the killing fields for the whole of the Third Reich. Under the hierarchy of oppression developed by the Nazis, the Jews were to be eliminated and the Polish population, suitably depleted by massacre and starvation, was to become a slave race. These slaves were to be *Untermenschen* with no education, no language, no intellectual life and certainly no monuments. Its former capital, Warsaw, was slated for eradication under a campaign of erasure against Polish material culture. The task was not just to deprive the Poles of a future but to suppress their memory of a different, independently spirited past. They were to be ignoble savages. Conquest, if it is to become a permanent state, needs at the very least acquiescence by the conquered. But this in itself may be dangerously insufficient. If the takeover is hostile, subjugation to the new master is essential. Simply disarming and policing matters only at the point immediately post-conquest. If hearts and minds cannot be won they must be broken; defeat must be a state of being not solely a military outcome.

In the wake of Columbus, Spain's conquistadors brought their priests to the New World to undertake this task. To ensure that there was no backsliding into dreams of previous glory or lapses into old religions, the treasures and relics of that previous world were trodden underfoot and any reminders buried. Monuments were razed, languages stifled and traditions killed. Conquerors in the twentieth century were no less crude, especially where, as in the conquest of the New World, territorial acquisitiveness has been coupled with ideological zeal. The Nazis' enslavement of the Poles, the despoliation of Slavic Eastern Europe in the wake of Operation Barbarossa and the annexation of Tibet by China are vivid instances of this tendency. Although in no way comparable to the genocidal crimes of the Nazis or the murderous Sinofication of Tibet, the transformation of British Mandate Palestine into the State of Israel has betrayed a similar desire to make its conquests permanent and irreversible at the expense of the existing inhabitants of the land.

One concept all these campaigns have shared is the use of architecture as a weapon, in particular the destruction of indigenous architecture as a means to reorder newly won lands. Polish, Russian, Ukrainian, Palestinian and Tibetan built heritage have all borne the brunt of the desire to tear down the previous cultural edifice and build anew. The architectural record of cities such as Warsaw, Lhasa and Jerusalem has been reshaped by conquerors at great cost to their built fabric. Cities such as Beijing, Moscow and Bucharest, on the other hand, have suffered at the hands of conquerors from within, their historic buildings decimated by revolutionary zeal in the wake of the victory of one establishment over another. Under liberal democracy, capitalist cities too have had their faces transformed by demolition and development in the interests of the powerful or in the name of modernity, but destruction for destruction's sake has, in the late twentieth century, been far more rare in democratic states than under Stalinism, Maoism or Nazism. It is the violence of the totalitarian vision, both in its ends and the thoroughness of its means, that created what was a storm of conflict for architecture when compared to the milder climate in the West.

The Nazis had no interest in the hearts and minds of those living to their east; this was apparent from the very outset of their invasion of Poland: the savagery of total war was not simply military in its intent. During the invasion residential areas were unnecessarily levelled, monuments destroyed, museums sacked and Warsaw savaged. Occupation proved more destructive still. Poland had vanished and Poles *as Poles*, a people with a collective identity and history, were marked for oblivion. Poland could see the threat before the war – valuable art collections were moved and moved again, bricked up in cellars and evacuated out of the country altogether. Churches, synagogues, monasteries and museums hid their priceless artefacts. Many of the hiding places were discovered and the Nazis began methodically looting the country of any art treasures they valued, before destroying the little that was left.

After the conquest, the regions of Poland now under German control were divided up into those to be annexed directly into the Reich, other regions set to become Germanized provinces, and the *Generalgouvernement* centred on Kraków – the zone where Poles, as migrant and seasonal work fodder for the Reich, were to live a basic existence. A campaign of genocide and cultural cleansing was instituted to reflect these new boundaries. Poles were to be forcibly resettled into the *Generalgouvernement* – apart from the few designated as ethnic Germans by the bogus virtue of their racial characteristics. Otherwise it was the land and its history that were to be Germanized, not the people – who were disposable.[1] All over the country Polish architecture and monuments were destroyed and Polish homes and businesses handed over to incoming ethnic Germans from other parts of the Reich. Those monuments the Nazis deemed to have Germanic antecedents were spared. Kraków, where the Nazis perceived Germanic characteristics in its medieval monuments, was particularly fortunate in this regard. The German academic Dagobert Frey, who provided a good deal of the skewed rationale for this Germanification of Polish architectural history, described Kraków as 'an Eastern outpost of Nuremberg art', and published the volume *German Architecture in Poland* expounding his theories. Even those monuments attributed to the German 'cultural tradition' did not always escape vandalism or plunder. The vast Veit Stoss carved altarpiece from Kraków's church of St Mary, for instance, was shipped off to Nuremberg on a specially built railcar.[2]

Warsaw was especially singled out for destructive attention. The capital had, in Nazi eyes, no future as a Polish city and it was steadily reduced to rubble. The initial invasion killed some 40,000 Varsovians and destroyed some 12 per cent of the city. Following occupation, Polish conservators attempting repairs to the bomb-damaged Warsaw Castle were dismissed and it was stripped of its internal fittings using forced Jewish labour. Its painted ceilings were torn down and the panelling removed. The remaining shell was drilled to take the explosives that were eventually to blow it apart. Monuments and statues to poets, composers and national heroes, including the giant monument to Chopin and the revered figure of King Sigismund in Castle Square, were torn down. Chopin was cut up and carted away.[3]

At the same time the round up of Jews and other citizens began, with many Poles being transferred for slave labour to Germany or, with the Jews, directly to work and death camps in Poland. In 1940 the Jewish Ghetto in Warsaw was created (see chapter Two) and the mass murder of Polish intellectuals (doctors, lawyers, teachers, artists and writers), the clergy and the nobility gathered pace. Anybody who had a role in the perpetuation of Polish culture or could be looked to as a potential community leader was in danger. Thousands were shot in the Palmiry Forest outside the capital and many more died in Auschwitz. A report from one Polish diocese, Poznań-Gniezno, found that only 31 of its 505 churches and chapels remained open. Many had been converted into farm buildings, warehouses or dancehalls.[4] In the *Generalgouvernement* a limited Polish 'culture' was to be allowed under the new regime: '[It is necessary to satisfy] a primitive need for entertainment and amusement: Operettas, light comedy . . .', but no art exhibitions, and no classical music, folk or patriotic songs could be performed.[5]

The German decision not to rebuild the half-ruined Warsaw was taken formally in October 1939. A team of Nazi town planners, based in Würzburg and headed by Friedrich Pabst, drew up a series of plans to build a small German garrison town on the rubble of the Polish capital – 'die Neue Deutsche Stadt'.[6] It would have only 5 per cent of the land area and 10 per cent of the population of the pre-war city of 1.3 million. Only a few select existing buildings would remain for German use. On the opposite side of the Vistula would be a slave camp for 80,000 Poles. Changing war priorities gained Warsaw a temporary reprieve, broken first by the destruction of the Jewish Ghetto in 1943. The following year, however, with Soviet troops pushing back German forces in the East, the Warsaw Uprising broke out on 1 August 1944 with the aim of liberating the city. The Soviets halted their advance and failed to intervene as the Nazis implemented their plan for razing Warsaw to the ground. Hans Frank, gauleiter of the *Generalgouvernement*, wrote in his diary: 'Warsaw will get what it deserves – complete annihilation.'[7] Himmler was of a similar mind: 'Warsaw, the capital city, the brain, the intelligence of this Polish nation, will have been obliterated.'[8] The systematic destruction of 700 years of architectural history began. Special annihilation detachments, the Vernichtungs-Kommandos, were set up to demolish the city street by street. Trees and telegraph poles were felled; mains, drains and tram tracks uprooted. Himmler gave orders to kill the remaining inhabitants, men, women and children. More than 250,000 people died.

Of the official pre-war list of 957 historic monuments in Warsaw, 782 were completely demolished and another 141 were partly destroyed. Only 34 survived because the Germans did not have time to set the charges once the Soviet advance resumed. When the fighting was over, even the course of street upon street in the old city could barely be traced. The most historic and aesthetically important buildings were burned or dynamited. Among the monumental losses were the national archives and national library, St John's Cathedral, the churches of St Jacek and Holy Trinity, Długa Street, and many more. Palaces destroyed included the Branicki, the Krasiński, the Radziwiłł and the Lazieński. The Treasury and the University, which had continued to operate underground, also fell, but the National Museum, which had been badly damaged during the German invasion, escaped the worst.[9] The Old Town, dating from the 1300s, and the fifteenth-century New Town, with all their medieval, Baroque and Neoclassical glories, were rubble and ashes. In December 1944 the ruined castle was finally blown to pieces. Of 3,708 million cubic feet of buildings in the city, 2,600 million had vanished. Warsaw's citizens had fought for their city and their culture and lost spectacularly. 'You may think I am a fearful barbarian,' said Himmler. 'If you like, I am one if I have to be. My orders were to burn down and blow up every block of houses. As a result, one of the biggest abscesses on the Eastern Front has been removed.'[10]

Had the Nazis not been defeated in 1945, there is no doubt that little of Poland's superb architectural legacy would today remain in any part of the country – apart from the occasional monument, suitably Germanified, in a sea of Teutonic redevelopment for ethnic Germans. This is precisely what has happened in Tibet, where, in the face of determined Sinofication, the barest scrapings of a culture more than a millennium old is clinging to the mountainsides.

When Chairman Mao's People's Liberation Army (PLA) marched across the border into Tibet on 7 October 1950 there were more than 6,000 monasteries across the theocratic state. The monasteries were at the heart of Tibetan life, serving as schools and universities, and training students in philosophy, medicine and architecture as well as religion. They acted as power-houses for, and repositories of, Tibetan language and culture. The state was rotten and corrupt; the religious institutions and noble Tibetan families presided over a system of serfdom across their vast estates, and for some, no doubt, the Chinese invasion may have indeed seemed a 'liberation' – as the Maoists claimed. There is little about China's Tibetan policy that could now justify the term.

Unlike the Nazis, Tibet's conquerors have stayed. Its entire religious edifice, as well as being a symbol of a separate national identity, was an affront to the atheistic, communist incomers set on revolutionary change. The Chinese set about dismantling Tibetan culture, demolishing its monuments, banning its language and smashing or looting its artefacts. The short-lived Lhasa Uprising in 1959 was the beginning of the end, resulting in a crackdown that forced the Dalai Lama into exile. Tens of thousands of ethnic Chinese have since been resettled in Lhasa and elsewhere in Tibet. By the end of the 1970s just ten monasteries remained open – sops to local feeling and, more importantly, honeypots for tourists. The cataclysm reached its full force under the Cultural Revolution (see below), which from 1966 convulsed China and Tibet in a frenzy of iconoclastic destruction. The goal was an end to the Four Olds: old thoughts, old culture, old traditions and old customs. Monasteries, including Ramoche, Norbulingka and Jokhang, temples and shrines were systematically destroyed or shut down. Tanks and aerial bombardments were used and even religious sites in remote Himalayan valleys were sought out and razed. The monastery towns of Drepung and Ganden, between them home to 13,000 monks, were just about flattened. Hundreds of thousands of Tibetans died and Buddhist monks, nuns and the intelligentsia were slaughtered. Thirteen hundred years' worth of religious artefacts and writings were smashed and burned. Only the thousand-room Potala Palace in Lhasa and twelve other designated key heritage sites were excluded from the ferocity of the Red Guards.[11]

The turnaround in policy at the end of the Cultural Revolution created something of a respite, certainly as far as religious architecture was concerned. A more liberal climate saw China financing the rebuilding and reopening of a limited number of monasteries. Monks have made their homes once again among the ruins. What remains, though, is just a shell of the former culture, heavily monitored and controlled by the Chinese. Rather than having a religious function, the monks' role is more akin to museum curators or tour guides. In many parts of the country, children of school age

The Chinese invasion of Tibet, the crushing of the 1959 Lhasa Uprising and the campaign of Sinofication that has followed have largely destroyed Tibetan culture, particularly its architecture. The Potola Palace in Lhasa, dating from 1648 with 1,300-year-old origins, is one of the few monasteries in the country that has survived half a century of cultural cleansing relatively undamaged. However, the World Heritage Site is now a tourist attraction rather than a religious house and seat of government, and poor conservation work by Chinese officials using alien methods has led to its deterioration and the recent collapse of one of its walls. The area in front of the Palace has been cleared of its Tibetan vernacular architecture to make way for a Tiananmen Square-style plaza.

Few of Tibet's former 6,000 monasteries survive. Here, a monk walks through the ruins of the Ganden, the monastery town established in 1409 on a mountain-top near Lhasa and razed by the Chinese army in the years following 1959. Recently, in the face of continued persecution, Buddhist monks have been returning to make their home in the ruins.

can no longer be taught in monasteries or even in the Tibetan language. Speaking and writing Chinese is essential to pursue a career. The majority of Tibetans remain illiterate and Chinese students form the main part of university entrants. Even these limited freedoms, set within a pattern of continuing human rights abuses, have been rescinded in recent years. China is alarmed at the vigour with which Tibetans have attempted to reclaim their past. The Dalai Lama has warned of the 'cultural genocide' underway in his country.[12] In the meantime, the deracination of Tibet's secular architectural heritage is, if anything, escalating. In part this is due to China's genuine desire to modernize and industrialize, whatever the price, but in much larger measure it is a desire to integrate Tibet into China – to bind it to the motherland permanently, eradicating tangible memories of a separate cultural and national past. Within four years of the invasion the Chinese had already completed such major infrastructure projects as the Tibet–Sichuan highway – along which thousands of Sichuan peasants have headed eastwards into Tibet, encouraged by financial incentives from the Chinese government.[13]

Lhasa remains the capital of the Tibetan Autonomous Region (TAR) but swaths of its former territory have been transferred directly to the Chinese provinces of Quinghai, Yunnan and Sichuan. A thoroughgoing reshaping of Lhasa has also been underway since the release of plans by the Lhasa Planning Bureau in 1980.[14] It envisages a Lhasa that will, apart from set pieces such as the Potala Palace, the Jokhang Temple and the Drepung and

Sera monasteries, bear little resemblance to the Buddhist city that has evolved since the seventh century. Already much has gone. The old Tibetan core has long been enveloped a dozen times over by the Chinese city, which is doubling in size every six years. The Tibetan population of 30,000 in 1949 now makes up only a third of the city's 380,000 (and rising) inhabitants.[15] The Tibetan character of the old city is being eroded apace. The historic wooden buildings of the Shol district below the Potala Palace have been removed and replaced with a concrete tourist village, with concessionary ersatz Tibetan applied details and a massive concrete monument to Tibetan 'liberation'. A large area of the district has been cleared to create a Tiananmen Square-style parade ground. 'The Potala Palace is being preserved very differently than in the past, as a museum,' argues Kate Saunders of the Tibetan Information Network. 'The most potent symbol of Tibetan Buddhism is being turned into a symbol for Chinese rule.'[16]

The oldest part of the city, the Barkor district, which was built around the circular pilgrims' path up to the Jokhang Temple, founded in AD 641, is gradually being destroyed. By the mid-1990s many historic timber and battered-wall buildings in the distinctive Tibetan vernacular and classical styles had already been removed along the route to make way for a new Chinese department store and other projects. Among the buildings demolished was the historic Surkhang House, a former noble's residence. The crude forms of the new buildings pay little or no regard to the historic grain or architecture of the city. The developments have been criticized by both the UN and UNESCO. Even Chinese architects have spoken out against the new developments.[17] In 2002 four more historic blocks near the house of the eleventh Dalai Lama were demolished. Tenants losing their housing often have little warning and are relocated well away from their original homes. The destruction is an ongoing attempt to achieve the Sinofication of Tibet.

This is not a battle between traditionalism and quality contemporary architecture – it is between an architecture of intrinsic quality that has local meaning and the crude concrete boxes that have characterized so much of China's recent regional architecture in its drive towards homogeneity. Even where restoration has taken place, such as at the Potala, the workmanship has been shoddy to the point where, in 2001, a section of one if its main walls, more than 9 m by 18 m, collapsed. In August 2000 the Tibet Heritage Fund, an NGO that has helped restore 76 historic buildings since 1996, was expelled from the country on the flimsy grounds of not having a proper licence to print its brochure.[18] As a consequence of this reshaping of the capital, 130 out of Lhasa's 330 remaining historic religious and secular buildings had vanished between 1995 and the turn of this century.[19]

The transformation of Tibet is set to continue, with the Chinese alarmed at the continuing 'splitist', that is, nationalist, attitude of Tibetans unwilling to be assimilated into China and desperate to hold onto their culture and traditions: their very identity as Tibetans. The climate of economic liberalization across China and Tibet is not matched by cultural or political freedoms. This is perestroika without glasnost. The revived campaign against Buddhism has seen the numbers of monks and nuns severely limited and the destruction of their makeshift cells built around ruined former temples and monasteries. It is thought that the defection in 2000 of two senior lamas whose presence gave some legitimacy to Chinese rule has, in part, been the catalyst for the clampdown. In 2001 thousands of monks' and nuns' homes were demolished at the Larung Gar religious community in Sether. A few months later parts of the Yachen monastic encampment, housing 800 devotees, met the same fate. The monks and nuns were ordered to demolish their own adobe-built shelters or face fines.[20]

Religious monuments and their contents are themselves continuing to disappear. These include the treasures of the Potala Palace itself, once home to 70,000 artefacts dating back beyond its rebuilding in the seventeenth century to its foundation in the seventh century. In 2002, a 5 m high bronze and gold statue of Maitriya, the future Buddha, was removed from the Palace to Shanghai. Many other objects have found their way onto the international art market via China.[21]

The renewed cultural offensive in Tibet is echoed in other national minority areas on China's fringes. It is part of a campaign launched in 2001 to 'strike hard' against 'crime', which in the Muslim region of Xinjiang, north of Tibet, means the 'three evils of separatism, terrorism and religious extremism'.[22] The collapse of the Soviet Union and the creation of the Central Asian Islamic republics may have been the initial trigger for China's growing suspicion of nationalist unrest, but 11 September has only heightened these concerns. The result is that the Chinese are busy demolishing the historic Silk Road city of Kashgar, while sprucing up a few set-piece monuments for tourists and binding the periphery of their empire to its core with infrastructure projects. This is not simply a wish to bring development and economic growth to some of the remotest cultures in the world: it is a desire to stop their conquests from peeling away. Destroying local distinctiveness – a memory of a separate identity and past – is as important for China as it was for German-occupied Poland. In 2005 the Dalai Lama dismayed many of Tibet's supporters when, in an interview with Hong Kong's *South China Morning Post*, he appeared to succumb to Chinese pressure and spoke out against separatism, declaring that 'Tibetan culture and Buddhism are part of Chinese culture. Many young Chinese like Tibetan culture as a tradition of China.'[23] The climb-down would appear to be an attempt to find a middle way between unsuccessful resistance and total absorption by China that allows some measure of Tibetan distinctiveness to remain.

If the eradication of difference and the subjugation of religious nationalism have governed Chinese attitudes towards its conquest of Tibet, the opposite is true in Israel, where religious nationalism has triumphed and the exacerbation of difference between Israel's Jews and its gentile population, specifically the Arab population, has been endemic in Israeli government policy decisions. This would come as something of a surprise to early twentieth-century Zionists who agitated successfully for the building of Israel out of the ruins of the Ottoman empire. While religious Jews had been resettling in Palestine in growing numbers since the nineteenth century, the vision of those who eventually came to conquer the country, following the unparalleled horrors of the Holocaust and the reparative 1947 UN partition plan, was essentially secular, forward-looking and, for many adherents, a form of ethnic socialism. A strange sort of socialism perhaps – one that looked to the backing of the great powers rather than working with the Arab inhabitants of the land to achieve their goals – but in many ways a progressive ideology none the less. Despite the Diaspora dream of a return to Jerusalem, the ritual sorrow at the destruction of the Herodian Temple in AD 70 and the Jewish people's subsequent exile, it is doubtful, given this secularist agenda, whether many Zionists at the point of Israel's creation would have envisaged that Jerusalem would become the focus for Israeli identity and that, within Jerusalem, Temple Mount would be the most intractable obstacle to cementing their conquest.[24] Many early Zionists regarded the city as a backwards, superstitious place full of conservative 'hill people'. Modern Tel Aviv, Haifa and Beersheba in the Negev desert were all put forward as alternative capitals.[25] Similarly, while pre-partition Muslim Palestinians revered Jerusalem as Al Quds (The Holy), it was to the larger region, to Cairo and Damascus, that Palestinian Arabs looked politically until the emergence of Palestinian nationalism in the period between the World Wars. Yet almost immediately following the creation of the State of Israel, the sacred geography of the past was employed to legitimize the present and to reinforce the status and identity of the Jews as the natural and continuous owners of Israel in general and Jerusalem in particular. The erasure of architectural and archaeological evidence to the contrary has been regularly employed in achieving this aim.

Israelis may have been handed their state by international agreement but they still had to fight for it. Both Israel and the Western powers that carved up Palestine may have regarded it as an empty land, but it was the Zionists that made it so in reality. This may not have been their goal at the outset but when, after years of increasing Arab-Israeli tensions full-scale war broke out following the UN's partition declaration and as the neighbouring Arab countries tried to prevent the establishment of the new state, more than 700,000 Palestinians fled Israel's towns and villages and out of the new country altogether. Atrocities were committed on both sides but Israeli military ruthlessness created a climate of fear in which, if the Palestinians were not actively forced out, as was often the case, they fled their homes in terror. To this day exiled Palestinians know the loss of their ancestral lands as *al-Nakba* – the Catastrophe.[26]

In their absence, Israel's new leaders appropriated Arab property and began to reshape the land in their own image – an uncomfortable combination of a desire for a modern European democracy, but one justified by scriptural antecedents. As the historian Erna Paris said of the South African Afrikaner founding myths: 'Attaching God to history is the most powerful nationalism of all.'[27] The map was literally redrawn. Place names throughout the country were rendered from Arabic into Hebrew or renamed based on biblical or pseudo-biblical antecedents (a process reversed in the case of Sodom, which was deemed contaminated by its embarrassing scriptural associations).[28] Between 1948 and 1950 at least 400 Arab villages were destroyed by bomb or bulldozer. Many vanished altogether and their ruins buried under Jewish settlements or hidden in newly planted forests. Far from making the desert bloom, ancient olive groves and orchards were grubbed up.[29] Some of the more aesthetically pleasing Arabic homes were gussied up as Jewish housing or as arts centres, but the general pattern was one of destruction. Mosques all over the country were demolished, closed or converted to other uses, from synagogues to cow byres. Even today, efforts by Palestinians to reopen or rebuild their crumbling sacred buildings are resisted by the Israeli authorities. Many villages have now been removed from the maps altogether, as if they never existed. Historic Arabic cities such as Acre, Haifa and Jaffa lost up to 90 per cent of their Arab residents and many of their Arabic buildings.[30]

In his authoritative survey of these rural losses in Israel, *Sacred Landscape*, Israeli historian Meron Benvenisti also notes the destruction of some urban Arabic monuments. In the Old City of Caesarea and the village of Kawkab al-Hawa, for instance, historic Arab buildings have been cleared and the surrounding Crusader-era walls restored. As Benvenisti puts it:

> In the Israeli context, it is preferable to immortalise those who exterminated the Jewish communities of Europe (in the late eleventh and early twelfth centuries) and murdered the Jews of Jerusalem in 1099 than to preserve the relics of the local Arab civilisation with which today's Israelis must supposedly co-exist.[31]

But then the Crusaders are not living dispossessed across the border, nursing their grievances and the keys to their former homes; such dangerous proximity can prompt the desire of the conqueror to leave nothing recognizable for the exiled to return to.

It was not until the territorial gains of the 1967 Six Day War, however, that the Israelis finally gained control of the Old City of Jerusalem and Temple

Mount. It had been a long wait – two thousand years. The army rabbi accompanying Temple Mount's conquerors symbolically carried a Torah scroll and blew a shofar within the precincts of the Islamic Haram al-Sharif. It was suggested that the al-Aqsa Mosque be dynamited, then and there, but the Israelis contented themselves with flying the Israeli flag briefly from the Dome of the Rock (where the conquering Crusaders had once installed a cross) before handing the keys back to its Muslim guardians.[32] A photograph of three young Israeli soldiers gazing in wonder at the Wailing Wall, which they had just captured, is now an Israeli icon. It has since been used to sell cigarettes, chocolate and wine, before being resurrected as a campaigning image by Israel's right wing. Its photographer, David Rubinger, is unimpressed, saying recently: 'Stones become holy. Temples have become holy. Mountains become holy, and now pictures. The trouble is that people die because something becomes holy.'[33]

It is hard to imagine another stretch of wall in history that has caused so much trouble. The symbolism of Berlin's division pales beside this Western Wall of the Herodian temple, the retaining wall of Temple Mount or, viewed from the Arab side, the al-Boraq wall of the Haram al-Sharif. The wall is the only visible survivor of the Temple precinct following its destruction by the Roman occupiers in AD 70 after a failed Jewish revolt. The Romans razed the whole city, including the Temple, and built in its place a classical grid garrison town they named Aelia Capitolina. Over the next six years the Jews were killed or enslaved overseas. The Diaspora had begun.

Jerusalem's recorded origins go back some thousand years before the Hebrew military leader David successfully seized the hill of Zion from an obscure Canaanite tribe, the Jesubites, who had named their city 'Rushalimum' after their god Shalem.[34] The first Jewish temple was raised on the site of the pagan altar. It became the ultimate focus of the Jewish faith:

> The land of Israel is the middle of the earth, Jerusalem is the middle of the land of Israel. The Temple is in the middle of Jerusalem. The Holy of Holies is the middle of the Temple. The Holy Ark is the middle of the Holy of Holies. And the Stone of Foundation is in front of the Holy of Holies.[35]

Solomon's fine temple with its cedar of Lebanon lining was destroyed by the Babylonians in 586 BC, along with the rest of the city, and then rebuilt on a more modest scale after the exiled Jews returned from Babylon. Although constrained by the limitations of the site, it was this structure that was rebuilt under Herod the Great (providing a venue for Jesus to make trouble) in an 80-year project to create the largest temple in the ancient world. The magnificent building, incorrectly but commonly known as the 'Third Temple', had been completed for only ten years before the Romans destroyed it for good. Its destruction is remembered at Jewish weddings with the breaking of a glass and in everyday prayers. After 3,000 years the site remains at the heart of the Arab-Israeli conflict both symbolically and physically. It is at the core of Jewish claims to contemporary Jerusalem and central to Judaism. The problem is that the site on which it stands, the Haram, the 'Noble Sanctuary', is only slightly behind Mecca and Medina in its sanctity to the Muslim world. It is here, the al-Aqsa, the 'farthest mosque', that Mohammed is said to have ascended on his night-time journey into Seventh Heaven and the presence of Allah. He tied up his winged steed al-Boraq to the al-Boraq Wall (once the Western Wall of the Temple, now the Wailing Wall). The Temple's Stone of Foundation is, at the same time, the place where God ordered Abraham to sacrifice his son and the rock from where Mohammed stepped up on his journey, leaving his heel mark imprinted in the surface.[36]

It was the conquest of Byzantine Jerusalem by Muslim forces in AD 638 that provided the opportunity to build the Haram's mosques, the al-Aqsa and the Dome of the Rock (the Mosque of Omar), on the Temple platform. The Temple site, in a calculated insult, had been used as a rubbish dump in the centuries since its destruction by early Christians, for whom the whole city had become holy in their tracing of Jesus Christ's Passion. The Christian pilgrimage route, which has changed over the centuries, now culminates at his tomb, over which was built the predecessor of the Church of the Holy Sepulchre on a site occupied in the intervening period by a Roman temple. Under Christianity the sacred geography had thus shifted across the Old City before Islam restored the spiritual centrality of Temple Mount. As another 'people of the book', Muslims too revere the prophets of the Old Testament and sited their monuments accordingly. After their conquest, the Muslims allowed the Church of the Holy Sepulchre to remain and, apart from during the Crusader period when the Dome of the Rock was ungratefully converted into a church and returned Jews were murdered or expelled, the Muslim Arabs ruled over these holy places and its Christian and Jewish population until the British Mandate and the subsequent seizure of the Old City by the Israelis in 1967. For well over a thousand years Jerusalem, ultimately as part of the Ottoman Empire, had been an Arab city with, for much of this time, a minority population of Jews and Christians. A Jewish majority emerged in the second half of the nineteenth century.[37]

Today, without the tourist trade to oil the quarters of the Old City, Jerusalem's streets and alleys are, by turns, viscous with local people and lifeless lacunae. The souk of the Arab Quarter is alive with Middle Eastern vigour with little room to move between the shoppers. But over at the massive square created in front of the Wailing Wall the crowd is only at its foot – as if it were a shaken container, its contents tipped to one side. Third Temple extremist touts in the plaza pull me in to see the treasures of their planned new temple and to explore the tunnels under Temple Mount. Despite the heavy police presence and repeated identity checks, there seems little to fear in the city, for a non-Arab at least. A few steps and corners away from the main streets, however, the smells of the stalls and the sounds of bartering fall away and you are in empty alley-ways surrounded by high walls, shuttered doors and silence, apart from the occasional shout of a child in a darkened room up above. Houses here and there are hung with blue and white Israeli flags many metres across, where Jewish settlers have forced their way into the Arab and Christian quarters. A rock lands at my feet, then, shortly after, another. I can't see who has thrown it – Palestinian or Israeli? – but the message is clear and I retreat back to the mainstream. This sense of a hidden life is true of many traditional cities of the Middle East where existence goes on behind high walls, but here there is a palpable, ongoing tension, sometimes hidden, sometimes bursting out in destructive fury.

Under the United Nations partition plan that carved Israel out of Palestine, the intractable issue of Jerusalem was to be solved by creating a *Corpus Separatum*, an international zone encompassing the city with access to all faiths. The Israeli conquest of, first, part and then the entire city has made this still-maintained UN position a sadly remote possibility. In 1980 the Likud government sought to have the final word on the matter by passing a 'Basic Law' declaring Jerusalem to be 'the eternal undivided capital of Israel'.[38] Using similar tactics to those adopted in the rest of the occupied West Bank and Gaza (see chapter Five) – the building of encircling Jewish settlements, the demolition of Palestinian homes, the shifting of boundaries and discriminatory planning measures – Israel has steadily tightened its grip in an attempt to ensure that the aspirations of the 'Basic Law' will not be rolled back. The razing and raising of structures in and around the Old City over the past half-century is both a microcosm of the Arab–Israeli conflict and its epicentre.

In the years leading up to the declaration of the State of Israel, vicious sectarian attacks were already being carried out by opposing forces in Jerusalem. Among the architectural casualties of the bombings and shootings were the *Palestine Post* newspaper offices, the Jewish Agency and the main shopping area, all attacked by Arabs, and the British Army headquarters at the King David Hotel, where a bomb attack by a Jewish terrorist group killed 91 people. Ethnic cleansing was rife as the city rapidly segregated itself into a Jewish West and a Palestinian East that included most of the Old City. The partition announcement itself was met with a pogrom on Jewish businesses in the New City.

In the war that followed immediately upon independence, the Israelis failed to gain control of the Old City. Jordanian forces, which had occupied East Jerusalem and the West Bank, pounded the historic Jewish Quarter into rubble, systematically demolishing houses, expelling the population of

Formerly named for its founder, Rabbi Yehudah HaChassid, the Hurva ('ruined') Synagogue in the Jewish Quarter of the Old City of Jerusalem in 1942 before the creation of Israel and the occupation of the city by the Jordanian army during the first Arab–Israeli war. The huge 19th-century building replaced an earlier structure. Its dome was a notable feature of the city skyline.

2,000 religious Jews and destroying 27 synagogues, including one of the glories of the Jerusalem skyline, the Hurva Synagogue.[39] The resulting division of the city meant that for the first time in many centuries the Jews were denied access to the Wailing Wall. Under Ottoman rule the Jews were allowed to pray at the Wall, even if they had to suffer as second-class citizens and were subject to periodic harassment by Muslims from the Haram-al-Sharif above.

When Israeli forces finally conquered the Old City in 1967 they lost no time in staking their claim and exacting revenge. The first architectural casualty was the ancient Maghribi (Moroccan) neighbourhood adjacent to the Wailing Wall. This Arab quarter was bulldozed within two days of victory to create a plaza facing the Wailing Wall. More than 100 historic buildings were dynamited and hundreds of Palestinians left homeless at three hours' notice.[40] Within a week the nearby Sharaf neighbourhood was levelled too. Around 700 buildings, including two mosques, were demolished and 6,000 Palestinians expelled. The plaza has since become the focus of militant Jewish religious nationalism – not just a place of worship but where soldiers are sworn in and have their guns blessed.[41]

The Islamic world was horrified at the perceived threat to one of its holiest sites. They feared, and still do, that one day the Jews would destroy the Haram-al-Sharif with its glorious mosques and shrines to rebuild the Third Temple, as some Jewish extremists have vowed to do. Israel's mainstream politicians wouldn't countenance such a proposal and the official Jewish religious position is that any attempt to rebuild the Temple by earthly hands would be a gross blasphemy. Only the coming of the Messiah will cleanse the site and allow the Jewish people to enter the rebuilt Temple once more. Until then the Wailing Wall is the limit. This rabbinical and political censure has not stopped small groups of hardliners, furious at being excluded from the physical embodiment of the heart of their religion, the only site on earth where the presence of God resides, from repeatedly attempting to destroy the Noble Sanctuary.

The first attack came in June 1968 when a deranged Jewish tourist set fire to the al-Aqsa Mosque, burning the pulpit from which Saladin (the builder of Jerusalem's walls) spoke. There have been at least five attempts since to blow up the mosques, often timed to undermine crucial junctures of the Arab–Israeli peace process. A holy war has been averted each time by Israeli security forces.[42] In addition, Third Temple activists have regularly tried to storm Temple Mount to pray (even though the whole of its 35 acres is a de facto outdoor mosque). An annual attempt by the Temple Mount Faithful to lay a 4.5 tonne marble foundation stone for the Third Temple on the ninth day of Av (the anniversary of the Herodian Temple's destruction) has resulted in violence and deaths. The most sophisticated attempt at destruction, in the early 1980s, was led by Yehudah Etzion, an explosives expert who planned to destroy the Dome of the Rock. In an interview with journalist Con Coughlin, Etzion explained how the 70 kg of Semtex would be placed:

> The whole operation was very carefully planned because we had to be careful not to touch the rock inside. We planned it in such a way that

A commemorative arch built following the capture of East Jerusalem by Israeli forces in the '67 War marks the destruction of the Hurva Synagogue and the Jewish Quarter of the Old City in 1948 by the Jordanian army. The Israeli government has recently given approval to rebuilding the synagogue in replica. An earlier scheme for a Modernist synagogue on the site by architect Louis Kahn was never pursued.

only three columns would be destroyed. This would cause the dome itself to fall onto the rock and protect it from all the other masonry.[43]

Further attempts on the buildings have been made since. In September 2003, Israeli secret police arrested Jewish extremists who had been planning a coordinated attack on a number of mosques (including the Dome of the Rock) during a single day.[44] Another body, the Temple Mount Institute, is busy, like the Hindu activists of Ayodhya in India, preparing ritual objects for a new temple, including a US$1.7 million golden menorah, a replica Ark of the Covenant, harps and elaborately embroidered vestments. The Institute's founder, Rabbi Yisrael Ariel, has repeatedly called for the destruction of the whole of the Haram-al-Sharif. His activities are supported by grants from the Israeli government, the city council and Christian fundamentalists who believe that the building of the temple will fulfil the necessary prophecies for the Messiah to return.[45]

If such activities were confined to a lunatic few it would be easy to see Muslim fears as paranoid; however these goals have wider support in Israel. According to one opinion poll conducted by Gallup Israel, the attempts by the Temple Mount Faithful group to lay the foundation stone for the Third Temple enjoy the support of 30 per cent of Israelis.[46] This figure seems high, given the obvious consequences of a genuine attempt at removing the Haram; it may reflect simply a generalized aspiration for the Temple to be eventually rebuilt rather than a realistic desire to act.

Muslim worries, though, are stoked by the reality that, since the creation of Israel, many Islamic shrines have been appropriated for Jewish worship. These include Nabri Rubin, a key Muslim shrine and focus of an important Islamic religious festival that used to attract tens of thousands of pilgrims annually. Following the 1948 war and the expulsion of the Palestinians, the site was left to decay to the point where its minaret was demolished in 1991. It was reconsecrated as a Jewish shrine despite there being no previous tradition connected to the site.[47] Elsewhere, the grave of Sheikh Gharib became the grave of Samson under the Israelis, before in the 1960s it was again reidentified as the grave of Dan and made a Jewish pilgrimage site. Similarly, in the northern Israeli town of Tiberias, the miraculous grave of Sitt Sakina, a member of Muhammad's family, was transformed into the tomb of Rachel, the wife of a celebrated Rabbi.[48] A large number of other sites have also been appropriated or encroached upon, most notably the Ibrahimi Mosque in Hebron (see chapter Five). Within the Old City of Jerusalem itself, an historic mosque in a fortress now called David's Citadel is part of a museum that tells the story of the city from the Israeli point of view. Its exhibition glosses over centuries of Arab civilization. In the same vein, government publications promoting the city stress the biblical past at the same time as being extremely economical with the truth regarding its Islamic heritage. Beyond the Old

City walls former Palestinian neighbourhoods have become Jewish and old Arab villages have vanished under Israeli building projects including the Knesset, government ministries and Independence Park – all of which have been built on confiscated Palestinian land.

The sense of a 'power of place' remains palpable in Jerusalem; it sags under the weight of memory and meaning. In the tiny inner sanctum of the Church of the Holy Sepulchre, the reputed site of Christ's tomb, I watch in awe as a smartly dressed, middle-aged pilgrim, squeezed in there with me, kneels, fishes some postcards of icons out of her plastic carrier bag then puts her head on the cold slab and wails, at the same time wiping the cards through the pool of tears and dust on the stone. Private grief or religious passion, who can say? The term 'Jerusalem Syndrome' has been coined by clinical psychiatrists to explain the intense religious delusions and erratic behaviour that affects some Jewish and Christian visitors to the Holy City. It is a relief to escape beyond the city walls to the scruffy streets of Palestinian East Jerusalem, where the tang of motor-oil and the hiss of compressed air from the many makeshift garages replaces the fervour of swinging censors and murmured invocations.

In an atmosphere that is a forcing frame for religiosity, it is not surprising that any development activities above, below or around Temple Mount are hugely provocative. Israeli archaeologists and politicians were outraged by recent excavations carried out by the Islamic religious authorities, the Waqf, beneath the Haram-al-Sharif, and Jewish excavations around the city have also been repeatedly condemned by UNESCO. There seems little doubt that Herodian levels of archaeology below Temple Mount are being disturbed and, perhaps, erased under the Waqf's control. Leading Muslims have often unhelpfully asserted that there is no evidence for a Jewish temple ever having existed. It may be that they want to make sure this is now the case. An unholy row has blown up over the creation of an enormous underground mosque below the al-Aqsa with a capacity of up to 20,000 and with two new emergency exits. The works are, in part, a modification of existing underground chambers known to the Crusaders, who kept their horses there, as Solomon's Stables. Jewish archaeologists sifting the rubble from the Waqf excavations claim it contains pottery shards from the First Temple era. In 2001 right-wing Christian representatives in the US Congress moved to block all funding to the Palestinian Authority if the digging continued.[49] The excavations have also been blamed for an alarming bulge that developed in the southern retaining wall in 2002 and threatened to undermine it. The Waqf refused access to Israeli archaeologists, which they saw as an attempt to assert control over the site. One Israeli group called on prime minister Ariel Sharon to allow the wall to collapse in order to destroy the 'pagan Arab presence' on the Temple Mount.[50] In February 2004, with the Israelis and the Waqf still at an impasse over repairs, a small section of the wall collapsed with each side blaming the other's building activities. A small earthquake may have been the cause of the collapse.[51]

At the same time, the Israelis have been busy burrowing their own tunnels by the Wailing Wall, expanding existing passageways and chambers and establishing a subterranean synagogue near the Noble Sanctuary. A proposal to build an exit to the tunnels caused political turmoil for years with the Palestinians fearing some literally underground plot to undermine the mosques above. The exit was finally opened in the dead of night in September 1996, with Jerusalem mayor Ehud Olmert swinging a hammer himself. When the work was revealed, resulting riots left 68 Palestinians and 15 Israelis dead.[52] Investigations by UNESCO have since confirmed that this Israeli tunnelling has affected the foundations of four historic Islamic buildings (three of them madrasas), endangering their stability.[53] The same report criticized the Israelis for their poor treatment of the unearthed remains of Islamic Umayyad-era palaces: 'Today's presentation [of the ruins] ... in the guise of highlighting the remains of previous periods, indisputably trivialises the Umayyad palaces, major monuments in the area.' It goes on to quote Israeli writer Amos Elon: 'Profound psychological reasons no doubt underlie the characteristically political and sometimes even chauvinistic approach . . . Patriotic archaeology, like faith in Freudian analysis, has a therapeutic effect; people overcome their doubts and fears and feel rejuvenated once they have rediscovered their origins, real or supposed, which are always hidden.'[54]

Elsewhere in the city, when important Islamic remains have been unearthed they have often been either destroyed or buried under new developments. By contrast, it sometimes seems as if every fragment of ancient Hebrew archaeology has been lovingly preserved. Similarly with cemeteries; every Jewish grave is held to be sacred *in perpetuity* and Jewish burial sites around Jerusalem have been carefully safeguarded from development. The Israelis were understandably outraged when they regained control of the Mount of Olives in the 1967 war and found that 80 per cent of the tens of thousands of Jewish graves had been desecrated or cleared for road and building projects. Yet, since then, Muslim cemeteries have repeatedly been cleared and redeveloped by the Israelis.

Jerusalem has been an Arab city for more than a millennium, but the demolitions and the new Jewish settlements built like ramparts on the surrounding hills have now transformed it into an emphatically Jewish-majority city – even if not to the extent the Israeli government would wish. Now only 13.5 per cent of East Jerusalem is occupied by Palestinians.[55] The Christian community, too, has dwindled to the point where there are very few followers left living in the Old City. Its various sects have not helped themselves by squabbling for centuries for control of the holy sites, to the point where the roof of the Church of the Holy Sepulchre was in danger of collapse because their rivalry prevented repairs. The Greek Orthodox, Latinates, Armenian, Ethiopian, Coptic and Syrian monks, who inhabit different parts of the building and have strict rules regarding which faith group can clean which step, window sill or column at different times of day or year, took decades to agree on a repair programme for the building. The recent experience of the Western Wall echoes this farcical situation.[56]

Notwithstanding the Christian groups' own shortcomings, the Christian built heritage of the city has not been conserved with any vigour by the Israelis. When, for instance, the remains of two of the largest Byzantine monasteries in the Middle East were discovered beside the Old City they were simply buried under a new road scheme. A Byzantine chapel discovered outside the Jaffa Gate, complete with frescos and mosaics, was cleared to make way for a car park. Extremist religious Jews have vandalized the archaeological remains of historic churches, in one instance pouring tar over a sixth-century mosaic floor.[57] By contrast, tiny fragments from the far end of the Western Wall that were removed to put in supports for structures above were seized by ultra Orthodox Jews, put into urns and carried away in a funerary procession for reburial at the Wailing Wall. The Christian churches have protested at this double standard to no avail. In his account of his journey through the surviving remains of the Byzantine Middle East, *From the Holy Mountain*, William Dalrymple notes that criticism of this policy has also come from liberal Israelis (as indeed has much of the material relating to Jerusalem in this chapter).[58] Dalrymple quotes Israeli archaeologist Shulamit Giva, who in 1992 described Israeli archaeology as 'a tool in the hands of the Zionist movement'. Archaeology, she said, had 'lost its independence as a scientific discipline and become an executive arm of an ideological movement, a nationalist and political instrument which provided "roots" for the new state'. The same is true of architecture, planning and conservation. This is the falsification of history; the erasure of evidence, of memories and daily reminders of a more complex and heterogeneous past.[59]

It is not just 'dead' buildings, uninhabited for centuries, that are disappearing; the living fabric of Palestinian-dominated areas in the Old City and East Jerusalem is in a poor state and the national and municipal governments' spending priorities dictate that little in the way of funding goes to Arab areas. Some 88 per cent of all housing units built in and around the city since 1967 have been for Jewish residents only.[60] Palestinian buildings have been demolished because they had been built without the necessary permits, which the Israelis will not grant. Palestinians are being forced to live at twice the density of the Jewish population[61] with a decaying infrastructure. As well as hundreds of houses, these losses include the Bourge Luc Luc Society building, set up to serve disabled people in the Old City. It was bulldozed at 4 a.m. on 27 August 1996. The supposedly 'liberal' former mayor of Jerusalem, Teddy Kollek, has boasted about his discriminatory polices:

What did I do [for East Jerusalem]? Nothing! Sidewalks? Nothing. Cultural institutions? Not one. Yes, we installed a sewerage system for them and improved the water supply. Do you know why? Do you think it was for their good, for their welfare? Forget it! There were some cases of cholera there, and the Jews were afraid they would catch it.[62]

Extremist Jewish groups have, during this time, taken over homes and other buildings in the Old City by legal and illegal means, including by force. They are the vanguard for the conquest of the remaining Arab quarters. Ariel Sharon is among those who have a house here. Armed troops and police patrol the streets and protect the settlers. In Jerusalem, as in the West Bank, the Israelis are busy creating new facts on the ground. For the Palestinians, meanwhile, 'Al Quds', has come to represent their national struggle: a resistance to conquest. Religious affairs writer Karen Armstrong describes it thus: 'Jews see Jewish Jerusalem rising phoenix-like out of the ashes of Auschwitz; Palestinians see the city, now surrounded by Jewish settlements, as a symbol of their own beleaguered identity.'[63]

The historic fabric of the world's greatest assemblage of sacred architecture will continue to suffer in the struggle not just to downplay the unpalatable (to Israeli taste) reminders of the city's Islamic past but in order to create a new and partial history. The primary determinant over what is cherished and protected and what is discarded and destroyed depends on how it fits into the narrative being created of Jerusalem as the eternal (and united) Jewish capital since the time of David. The manipulation of Jerusalem's built record can be seen, following Eric Hobsbawm's schema, as the invention of tradition by architectural means. It is important not to overstate the case (the Dome of the Rock is probably quite safe unless a maverick Israeli bomber makes it through the security net) but the city's pluralist history, as expressed in its structures, is not valued and there is no doubt that it is slowly being supplanted by a mono-cultural Israeli built narrative. This tendency is not confined to Israel but it is especially true of new nations, or where a tradition has escaped from beneath the whip of foreign domination; both Greece and Saudi Arabia, for instance, are culpable when it comes to the destruction of Ottoman heritage within their borders. The difference in Israel is that the meanings are being contested vociferously from within.

By no means, though, are all conquests territorial. Revolutionary situations – the making of new orders and the defeat of old ones – have always been climates of conflict in which much is torn down and much erected. The architectural megalomania that appears synonymous with tyranny is explained in part by this desire to erase, renew and control. The architecture produced by such regimes has been researched widely and will not be dwelt on here, but those structures deemed expendable or expressly singled out for destruction should not be forgotten, since they are as revealing as what has been built in their stead. Stalin's campaign against religion, national minorities and their architectural inheritance in the Soviet Union is a case in point.

Immediately following the 1917 October Revolution, different tendencies emerged among the Bolsheviks with regard to architecture and architectural heritage. The ultra-left of the party wished to destroy every last vestige of a bourgeois cultural past, including their buildings, and establish a *proletkult* representative of workers' (supposed) interests, while the party's right, which eventually emerged victorious, imposed a centralized homogenous national chauvinism as a means of building 'socialism in one country' following the failure of other European revolutions. A third, more sophisticated, position supported an avant garde that learned from and built upon the previous civilization's artistic achievements: the revolution meant that culture was now simply human rather than bourgeois. Trotsky articulated this position using architectural imagery:

> The Renaissance only begins when the new social class, already culturally satiated, feels strong enough to come out from under the yoke of the Gothic arch, to look at Gothic art and on all that preceded it as material for its own disposal, and to use the technique of the past for its own artistic aims.[64]

It was, unfortunately, a stance repressed following the death of Lenin and the rise of Stalin. Yet Trotsky's own position did not stem from a sort of Bolshevik liberalism (if such a contradiction in terms can be allowed), for Communism could not be ushered in without using the methods of the old society; violence, destruction and annihilation. 'The revolution saved society,' he wrote, 'but by means of the most cruel surgery.'[65]

Old Moscow survived almost intact until Stalin consolidated his grip and began his first Five Year Plan in 1928. Before this the Bolshevik regime had put architects to work repairing architectural masterpieces damaged in the civil war. But this conflict and the lack of resources in the country had only delayed redevelopment schemes for the city that had 'Socialist Man' in mind. After 1917 various plans had been prepared for the rebuilding of Moscow as either a garden city or as a rationalist Modernist Utopia. It was, though, a pompous metropolis characterized by the giantist architectural equivalent of heroic Socialist Realist art that emerged from the late 1920s onwards – to be followed in later years by low grade system-building. Vast swaths of the city, whole neighbourhoods, churches and palaces were destroyed in the 1930s to make way for the self-aggrandizing vision of Joseph Stalin.[66]

Given the Bolshevik hostility to religion it is not surprising that sacred architecture felt the full force of Stalin's destructive power. Churches, synagogues, mosques and monasteries were shut down in the immediate wake of the Revolution. Many were converted to secular uses or Museums of Atheism (anti-churches), whitewashed and their fittings removed. Many more were demolished across the Soviet empire from the late 1920s and throughout the 1930s. Moscow's biggest loss (if not the most meritorious architecturally) was the Cathedral of Christ the Saviour. The equivalent of 30 storeys high and 45 years in the building, it had finally been consecrated in 1883. Its dome weighed 176 tonnes, its bells 140 tonnes. Inside, a huge iconostasis needed 422 kg of gold to gild it. It was a shrine to Tsarist military prowess and was as much war memorial as church. Its replacement, announced in 1931, was to be the equally domineering Palace of the Soviets. Designed to be the largest building in the world, it was to be equivalent in volume to 1930s New York's six biggest skyscrapers combined. The 100 m high statue of Lenin crowning its 150 floors would raise its index finger a further 6 m. Lenin's feet would have been 14 m long.[67] The whole edifice aimed to demonstrate the superiority of the new socialist order. As Ryszard Kapuścinski points out in his travelogue *Imperium*, there were many other sites available in Moscow to build the Palace, but the replacement of the House of God with a House of the Party had obvious symbolism.[68] It was never built, though, and for many decades the remodelled foundations of the dynamited church served Muscovites as a swimming pool, steaming away through the Russian winters. St Basil's Cathedral in Red Square, surely the most obvious symbol of the city, also narrowly missed demolition as part of a scheme to improve the space for May Day parades.

This secularist iconoclasm (from without the Church rather than the result of doctrinal differences within or between faiths) has its counterpart in the anti-clericalism and smashing of churches in revolutionary France and in Republican Spain, where, as usually occurs, the Church was allied with the old order, conservatism and superstition. In Russia, an estimated 20–30 million painted icons were destroyed – used for fuel, chopping boards, linings for mine workings and crates for vegetables.[69]

Stalin's ferocious campaign of conquest against the architecture of the old order reached its zenith as part of the wider Terror that aimed to destroy any semblance of dissent or secessionist tendencies among the nationalist groupings that made up the Soviet Union. Crimean Tartars, Chechens and Ingush at the territorial fringes of the state and potential enemies of Pan-Slavic unity were brutally relocated thousands of miles to a desolate East and their abandoned homes and monuments destroyed. Collectivization and the desire to build and feed an urban proletariat at the expense of the peasants also led to the deaths of up to 10 million people in what were essentially manufactured famines. National cultures, languages and histories were quashed and distorted to create a new history, including an architectural history, compatible with the Russification of the Soviet republics. Ukraine suffered severely as a result of these policies. Its peasants starved, its intelligentsia was murdered and its cities despoiled. Publishing books in Ukrainian was forbidden and millions of native Russian speakers were resettled there. The once beautiful Kiev, the heartland of the Ukrainian Church and Ukrainian nationalism, had its monuments murdered too. More than 254 of Kiev's historic buildings, both secular and religious, were razed. Among the monuments destroyed were jewels of Ukrainian architecture dating back to the eleventh century, including the twelfth-century monastery of St Michael of the Golden Domes, demolished in 1935, and the late seventeenth-century church of the Epiphany, demolished in 1934.[70] Some Ukrainian nationalist symbols were retained if they displayed elements of the medieval, pre-Cossack Kyivan Rus' style that fitted the concept of a Pan-Slavic brotherhood; St Michael was too altered to qualify. Other elements of Cossack culture were promoted but defanged – fearsome Cossack warriors became an exportable jolly dance troupe.[71] The eleventh-century cathedral of St Sophia became a museum, as did the cathedral of the Dormition in Pechers'ka lavra, until it was destroyed in mysterious circumstances in 1941. The Russians blamed the invading Nazis, who perpetuated Stalin's terror and despoliation for their own ideological ends; the Nazis blamed the destruction of the cathedral on the retreating Russians.

During the course of the twentieth century as many as 10,000 historic Ukrainian monuments vanished in the face of the new orders being forged by Stalin and Hitler. Operation Barbarossa, Hitler's campaign against the Soviet Union, was as savage and intense as his dismemberment of Poland. The Jewish population of the region and its culture suffered accordingly. Initial German proposals that the Ukrainians might be spared a similar fate by employing Ukrainian nationalism as a bulwark against Bolshevism did not stand up long to a Nazi race theory intent on killing or enslaving the Slavic people and eradicating its culture. 'Kiev would be proof of that,' writes Lynn H. Nicholas in *The Rape of Europa*, her distinguished account of the looting of art during the Second World War:

> After its fall on September 17 [1941] its museums, scientific institutes, libraries, churches and universities were taken over to be exploited and stripped. Everywhere in the USSR special attention was given to the trashing of the houses and museums of great cultural figures: Pushkin's house was ransacked, as was Tolstoy's . . . where manuscripts were burned in the stoves . . . The museums honouring Chekhov, Rimsky-Korsakov and Tchaikovsky received similar attentions, the composer of the 1812 Overture being particularly honoured by having a motor-cycle garage installed in his former dwelling.[72]

By the end of the war it was not just Kiev that was in ruins. The retreating Germans' scorched earth policy had created a wasteland stretching from Leningrad to the Crimea. No quarter was given to the culture of the Jews or the Slavic *Untermenschen*. Between Stalin and Hitler a thousand years of architectural history had been laid waste in little more than ten.

Calculated cultural destruction on this scale was not seen again until another personality cult masquerading as Marxism unleashed the Cultural Revolution on China and its satellites in late 1965. With one of Mao Tse Tung's own sayings being 'Destruction before Construction', it was inevitable that China's revolutionary change would not be of the type that built on previous cultures. The attacks on monuments began well before the Cultural Revolution proper in the post-victory drive to modernity; feudalism and everything associated with it would be suspect in the new peasant Utopia. The erasure of traditional Beijing began in 1950s and continues to this day. The first of the city's architectural casualties were the pailous, the ceremonial archways that spanned the city's streets and commemorated pre-revolutionary figures, which were all pulled down. Countless city blocks were cleared to make way for socialist avenues and parade grounds. It then took twelve years to demolish Beijing's long-venerated city walls, laid out, as was the whole capital, using the principles of sacred geometry.[73]

Despite the upheavals of this Great Leap Forward, by the early 1960s Mao was impatient with the rate of progress being made. Corruption was endemic and, at a local level, incipient capitalism was making its quiet return. Intellectuals were the first to be targeted in Mao's campaign against backsliding. Writers and artists were identified as 'harmful bourgeois influences' on the 'brink of revisionism' and the purges began.[74] Rich peasants were another target, a particular affront to Mao whose communism, unlike that of Western Marxists, had worked on the premise that the peasantry could be the motor of revolutionary change rather than a more advanced urban proletariat. Mao decided to set the masses in motion once again; in September 1965 the Great Proletarian Cultural Revolution was officially born. Its literal meaning in Chinese is 'a full-scale revolution to establish a working-class culture'.[75] Mao's chosen method was promoting chaos and rebellion among the young, the students and those who had failed to benefit from the changes to date. The Red Guards went into action and on their hit list was anybody in authority, teachers and parents for example, and anything representative of the 'Four Olds' that had caused such devastation in Tibet. Historic architecture was an easy target – demolish a building and you have a visible and immediately satisfying indicator of change – much easier to measure than the outcomes of compulsory denunciations and re-education. At the other end of the scale, even cultural markers as ephemeral as make-up, hairstyles and shoe fashions were eyed vigilantly by the Red Guards for any signs of bourgeois or individualistic pretensions. Although religious buildings suffered the brunt, during the next few years books, paintings, shrines, calligraphy, temples and museums were all variously burned, ransacked, torn to pieces or closed down. The Peking Opera was reduced to performing just six execrable Revolutionary Model Operas under the direction of Jiang Qing (Madame Mao). Western composers were too decadent, Soviet composers too revisionist and folk music too feudal. 'Destroy the Old and Establish the New!' was the diktat.[76]

Although the Forbidden City was spared, most of Beijing's remaining museums and monuments were not. The Daoist Temple of the White Clouds, one of the city's principal landmarks, was used as an army barracks and the remaining city gates were torn down. The thirteenth-century Buddhist White Dagoba Temple became a warehouse; the pagoda of the thirteenth-century Tianning si (Temple of Heavenly Peace) remains, but the Buddhist monastery attached to it was razed. Every museum was closed and other buildings, if not destroyed, were turned over to suitably proletarian new uses. The memoirs of one Red Guard who later defected, Dai Hsiao-ai, record how gangs of young Guards would ransack private houses and public buildings alike in the maelstrom, destroying anything in their path regarded as traditional, superstitious or simply old:

> Statues, paintings, and other objects in public parks, temples and cemeteries were quickly destroyed. We had no plan on these occasions but simply roamed the streets looking for things. Someone would shout, 'Let's go to such-and-such temple', and we would all follow. Very often some other group would have been there first and left nothing but a pile of ashes or a group of statues smeared with paint. At least once a day, we would cart a statue to a large intersection and ceremoniously smash it to pieces. Passers-by would stop and watch us. Some would congratulate us, but most lowered their heads and hurried by . . .[77]

Another Guard notes that old artefacts became hard to find, even houses with overhanging eaves being regarded as feudal remnants and targeted to 'keep people from thinking of the past'.[78]

Simon Leys, the Belgian Sinologist, recorded the results of all this destruction in his book *Chinese Shadows*.[79] He criss-crossed China in 1972, describing the devastation he found there. The city of Hangzhou, immortalized in the proverb, 'Above is paradise, here below are Suzhou and Hangzhou', serves as a good example of the havoc wreaked.[80] This important historic city had already been damaged by foreign invasion in the nineteenth century and what remained was ravaged during the Cultural Revolution. The architectural losses were terrible: Buddhist cave sculptures from the tenth century were smashed with hammers; the Great Buddha temple and the Fang Sheng monastery vanished, the latter replaced by a public toilet; other temples lost all sculpture and decoration. Plans to destroy the Ling-yin Temple were fought, however, and it was saved, although its monks were dispersed. Even the 60 m tall Pagoda of the Six Harmonies, a thousand years old and the symbol of the city, was denounced as feudal and was only saved by the complications necessary to demolish it.[81]

All this destruction was designed as an act of propaganda (architecture as scapegoat) and a way of creating a climate of terror rather than genuinely helping pursue the goal of societal renewal. As Leys writes: 'What makes the Maoist vandalism so odious and so pathetic is not that it is irreparably mutilating an ancient civilization but rather by doing so it gives itself an alibi for not grappling with the true revolutionary tasks.'[82]

It seems that in the absence of clear dividing lines or enemies (in what amounted to a civil war) the only clear enemy was beauty. The Cultural Revolution was a war on aesthetics and on any individual creativity that marked out the particular from the mass. The Cultural Revolution was a Pyrrhic victory – only stones were conquered.

The iconoclastic legacy of Maoism was not confined to China and Tibet. Although Mao's attitude towards cities and the countryside, between the urban worker and the peasant, swung wildly depending on pragmatic political or security requirements, a suspicion of the citified intelligentsia and of the uncontrollable town was always simmering and spread across large parts of South East Asia. Just as China's Cultural Revolution wound down in the early 1970s ('victory' was officially declared in 1969) an even more virulent form of anti-urbanism arose in Cambodia under Pol Pot and the Khymer Rouge. Almost their first act on gaining control of the country in 1975 was the forced emptying out of the population of Phnom Penh and other cities into the countryside. Doctors and nurses were expelled from hospitals at gun-point mid-surgery. A neo-natal unit's staff at the Calmette Hospital were evicted leaving their charges to starve to death.[83] The regime's intense hostility to city dwellers, the educated, contemporary culture in all its forms and to religion in particular, turned quickly to genocide. Between 1.7 and 2.2 million out of Cambodia's 8 million people were executed or worked to death.[84] Teachers, doctors, lawyers, bureaucrats – anyone with more than a basic education – were killed along with ethnic minorities such as those from the Vietnamese-influenced Eastern Zone. Religious groups such as the Cham Muslim minority and Buddhist monks were killed in their tens of thousands.[85]

Along with the destruction of people came the destruction of architecture. Cities were generally left to rot but religious buildings were systematically flattened or turned to new agrarian uses. Within Phnom Penh itself, the cathedral and the National Bank were destroyed while the National Museum and National Library were vandalized and abandoned.[86] The aim was the creation of a new order of agrarian 'base people' who would begin society anew. Pol Pot stated that his aim was to 'abolish, uproot and disperse the cultural, literary, and artistic remnants of the imperialists, colonialists and all of the other oppressor classes. This will be implemented strongly, deeply and continuously.'[87] Khmer Rouge leaders had been educated in the French Communist Party's tradition – Stalinist but revised with heavy dollops of Maoist thought: the worst of both worlds. The Khmer doctrine held that only labour value had meaning. Cities, they believed, were parasitical on the countryside, extracting surplus value from their hinterlands.[88]

Architects and architecture had no place in such a society. There was one important exception, Angkor Wat and the related temple complexes of the ancient Khmer civilization. These buildings had a useful nationalist symbolism with which to bind people to the regime, while at the same time being temporally distinct from a living culture marked for destruction. 'The people who built Angkor Wat', said Pol Pot, 'could do anything.'[89] This did not stop the Khmer Rouge looting tonnes of statuary from the temple site to sell abroad and finance their erasure of a later civilization. And suitably for Pol Pot, Angkor was already in ruins, entirely non-urban and stealthily reclaimed by the jungle. Perhaps the Khmer Rouge were attempting to replicate this conquest of man's work by nature when, reportedly, they planted palm trees down the middle of Phnom Penh's streets? Pol Pot was attempting 'urbicide', the murder of a city, by starving it of its citizens rather than destroying the city buildings themselves.[90]

The notion of 'urbicide' was popularized recently by Bogdan Bogdanović, an architect and former mayor of Belgrade, who fled Serbia during the Bosnian war.[91] Cities such as Vukovar, Sarajevo and Mostar were 'murdered', he said. Cosmopolitan, pluralist, ethnically mixed and liberal, they were anathema to ethno-nationalist extremists bent on both territorial conquest and imposing an ideology of racial purity. Urbicide, argues Bogdanović, is the intentional attack on the human and inert fabric of the city with the intent of destroying the civic values embodied within it – the very spaces for interaction where cultures are generated and shared. Bogdanović also saw the attack on Dubrovnik as urbicide: the attackers were backwoodsmen from Krajina and Montenegro. The bombardment was 'intentionally aimed at an object of extraordinary, even symbolic beauty. It was the attack of a madman who throws acid in a beautiful woman's face and promises her a beautiful face in return.'[92] He sees such feelings as arising from an atavistic enmity: 'For the savage has trouble grasping that anything could have existed before him; his idea of cause and effect is primitive, monolithic . . . a malicious animus against everything urban, everything urbane.' It is an argument similar to that used by the writers of Dubrovnik (see chapter Three), but blaming peasant ignorance and mistrust rather than the perfidious Orient.

121

It was, too, the fear expressed by liberal Mostarians alarmed at the extremist attitudes of the Croatian peasant refugees forced into the city by the fighting in the countryside.[93] The notion of the uncivilized attacking the civic – the barbarian at the gates – has long been with us. It is the fear of the settled in the face of the nomadic hordes, the fear of inchoate, narrow tribalism by ordered heterogeneous city dwellers.

The co-mingling of mosque, Catholic and Orthodox churches in Sarajevo is an embodiment in stone of everything the Serbs were fighting against. Mostar's mixed marriages and egalitarianism were equally unacceptable to Croatian extremists wanting to cleanse the city of its Muslims and Muslim architectural heritage. Mostar's bridge was, like the Višegrad bridge in Nobel prize-winner Ivo Andrić's classic Bosnian novel *The Bridge over the Drina*,[94] a singular monument to this willingness to reach out to a community beyond one's own. Mostar's bridge had to go.

Urbicide, however, demands attacks on more than the individual buildings of representative communities; it is the aggregation of buildings that constitute heterogeneous shared spaces where people mingle that are the targets.[95] The architectural conditions that foster this heterogeneity have to be destroyed if an ethno-national or ideological homogeneity is to take its place. The space that cities allow for diversity and the exchange of ideas also means that authority cannot be uniformly imposed – power can never be absolute. Cities as a locus of tolerance and freedom are, to their detractors, dangerously uncontrollable, instinctively oppositional to authority, constantly changing and evolving in new and diverse ways. Because of this the city is also the City of Sin. Babylon. The cities of Sodom and Gomorrah were condemned for widespread homosexuality (or, as textual revisionists would have it, the sin of a failure in hospitality), inviting God's wrath and destruction. Koranic and Vedic writings also betray a suspicion of the city as encouraging vice. The wartime destruction of cities in Classical times was sometimes blamed on insufficiently observant citizens: gods not sufficiently propitiated or, as in Rome, on citizens too weakened by libidinous behaviour to resist their overthrow, *pace* Gibbon.

More recently, Afghanistan's peasant Taliban overthrew the decadent, sinful city. The movement has now joined the Goth, the Vandal, the Mongol and the Hun in the pantheon of the uncivilized and barbarous. The destruction of the Bamiyan Buddhas was the nadir of their cultural policy. Set within a niche in a 90 m cliff, the statues, roughly 40 and 55 m high, were blown up in March 2001. The destruction of the monuments, probably at least 1,500 years old, was announced in advance by the Taliban and proceeded despite world-wide appeals to save them, including many petitions from Islamic clerics, by no means all of whom shared the Taliban's interpretation of the Hadith's proscription of idols. Thousands more statues and painted images

Lot and his Daughters (1520) attributed to Lucas van Leyden. This depiction of the fall of Sodom, with its intimations of incest, has been a popular subject for artists. The destruction of sinful cities and a suspicion of the urban is found throughout Vedic, Koranic, Classical and Judaeo-Christian texts. Similarly, present-day notions of 'urbicide' – attacks on the cosmopolitan and multi-cultural – have been used to explain assaults on cities such as Dubrovnik and Sarajevo.

The larger of the two Buddhas of Bamiyan, blown up by the Taliban (apparently with the urging of al-Qaeda) in March 2001 was, at around 55 m high, the tallest standing Buddha in the world and at least 1,500 years old. It was not simply an iconoclastic brand of Islam that led to their destruction; the statues were felled during a campaign of ethnic cleansing of the Hazara people of the area who resisted Taliban rule and regarded the statues as a symbol of their region. Hazari prisoners were dangled on ropes to set the explosives.

across Afghanistan were smashed in the Taliban's campaign against idolatry. Few of the contents of Kabul Museum survive. Figurative work, of course, suffered most. Statues and pottery were smashed with hammers and axes. Some of the museum's paintings were saved by a dexterous Afghan artist, who used washable paint to hide images of women and children by turning them, temporarily, into painted bushes and trees. They were restored by washing off the paint in public after the defeat of the Taliban.[96]

Although there is clearly an iconoclasm driven by scripture at work here (the history of which is largely outside the scope of this book), the dynamiting of the Bamiyan Buddhas was more than this; the statues were entangled in a process of ethnic cleansing and conquest. Although Muslim, the Shi'a Hazara minority, who resisted Taliban rule, had adopted the Buddhas as an emblem for their region. They called one statue 'Solsol' ('year after year') as a symbol of permanence and continuity.[97] The statues were the victims of a political and military campaign of conquest, not simply religious prejudice. The Taliban methodically devastated the Bamiyan region. It was not just the Buddhas that were razed, much of the town of Bamiyan itself had been flattened, building by building, two years before. Thousands of Hazaras were killed or escaped to live in the ancient monks' caves near the Buddhas. The town of Yakowlang and many villages were also burned to the ground.[98] It was thirteen imprisoned Bamiyan men who were forced to descend ropes at gunpoint to set the explosives around the statues' niches.

The Taliban's Mullah Omar had been equivocal about the future of the Buddhas. In 1999 he had declared them to be rare ancient monuments and, since there were no Buddhists left to worship them, they were excluded from the Taliban's campaign against idolatry. This changed in 2001 when he condemned them as 'shrines of the infidels'.[99] It was claimed that the pressure to destroy the statues came after lobbying from the foreign militants gathered around al-Qaeda, supported by fatwas from Whahhabi clerics in Saudi Arabia who, it has been argued, are resistant to the incorporation of items of material culture under Islamic control into universal (i.e. Western-imposed) notions of art-historical value.[100] Here it is difficult to separate out the religious from the political. Historically, the episodic destruction of images under Islam has sometimes been linked to anthropomorphic notions of power being embodied within a statue, hence the beheading, defacing, whipping and humiliation of figurative works of art as seen, for example, under early Islamic rule in the Indian subcontinent. In this context it is interesting that contemporary Hindu extremists in India responded to the destruction of the Bamiyan Buddhas with a threat to raze mosques in their country, while a Taliban spokesman subsequently justified its actions at Bamiyan as being a much delayed response to the levelling of the Babri mosque at Ayodhya.[101] It has also been suggested that the toppling of the idols was 'a first strike in bin Laden's 9/11 masterplan'.[102]

The concept of the cosmopolitan, of living companionably with the artefacts of another culture, even a long dead one, was something the Taliban (and certainly al-Qaeda) could not tolerate, either in Bamiyan or the once beautiful and multi-faith Kabul. It was the 'malice of hill-dwelling zealots', said the writer Philip Hensher, echoing Bogdanović, of the Pashtun-speaking Taliban.[103] Kabul was as much the victim of urbicide as Sarajevo. Bogdanović notes the work of the nineteenth-century Serb linguist Vuk Karadžić, who propounded the view that the Serbian spirit was rooted outside cosmopolitan and impure cities.[104] Such ideas have their equivalent in the philosophy of Heidegger – a belief that rootedness in a native soil rather than in cities was an essential component of cultivating a national tradition.[105] It is an idea that was easily incorporated into Nazi ideology: 'the soil and blood of the Volk'. This was the other side of the coin spun by Hitler in his grandiose schemes for Germania, his new capital on the site of Berlin. (Jewish districts were among the first to be razed in preparing the ground for the planned monumental dystopia.) The pastoral Teutonic homeland was a recurrent image in Nazi propaganda. Cosmopolitanism was not part of the plan for either town or country.

Empires and tyrannies have always been drawn to vast and monumental rebuilding programmes – architecture on a scale that reflects both their massive ambitions and a desire for the parade grounds and spaces for rallies where their power can be witnessed by the awestruck masses. Equally, as has been widely observed, the Haussmannization of Paris, which destroyed so much of the old city, was as much about surveillance and military control of the boulevards as it was an exercise in beautification and economic regeneration. The same could be said of Beijing today, where the vernacular *hutongs* (courtyard houses) that make up the fabric and character of the historic city are still being steadily bulldozed. The eminent architect Liang Sicheng failed to persuade Mao that the new Beijing should be built adjacent to the ancient, sacred city; the obliteration of the past was as much a consideration as the building of the new. The desire to create a socialist man and a socialist city, or a fascist man and city, has built within it a desire to bring about that change through the very act of destruction and rebuilding – the violent *process* of change.

Le Corbusier's Modernist vision of building a new society through new cities, his desire to 'kill the street', has by contrast been seen generally as progressive rather than as urbicide with a human face. The oftquoted final line from his 1923 *Towards a New Architecture*, 'Architecture or Revolution. Revolution can be avoided', places the built form of cities at the root of social unrest.[106] Le Corbusier was advocating a technocratic top-down act of destruction and rebuilding as a substitute for grass-roots action by people themselves. In this, despite its well-meaning idealism, it is essentially a reactionary rather than a revolutionary concept and, as such, was taken up with gusto by post-war communist Eastern Europe as easily as by Western democracies. Remaking architecture can never be a short cut to Utopia but this does not stop attempts to make it so.[107] And although failed Modernist planning is a common feature of the peacetime cities of the capitalist West, it was among totalitarian regimes behind the Iron Curtain where the centralized power over the redevelopment of the built environment and the overt desires of radical ideology came together in a way that allowed the violent implementation of such ideas on a massive scale.

In Ceauşescu's Romania the planned mass murder of the country's historic and vernacular architectural heritage in both town *and* country is remarkable in both its scope and comparative recentness. Despite some appallingly inappropriate rebuilding of historic centres in the 1960s in the name of modernity, until the mid-1970s Romania had a relatively sophisticated system of building conservation. Ceauşescu's desire to modernize and industrialize what was still largely an agrarian economy was balanced by a will to preserve the nation's rich architectural tradition. All this changed when the dictator conceived a plan to eliminate virtually all traces of historic Romania in his drive to create a new systemized and industrial society that completely broke with the past. In 1974 an Urban and Rural Systemization Law was passed creating the legal framework for the wholesale razing of Romania's towns and villages. The March 1977 earthquake that badly damaged Bucharest and the surrounding region served as the excuse to implement the plan in earnest. In November that year the government's own Directorate of Historic Monuments was closed down and its architects, engineers and craftsmen disbanded. With the bulldozers moving in they were no longer needed.

The 19th-century Minovici Institute for Forensic Science sat on a triangular site in a historic district of Bucharest that was razed to the ground as part of Ceaușescu's country-wide programme for the destruction of historic buildings. Many thousands of churches, mansions, historic monuments and entire towns and villages were destroyed and redeveloped.

The Institute was demolished in August 1985. The frontage buildings in the top photograph have already gone – the leveling of the chapel and the rear wing followed in September. Not an important building in its own right, but the Institute is typical of the quality architectural fabric that was regularly erased by the regime.

By the time Ceaușescu's regime fell in late 1989 an architectural slaughter had occurred. Whole quarters of historic Bucharest had been torn down and a further 29 historic towns had been utterly rebuilt with only a rare monument left standing. At least 37 more centres were in the midst of being razed and redeveloped. Up to 90 per cent of their historic fabric was scheduled for clearance. Work had also begun to systemize the villages. Between seven and eight thousand villages were slated for demolition out of a total of 13,123. Instead of the centuries-old peasant homes with vegetable gardens that were such a pervasive feature of Romania's towns and villages, there would be just 500 agro-industrial centres made up of prefabricated communal tenements around a shopping and service zone. The village programme would have meant moving 11 million people from their houses to flats. It has been calculated that, at the rate of demolition achieved, there would have been only 17,600 pre-1900 buildings left in the whole of Romania today.[108]

What prompted such destruction, such an urge to conquer the past? This was not urbicide based on a fear of the urban – quite the contrary, the country would have been almost wholly urban – nor was it simply collectivization on the Soviet model. Various writers have put forward psychological analyses to explain Ceauşescu's state of mind. Doina Petrescu invokes Freud's *Neuro-Psychosis of Defence*, the urge that 'disavows reality and tries to replace it'.[109] Petrescu argues that the Bucharest clearances and the building of Ceauşescu's mad 'wedding cake' House of the People, in the place of street upon street of the historic city, was an attempt to deny 'an oppressive reality and the replacement of it by a "wonder"'. The kitsch, Neoclassical monster, with its 330,000 square metres of floor-space and a 3.5 km monumental boulevard leading up to it, is, as a building, second in size only to the Pentagon.

Bucharest's Văcăreşti monastery built 1716–22 was regarded as 'the most outstanding achievement of 18th-century Romanian architecture'. Its restoration was completed in 1977 by the Historic Monuments Directorate, which was disbanded the same year. Demolition began in December 1984, shortly before this picture was taken.

The western façade of the Văcăreşti monastery after its three towers were demolished. Destroying the complex, including the main church, a chapel, palace and galleried cloister, each a listed historic monument, took nearly three years. Some of the rubble was dumped in the courtyard of the Mogoşoaia Palace 20 km away.

More straightforwardly, the vanquishing of Romania's architectural heritage, with all the diversity, richness and idiosyncrasies of buildings from before the age of mass-production, was a desire to create a new Romanian worker shorn of an individualistic peasant past, religious conviction or ethnic heritage. An important aspect of Romanian communism was an attempt to homogenize the state, creating an industrialized urban proletariat whose strong regional elements (German, Hungarian, Jewish, Roma, Greek, Serb and Ukrainian) had to be suppressed. Individualism and divergent cultural heritages were unacceptable, as was any architectural evidence of them. Stalin would have understood.

The House of the People stands on the site of the early seventeenth-century Mihai Vodă monastery. The religious complex and the Uranus Hill on which it sat were levelled to create a space for it. The monastery church itself was saved but moved in 1986 to a new location suitably hidden among new slabs of state housing. The church's reprieve may have been due to the fact that it was founded by Michael the Brave, a warrior king favoured by Ceauşescu for his temporary unification of Romania's principal constituent parts (Moldavia, Wallachia and Hungarian-dominated Transylvania) in 1600.[110] Dozens of other historic city churches, palaces, public buildings and private homes – many listed monuments – did not escape his mania. Major losses included the Văcăreşti monastery (1716–22), 'the most outstanding achievement of 18th-century Romanian architecture', the demolition of which took three years to complete.[111] Art historians sent letters protesting the destruction: 'Every nation legitimises its existence through its creativity,' wrote one. 'When evidence of this creativity is suppressed, piece by piece, the very identity of a nation is gradually lost.'[112] The appeals were ignored. In the regional towns and villages centuries-worth of vernacular buildings reflecting, in their various styles and urban morphologies, the ethnic jigsaw of Romania vanished and a mythical national unity with its origins in Roman Dacia promoted.

It was another Cultural Revolution of a sort. Another erasure of various group memories in order to redefine a nation's idea of itself and forge a new unified collective memory reinforced by the facts on the ground. The very process of this overwhelming change to a familiar and treasured physical environment must also have been profoundly dislocating and inculcated a sense of fear about the power of the state, transforming people into 'impotent spectators'.[113] Ceaușescu's aim was the obliteration of difference. A uniform Romanian worker was to come off the production line. Systemized, standardized, terrorized. Controlled, deracinated and conquered.

5 Fences and Neighbours: The Destructive Consequences of Partition

Before I built a wall I'd ask to know
What I was walling in or walling out,
And to whom I was like to give offence.
Something there is that doesn't love a wall . . .
ROBERT FROST, 'MENDING WALL'

Visiting West Belfast again in 2002, I could not fail to notice that the streets that summer were awash with more than the usual number of flags. As well as the nationalist tricolour, hundreds of Palestinian flags had appeared on lampposts and buildings, even poking out of chimney pots. Soon after, the blue and white colours of the Israeli standard with its Star of David were decking the brick terraces of the Loyalist areas of the city.

Belfast has long had a penchant for militant iconography – from flags and murals to painted kerbstones; they are a defining image of the city. They serve many functions, not least as territorial markers delineating the enclaves of the divided community.[1] In identifying with the Palestinian liberation struggle, I was told, Belfast's Republicans were pointing out powerful parallels between the Occupied Territories and the province; division, military occupation and resisting a powerful neighbour. Loyalist sentiment may simply have been reactive, but an identification of the Republican movement with terrorism and a horror of state fragmentation no doubt informed their own appropriation of Zionist regalia.

Belfast's empathetic flag-waving began soon after the Israeli Defence Force (IDF) invaded the West Bank cities in pursuit of suicide bombers, causing devastation in their wake. The incursions effectively ended the tentative Palestinian autonomy that emerged after Oslo II in 1995. The past century, and especially the past 30 years of The Troubles, has seen Belfast, like

Jerusalem, become an increasingly segregated city. Attacks on homes, intimidation and violence mean that mixed areas of Catholics and Protestants now barely exist in the inner city. In Israel's Occupied Territories, the pattern of Jewish settlement building and the destruction of Palestinian homes, infrastructure and heritage intensified under the al-Aqsa intifada, since attempts to forge peace are bound up with territorial manoeuvres and segregation. Israelis on the right have been determined to prevent the unravelling of the land-grab gains made in the Six Day War of 1967, which saw East Jerusalem and the Old City and the (then) Jordanian West Bank come under their control. The feeble mosaic of semi-sovereignty established by the Palestinian National Authority was effectively ended. Nablus, Hebron, Ramallah and Bethlehem were wrecked.

Partition has immense consequences for the built environment. The enforcement of divisions, borders and segregation means both creating physical 'facts on the ground', as the Israelis call it, and marking that delineation with walls, fences and voids where the two communities rub up against each other. Berlin had its 155 km long 'Anti Fascist Protection Rampart', Belfast its 'peace walls' (now called interface zones by the city's socio-geographers), and Israel has recently begun construction on its 'Seam Area'. The political motivations for this segregation, and the military methodologies enforcing it, are not so much directed at opposing armies as the mass of people either side of the divide. The first architectural casualty is, for the most part, housing, destroyed by low-tech arson and bombings or by armoured bulldozers and Apache helicopters . . . or by decree using planning regulations and building permits to bureaucratize demolitions. Zones of segregation and differentiation, however, often ripple out from totemic individual structures, whether it be the Dome of the Rock in Jerusalem or the Babri mosque in Ayodhya, India, the destruction of which is emblematic of the failure of the Indian subcontinent to resolve its tensions 50 years after the Partition that violently severed the subcontinent.

Berlin is, perhaps, unique in that it was the *Mauer* (which in German means 'barrier', not simply 'wall') itself that became symbolic, not just of a city divided but of two opposing global ideologies glowering at each other over a stretch of concrete and barbed wire. The process of building the Wall and of its own destruction is enormously revealing of the physicality of politics. Was West Berlin besieged or a salient? By contrast, Nicosia, which was divided for three decades by an impenetrable barrier, has largely gone unremarked until the recent Turkish and Cypriot bids to join the EU. In the intervening period, cultural cleansing has decimated the divided island's built heritage many times over.

Where issues of delineation are concerned, the demolition of architecture is often closely linked to issues of rebuilding and intensified by proximity either side of the line. Where they are in competition, two cultures, ethnicities, ideologies or races existing side by side, but not mixing, create a heightened architectural consciousness regarding the past and future on both sides and along the border zone itself, however 'artificial' that zone is historically (or maybe especially so). Memories are vying for physical expression, creating, as one Israeli historian puts it, 'intimate enemies'.[2] In general such divisions are about making displacement, uneasy truces or partial victories into concrete statements of possession and validation. Differences are made manifest to intensify ownership. The perception of 'otherness' of those beyond the line is encouraged and fostered, and homogeneity on one's own side reinforced. The self is defined in relationship to the 'other'. All that is air hardens into solidity.

In the anti-Muslim riots that swept the Indian state of Gujarat in February 2002, perhaps as many as 2,000 men, women and children died: hacked and beaten to death or electrocuted and immolated in their houses. Mosques, shrines, businesses and whole villages were destroyed. The riots were a response to the burning to death of 58 people on a train bringing Hindu extremists back to Ahmedabad from Ayodhya, where they had been engaged in efforts to build a new temple dedicated to the Hindu god Ram on the site of a mosque.

In 1992 a mob led by the right-wing Hindu Bharatiya Janata Party (BJP) and activists from the World Hindu Congress (VHP) finally succeeded in razing the sixteenth-century Babri mosque in Ayodhya. With picks, sledgehammers, chisels and their bare hands, they swarmed all over it and took it apart. It was one of the last Mogul buildings remaining intact in the city from its heyday as the capital of the Muslim Awadh region. Each year since there has been inter-communal violence in the city related to marches led by Hindu extremists. The *karsewaks* (Hindu religious volunteers) who attacked the mosque claim that it had been built by the Mogul emperor Barbur as a calculated act of architectural sacrilege on the site of a demolished temple that marked Ram's birthplace. A booklet published by the activists argues that the intention in building the mosque was 'deliberately offensive and meant to give an ocular demonstration of Hindu humiliation for all time'.[3] They are determined to rebuild it – or rather, build it, since there is no reliable evidence that the Ram temple ever existed on the site. Stonemasons' yards have been busy for years with craftsmen carving prefabricated elements for the new temple.

The Babri mosque, with its three Islamic stone domes, had been closed following Partition in 1947 (an ownership dispute had flared after Hindu activists placed Ram idols inside) and it remained padlocked until 1986, when Hindu worshippers were allowed entry. Various attempts had been made to remove the mosque through the courts and by direct action, but it was not until 1992 that the hardliners finally succeeded. Since then, the

The Babri mosque in Ayodhya, Uttar Pradesh, was built in the 16th century by the Mugal emperor Barbur, possibly on the site of an earlier mosque dating back as far as 1194. With very little evidence, Hindu extremists have long argued that it stood on the site of a temple marking the birthplace of Ram, whose destruction was an act of iconoclasm by Muslim invaders. The three-domed stone structure was finally demolished in December 1992 by activists intent on 'rebuilding' the temple. A political lightning-rod, the issue is deadlocked but has sparked murderous anti-Muslim riots and the destruction of Islamic monuments and mosques across India.

demolition site has been heavily guarded, but in 2002 a pair of pillars for the new temple was ceremonially erected by militant Hindus. The presence of a 37,000-strong security force meant the extremists were forced to make their statement a mile away from the rubble of the mosque, but the point was made. A local Hindu saint had declared the entire area of the city *ramkot* ('Ram's place') as a justification for the wayward foundation ceremony, but that has not stopped them demanding that the actual temple must be built on the actual site of the mosque. The intention appears to be, as well as supposedly reversing the perceived humiliation at the hands of Muslims caused by the building of the mosque in the first place, to force the Muslim and Hindu communities apart. It is part of a campaign against pluralism and a multi-ethnic society. The slogan of Hindu Indian hardliners then, and at the time of partition, was 'Pakistan or Kabristan' – Pakistan or the graveyard. Muslims can take their choice.[4]

Communal strife has long had a place on the Indian subcontinent. However, up until independence and the 1947 Partition that created the states of Pakistan and India, these eruptions between Hindus, Sikhs and Muslims had, for long periods, usually been minor affairs. The different religions and their monuments had largely coexisted side by side, as in Bosnia. Although British colonialists had sought to exploit divisions between communities during their rule, when it came to the struggle for Indian independence the debate was dominated by pluralists; extreme Hindu nationalism had little part to play in the Indian National Congress, although Hindus provided most of the leaders and formed the majority of its members. Even so, Muslim leaders at the time remained wary of becoming an eternal minority group in a Hindu-dominated independent India. Partition, when it came, saw communal clashes and brutal ethnic cleansing on a vast scale. In the region of two million people were killed and another 12–15 million were shunted across the new borders. In the process temples, mosques and the cultural patrimony of each religious group suffered severe damage. The fallout from partition still dominates politics in the subcontinent and has done so increasingly as nationalist and religious chauvinism has combined in an effort to shore up failing governments on both sides of the border.

In Pakistan the Muslim leadership rapidly abandoned secularism post-Partition and became a theocratic state; Islamic laws were embedded in the constitution of 1956. Indian post-independence governments, dominated by the Congress Party, succeeded for a long time in maintaining the semblance of a secularist and pluralist line. Key constituencies such as the Muslims and lower castes were wooed. The growing disenchantment of Indians with successive Congress governments, however, created a space where extremists could thrive, to the point where, by the mid-1980s, the mosque at Ayodhya was more than a contested monument: it had become, and still is, an indicative symbol of the future direction of Indian society. The issue was then used successfully by the Hindu chauvinists to propel themselves into government on a ticket that sought to unite various Hindu castes in a single political bloc. The Ayodhya crisis must also be seen within a climate of increased tension between India and Pakistan over the last decade regarding Kashmir, where mosques and temples are routine targets for opposing groups, and because of the testing of nuclear missiles on both sides of the border. The disputes have brought the two countries to the very edge of war. Muslims within India and minorities within Pakistan have suffered commensurately. Christian churches in Pakistan have also come under repeated attack from hard-line Islamists (as have the mosques of competing Islamic faith groups).

It is not just about Ayodhya any more, if it ever was. Increasingly Hindu activists are dredging up disputes over temple destruction going back many hundreds of years to Islamic rule in India following the wave of conquests that began in earnest in the eleventh century. They are seeking to portray Islam in India as inherently iconoclastic and intolerant, and Muslims as outsiders or, historically, as forcibly converted Hindus, in an effort to inflame the continuing rupture of Partition and the uneasy ethnic truce that followed. Claims of 3,000 or even 60,000 destroyed temples have been made. Among many examples, activists cite the Quwwat-ul-Islam mosque built by the first Islamic ruler of Delhi with stones and columns from destroyed Jain and Hindu temples, and the destruction of Buddhist and Hindu temples and monasteries across the Gangetic plain. The great university of Nalanda was also razed by the invaders. Mosques, they argue, were built on the site of temples in the holy cities of Benares and Mathura – the latter remains one of the vhp's principal targets for demolition.[5] While some of this destruction, many centuries past, is undoubtedly genuine, its extent, motivation and context has been seriously disputed, notably by historian Richard Eaton. His research suggests that the figure for temple destruction that can be claimed with any certainty is more like 80 and was linked to the practice of capturing a defeated ruler's state deity housed within a temple (and thereby a symbol of a Hindu ruler's authority) or as punishment for rebellion. Such acts were limited political statements rather than a pattern of widespread cultural cleansing. Eaton also argues that the practice featured in internecine conflicts between Hindu rulers and long predates the Islamic conquest or, for that matter, the concept of India as an entity.[6]

The use of this once dormant history of iconoclasm is the past emerging into the present to justify an architectural battle that in turn symbolizes a political conflict. The demolition of sacral buildings has become a key proxy through which post-Partition intercommunal strife is now expressed. Ayodhya is India's Twin Towers – a ground zero from which waves of violence are spreading to engulf thousands and potentially millions of people. The future of one building is intensifying segregation across India. Sacred sites are, of course, almost inevitably contentious given their role as

fixed physical nodes around which cultures shift temporally. Historic meanings are sustained or can be revived around these structures. Claims to
future identities are anchored in them. The importance of individual buildings can also wax and wane and may bear little relation to their intrinsic
architectural merits or historical signficance; Ayodhya's Babri mosque was
not Jerusalem's Temple Mount or even Amritsar's Golden Temple, but a
rather ordinary, provincial mosque. Yet the future of the site has implica-
tions for an entire subcontinent. It was the championing of the temple
builders' campaign by the BJP that led them into government. Members of
the BJP coalition cabinet were present in the crowd at the mosque's destruction. The party and related organizations like the VHP and RSS have their
roots in a proto-fascist ideology, Hindutva, which emerged in the 1920s
and '30s. Narendra Modi, the BJP chief minister of Gujarat, despite being
accused of supporting the anti-Muslim pogroms that convulsed the state in
2002 following the train burning at Godhra, increased his vote in recent
elections using anti-Muslim rhetoric. The state of Gujarat and its police
force have also been blamed for collusion in the killings.[7] Modi blamed
'public anger' for the pogrom, a claim that echoes misleading statements
about the causes of Kristallnacht. Instead, the suggestion of an element of
planning behind the attacks has been backed by the respected Indian
journalist Kudlip Nayer: 'The entire city of Ahmedabad has been mapped
out . . . areas, houses, shops and factories of Muslims were marked and the
specific task of killing, looting and burning was assigned to different
groups.'[8] As well as the thousands of Muslim deaths and Muslim families
forced from their neighbourhoods in this campaign of ethnic cleansing in
the Gujarat city of Ahmedabad and beyond, the state's Islamic architectural
heritage was widely desecrated. This is not destruction along the line of a
border, as such, but the specific consequence of the imposition of such a
divide: an attempt to instigate a vast ethnic mopping-up operation decades
after the fact.

It would be a great mistake to see India as an exemplar of intercommunal
peace before Partition and before the rise of the Hindu right in the past two
decades, but the country has been a pluralistic society for centuries (even if
at times fractiously so). These elements of tension and coexistence are, for
instance, built into the very fabric of the Old City at the heart of Ahmedabad,
which is made up of *pols* – dozens of intertwining cul-de-sac streets and
alleys, each leading off from a single entrance. Traditionally, each was home
to extended families or craft groups. Since religious riots in the early eighteenth century, the *pols* have become progressively more ethnically specific
(although crafts have, in any case, always had strong ethnic affiliations).
Serious riots in 1969 and in the 1980s accelerated this trend to segregation.
Gates at the entrance to each of these micro-ghettos could be closed in times
of trouble. At the same time, this web of territoriality is dotted with public

buildings and monuments of all faiths – ancient temples and historic mosques and shrines side by side.

It is the mix of modernity and medievalism that makes Ahmedabad, India's sixth largest city, such a fascinating place – although its 'sights', apart from spiralling historic step-wells drilled deep into the ground like inverted Towers of Pisa, are rarely majestic enough to divert tourists from the well-trodden route from the palaces of Rajasthan to the madness of Mumbai. Ahmedabad is often called the 'Manchester of the East' for its textile industry. Its core may be ancient but the wider city has massive boulevards and celebrated experiments in Modernist architecture by the likes of Le Corbusier, Louis Kahn, Balkrishna Doshi and Charles Correa. At the same time, veiled Rajasthani women in clashing hot pinks and lurid greens are working on the building sites carrying baskets of bricks on their heads. Wandering cattle, bullock carts and erratic family saloons make for a terrifying trip across the massive concrete bridges spanning its dribble of a river. It is as if the city woke up briefly to the future in the post-independence period, then settled back down with a dust-raising, reactionary thump.

During the 2002 violence, petrol bombs, acid and stones were hurled into Muslim *pols*. Communities and monuments across the state suffered. The Indian campaign group Communalism Combat has reported that 230 shrines, tombs and mosques in Gujerat were vandalized or destroyed in the 72 hours following the Godhra train fire.[9] Among the structures singled out were the graves of the celebrated poet Wali Muhammad (1667–1707, 'Gujarat's Geoffrey Chaucer') in Ahmedabad, and the musician Ustad Faiyaz Khan in Vadodara. Khan's grave was covered with burning tyres and badly damaged while Wali Muhammad's roadside tomb was demolished with pickaxes, despite his artistic appeal across religious divisions. Hindu activists built an impromptu miniature temple on its former site. 'We have broken a mosque and built a temple,' said one participant.[10] Two days later the city authorities laid tarmac over the whole area and incorporated it into the roadway, obliterating even the monument's site. Other damaged monuments of great significance include Ahmedabad's Dada Hari mosque, the carved stone screens and tombs of which were smashed and its collection of Korans burnt on a bonfire. The Malik Asin mosque and another sixteenth-century mosque in the city were completely bulldozed.

Despite the Ayodhya mosque's demolition, the replacement temple remains unbuilt: the matter is still in the courts. A highly contentious archaeological report into the history of the Babri site ordered by the court was delivered in August 2003. It appeared to support the belief that there had been a temple on the site, but this archaeological 'evidence' has been comprehensively trounced by archaeologists from both faith communities who are independent of the politicized Archaeological Survey of India, the government body who carried out the hasty dig and whose head was replaced by the BJP shortly before the investigation.[11] The BJP has since lost power at national level and the new government, a more secular Congress-led coalition, has challenged the BJP's 'saffronization' of history. Biased school textbooks are being withdrawn, among them one that claims that such indisputably Islamic structures as the Taj Mahal were designed by Hindus.[12] The new direction offers hope but the architectural impasse at Ayodhya remains and the dusty ideological whirlwind spinning out from the Babri rubble, which has already left thousands dead and more than 12,000 Gujarati Muslims homeless, still has the potential to intensify the forced segregation of Indian society across the country.

The impact of such a demolition, were it to take place in Jerusalem, or more specifically on Haram al-Sharif/Temple Mount, hardly bears contemplation. Sacred sites in the Holy Land arouse passions; they have launched Crusades. The present intifada was ignited by Ariel Sharon's stroll within the walls of the Haram al-Sharif – an unquestionable attempt to assert ownership and an act of encouragement to extremists within Israel. It is no coincidence that both the latest uprising, known as the al-Aqsa Intifada, and a Palestinian suicide-bomber organization, the al-Aqsa Martyrs Brigade, have taken their names from one of the Haram al-Sharif's mosques. International opinion matters, though, and the Israeli government would prefer to deal with a Palestinian national struggle rather than incur a Middle East-wide *jihad* by attacks on sacred sites. As would the Palestinian leadership, for that matter. Instead, with important exceptions, such as the incursions into Nablus and Hebron described below, it is the quotidian house that has been at the forefront of a war by architectural proxy over the past few decades. Outside the Old City of Jerusalem it is secular sites of contention that predominate in this battle, which is conducted along the putative lines of partition between the occupied West Bank and Gaza and Israel. Ariel Sharon's nickname is 'The Bulldozer' for good reason; it is Jewish settlements and Palestinian houses – the building of the former and the demolition of the latter – that matter in this demographic and territorial struggle between Israeli *hitnahalut* (settlement) and Palestinian *sumad* (steadfastness to place and land).

The mass expulsions and population flight from Arab towns and villages in Israel and the subsequent destruction of many villages in the war following the creation of the Israeli state are continuing today in the Occupied Territories but in a much more gradual, controlled and strategic way. It is ethnic cleansing and has been increasingly recognized as such by a new generation of liberal Israeli historians. This policy dates back to the 1967 conquest of the West Bank, Gaza and East Jerusalem in the Six Day War and beyond. Creating 'facts on the ground' is Israel's three-dimensional territorial policy. It is a strategy designed to flex the 1967 border as far as possible in Israel's favour ahead of any peace settlement.

Between 1967 and mid-2004 Israel demolished in the order of 12,000 Palestinian homes, evicting an estimated 50,000 people. Many of the families left homeless are refugees who first lost their houses in the 1948 war.[13] The rate of destruction has escalated radically in recent years. More than 3,000 homes, hundreds of public buildings and private commercial properties were destroyed by the Israeli army in Israel and the Occupied Territories in the three and a half years to May 2004.[14]

At the same time, at least 136 exclusively Jewish settlements (and on some counts up to 200) have been built within the Occupied Territories since 1967 in violation of international law and, when it suits, Israel's own laws. In the region of 200,000 Israelis now live illegally in the West Bank, with 200,000 more in East Jerusalem and, until recently, at least 6,000 in Gaza. The settlers tend to be composed of the most radical elements of Israeli society: those who would like to see Greater Israel extend at least to the Jordan river and perhaps beyond. With development and demolitions used as weapons, town planning has become central to Israeli nation-building. The entire state is planned and 93 per cent of land is state-owned. Tax incentives encourage Israelis into the new settlements and 'national priority zones'; a married Jewish couple with a child are entitled to a subsidized home loan worth £25,000 if they settle in the West Bank, compared to £10,875 in coastal Tel Aviv.[15]

The demolitions, together with the settlements and their related roads, checkpoints, residency permits and the security walls now under construction, are, say critics, a way of maximizing Israeli territorial expansion at the same time as ensuring that any future Palestinian state will be more akin to South Africa's apartheid-era Bantustans, dependent on Israel for everything from jobs to water. Lack of control over resources, limits on the freedom of movement and the fracturing of the territory into a barely contiguous mosaic of about 190 fenced-in Palestinian areas allows Israel to control the Palestinian population without having to absorb millions of Arabs into Israel proper (the consequence of full annexation) and thereby upsetting the demographic superiority of Jewish Israelis in the state.[16] The architectural manipulation of the region will also ensure that Arab East Jerusalem will become ever more isolated from its Palestinian hinterland. In this scenario, the continued maintenance of a sometimes porous, sometimes solid, but always flexing border between Israel and the Occupied Territories and the partitions within the Territories themselves are essential to Israel.

The Israeli state uses three justifications for the demolitions: a bureaucratic one that targets Palestinian houses without building permits; punitive destruction of family homes where a member is suspected or known to be involved in terrorism; and military clearances necessary to create security strips along borders, and around Jewish settlements and their roads. In the past the Israeli government has been unwilling to admit that demolitions by

Around 12,000 Palestinian homes have been destroyed by Israeli forces since the '67 war. The losses have been the result of both bureaucratic and military decisions and as retribution for the actions of known and suspected Palestinian suicide bombers. The Israelis have manipulated its architectural and planning policies to create three-dimensional 'facts on the ground'. Here, Sobhiya Al-Amour, 50, confronts an Israeli armoured bulldozer destroying two houses near the Jewish settlement of Kfar Darom in the Gaza Strip, 12 February 2001.

the military are acts of revenge for Palestinian attacks on Israelis – they are often disguised as security necessities – but more recently, attempts have been made to defend this policy publicly. The bureaucratic, or 'administrative', demolitions are conducted using different legal mechanisms to those of the military, even if the actual demolition work is carried out by the army, as is usually the case. The motivation – in addition to retribution – is to keep the expansion of Palestinian areas to a minimum at the same time as allowing the safe expansion of Jewish settlements. Apart from those in annexed East Jerusalem, the demolitions have taken place in Gaza and in 'Area C' of the West Bank, the more than 70 per cent of its area where Israel has remained in continuous control and occupation despite the establishment of the Palestinian National Authority. Israel controls the planning system well beyond its 1967 borders.[17]

Palestinians find it impossible to acquire the proper building permits here, in what are effectively frontier lands within their own territory, and so are forced to build illegally. A combination of British Mandate, Jordanian and Israeli planning laws is used to enforce this situation. It is ostensibly a civilian system but it is used to pursue war aims. The main West Bank planning bodies themselves are housed in military complexes that are unlikely to admit Palestinians, never mind allow them to pursue claims that are, in any case, almost always refused. Elsewhere, even if building permits are granted by civilian authorities, the military still has a right of veto. Significant obstacles to legal building also include the fact that land registration has been frozen for 30 years, so Palestinians cannot prove ownership and their permit bids fail. In addition, much of the land has been declared 'state land' by the Israelis; no Palestinian building is allowed. Palestinian authorities have planning control only outside Area C in zones that are tightly circumscribed around existing Palestinian urban centres as they were defined before 1948. Official development plans for these West Bank areas date back to the Mandate era and envisaged a much smaller local population. Building is illegal in the absence of an official plan. Since new plans have not been approved by the Israelis, no Palestinian can build outside the inner areas of the existing towns and virtually none can be built in rural areas.[18]

According to the Israeli human rights organization B'Tselem, the Palestinian desire to build is not a weapon in the same way the Israeli demolitions are: 'Their act is not intended as a political statement or as opposition to Israeli control in the area but rather to meet a need for housing for themselves and for their families that Israel's policy does not allow them to realize.' In 1990 alone, some 13,000 Palestinian homes had to be built illegally.[19] In Jerusalem itself fewer than 300 building permits a year are granted to Palestinians, even though they make up a third of the city's 670,000 population. Palestinian areas of East Jerusalem are also zoned so that extensions to existing houses are severely limited.[20] In July 2002, in an act that brought the issue to international attention, homes belonging to fourteen East Jerusalem Palestinian families near the Jewish settlement of Pisgat Ze'ev, and dozens more elsewhere in the Occupied Territories, were demolished in one week. Foreign governments were provoked to respond. The UK described the demolitions as 'provocative and inflammatory', the US as 'deeply troubling'. Jerusalem's right-wing mayor Ehud Olmert was defiant, saying that, in future, all unlicensed buildings would be demolished. The Palestinians, he added, must know that 'the glory days are over'.[21]

The extent of the demolitions rises and falls with changes in Israeli's political and security climate. Before the mid-1980s, long-standing illegally built houses had a good chance of remaining *in situ*, but since then 'administrative' demolitions (in addition to direct military clearances) have escalated. At the time of writing they are running at twenty a week, often occur without warning and have, on occasion, killed or injured occupants within.[22] These deaths have been vigorously denied by the Israeli government but there is now clear evidence to support the claims, including instances in Nablus (April 2002) and Gaza (September 2004).[23]

During the same period, thousands of Jewish homes, commercial and public buildings have been built illegally in the West Bank. Less than a handful have been demolished. Instead, most are given building permits retrospectively. In short, although Palestinians are responsible for an estimated 20 per cent of illegal house building, they suffer virtually all the demolitions for building without a permit.[24] Homes that have taken years to save for and build are destroyed in hours – often with personal possessions still inside. Families are forced into tents or relatives' crowded houses. Israeli politician Effi Eitam, leader of the National Religious Party, described illegal Palestinian houses as a 'jihad of buildings' creating 'uncultured . . . terrorist nests'. He went on to say that the Temple Mount mosques were a 'blight of universal proportions'.[25]

The effect on housing-need cannot be over-emphasized. The Palestinian birth rate is 7.73 per family (in Gaza) with the population of the West Bank and Gaza estimated to approach 12 million by the middle of this century.[26] At the same time, 70 per cent of Palestinians live below the poverty line, often in unsanitary conditions that the demolitions and the curbs on building maintain and intensify. By contrast, successive Israeli governments have continued to build settlements even while agreeing to a freeze as part of peace discussions, such as Oslo II or under the later ill-fated 'Road Map to Peace'. In 2003, for instance, building work in the illegal Jewish settlements increased by 35 per cent according to Israel's Central Bureau of Statistics. Yet building work within Israel itself was at its lowest rate for ten years.[27] In August 2004, while declaring that it would withdraw settlers from Gaza, the Sharon government said it would build 533 more homes in the West Bank settlements on top of the 1,000 construction tenders for houses announced the previous week. According to the Israeli pressure group Settlement Watch, the 2,167 West Bank building permits granted to August 2004 were more than those for the three previous years combined.[28] Settlement Watch coordinator Dror Etkes said: 'This is about redesigning Israel and moving the bulk of it eastwards onto the land on which the Palestinians want to build their state. It is the continuation of a process that has been going on for 40 years.'[29] The Gaza withdrawal looks like a tactical measure – a gesture of reasonable behaviour while the more intensive work of redeveloping the West Bank continues apace. The withdrawal, and the removal of a limited number of tiny outposts on the outer limits of some settlements, has infuriated extremist settlers. In response, they have not just demonstrated outside Temple Mount but, in some cases, have plotted to occupy the Haram al-Sharif or even, in the case of three members of an Orthodox Hassidic sect, to fire a shoulder-held missile at the Dome of the Rock.[30] In a highly symbolic move, Sharon agreed to delay the Gaza withdrawal so that it does not coincide with the annual period of mourning for the destruction of the Herodian Temple observed by religious Jews.

However unjustifiable, there is a greedy territorial and demographic logic to these administrative demolitions. And, in some cases, a military logic. Beyond this, however, the notion of demolition acting as collective retribution for Palestinian attacks on Israelis is bizarrely atavistic. It is as if the stones themselves are culpable. In November 2001, for example, Israel's security forces demolished the West Bank home of Nathir Hamad's family, accusing him of planning a gun attack, and in July 2002, more than twenty relatives of suspected bombers were evicted and their homes blown up by the military. The families were then threatened with expulsion from the country.[31] At the same time, the IDF destroyed the three-storey house of a Hamas commander accused of organizing an attack on the Jewish settlement of Emmanuel. A few years earlier, in the summer of 1997, dozens of Palestinian buildings were demolished in response to the bomb attack on Jerusalem's Mahane Yehuda market. Sometimes the retribution appears directed at any likely house near to an Israeli death at the hands of terrorists; at others the housing is inconveniently close to a Jewish settlement or the roads serving them. The focus of attack may be directly on the family home of a known or suspected bomber, or a demolition can encompass whole blocks of flats (such as an eight-storey apartment building in Hebron).[32] Up to 672 other cases of punitive demolition have been extensively documented by human rights organizations such as Amnesty International and B'Tselem.[33] The retribution works both ways and escalates the terrible violence on both sides. In January 2003 the al-Aqsa Martyrs Brigade claimed responsibility for two bombs that killed 23 people and injured more than 100 in an attack on a Tel Aviv bus station. The Brigade stated that the bombs were in retaliation for the demolition of Palestinian homes.[34] These punitive demolitions by Israeli forces are not even-handed though; the family home of Yigal Amir, the extremist Israeli who assassinated prime minister Yitzhak Rabin in 1995, remains standing. In February 2005 the IDF announced an end to the policy of punitive demolitions, ostensibly as part of a goodwill gesture following the death of Arafat and the election of Mahmoud Abbas as Palestinian leader, although it was also increasingly recognized by the army that the demolitions were generating more resistance rather than acting as a deterrent.

Military demolitions, however, are not confined to the identified houses of activists, which make up only a small percentage of the 12,000 Palestinian houses destroyed. Armoured bulldozers have been joined by jets and helicopter gunships in razing Palestinian buildings across the Occupied Territories. These attacks have been even more devastating and indiscriminate. On 10 January 2002, for example, the IDF demolished 60 homes in Gaza's Rafah refugee camp, leaving around 600 Palestinians homeless. The incident provoked an international outcry, especially since demolitions usually occur at night without warning when many residents are asleep. And, as elsewhere, the military grubbed up olive and citrus orchards, smashed glass-houses, dug up irrigation pipes and ploughed in crops. Palestinian agriculture has been badly damaged by these actions, which leave people without an income or a ready food source. The UNWRA calculates (as of February 2002) that during the course of the al-Aqsa intifada the IDF demolished 655 homes in the Gaza Strip alone. The Israelis admitted to half this figure (including farm buildings and walls) claiming 'pressing military necessity' and citing Palestinian attacks in the vicinity where buildings had been used as cover. In most instances, however, the demolitions have occurred up to weeks later or in another location, provoking accusations by human rights groups of grave breaches of the Fourth Geneva Convention relative to the Protection of Civilian Persons in Time of War and of illegal collective punishment contrary to the UN Convention against Torture.[35] More destructive incursions into Gaza by the IDF have followed, including 'Operation Root Canal' in October 2003, which wrecked a further 200 homes, and again in May 2004, by which time a total of 2,200 demolitions had occurred in the Strip since 2000 – one of the world's most densely populated urban areas.[36] Suhaila Ahmad Salim Barhoum, a widow whose extended family lost 11 houses, home to 75 people, in the Barahmeh district of Rafah in June 2001, told Amnesty International:

> I woke up at the sound of the army shooting and I ran off inside the camp with the children; other times when the army shot we ran away and waited until the shooting stopped to come back. But this time the tanks came up against the houses with the bulldozers. When they left there was only rubble and dust left in the place of our houses. I had a

nice house; four rooms, one for each of us, the kitchen, the bathroom and a hall. I built it four years ago. My previous house was demolished in 1982, when they established the border. Then my house was right where the border is now. After some time I got some compensation but it was not enough, and I had to wait to have enough money to build a new house. And now I won't be able to build another house again.[37]

Sharon has been unapologetic about a policy with which he has been involved for many years. As far back as 1953 he commanded Israeli forces that flattened the Palestinian village of Kibya. Sixty-nine Palestinians died in what was a revenge attack for the murder of a Jewish woman and her children. More recent attacks on Israeli settlements have led him to espouse the implicit policy explicitly. Asked how he would deal with Palestinians repeatedly shooting on the Jewish settlement of Gilo from Palestinian Beit Jela, he said: 'I would eliminate the first row of houses in Beit Jela . . . I would eliminate the second row of houses and so on. I know the Arabs. They are not impressed by helicopters and missiles. For them, there is nothing more important than their house.'[38] Despite the horrific attacks on Israeli civilians by Palestinian terrorists, it is the Israelis who have made bricks and mortar, construction and destruction, central to the struggle. Only a formerly exiled community with its Diaspora dream of 'next year in Jerusalem' could know the effect of such a policy. For Palestinian exiles, many of whom still cherish the keys to their former houses in Israel, returning home is a potent dream. 'Exile', said Edward Said, 'is strangely compelling to think about but terrible to experience. It is the unhealable rift forced between a human being and a native place; between the self and its true home.'[39] The Israelis have denied many Palestinians homes even in exile. It is no wonder that the bitterness of the conflict is intensifying.

In the West Bank the demolitions reached their climax in the spring of 2002 when the IDF launched Operation Defensive Shield, taking control of the major West Bank towns, ostensibly in pursuit of suicide bombers. The consequences have been devastating. It was the levelling of large areas of the town of Jenin in April 2002 that truly brought home the scale at which the Israelis have been willing to destroy housing. The deaths of thirteen Israeli soldiers attacking the refugee camp attached to Jenin in search of suicide bombers led the IDF to adopt a tactic of wholesale clearance in order to penetrate deep into the densely built stronghold. Bulldozers cleared an area 400 by 500 m. According to a UN report, much criticized by human rights groups for its underestimates (and conducted without full investigation on the ground in the face of Israeli opposition) more than 100 houses were destroyed – almost 10 per cent of the total. At least 50 Palestinians died amid accusations (unproven on this occasion) of massacres and people being buried alive under the rubble.[40]

Across the West Bank, the towns of Ramallah, Hebron, Bethlehem and Nablus were also ripped apart. Upwards of 490 Palestinians died in the incursions, both fighters and civilians, 1,447 were wounded. About 2,800 refugee homes were damaged, said the UN report, and 878 completely destroyed. Around 17,000 people were made homeless.[41] It was not only houses that were wrecked; schools, hospitals, universities, TV and police stations, Gaza airport and, most prominently, Yasser Arafat's Ramallah headquarters compound were also targeted for damage and destruction. It was a systematic demolition of the nascent Palestinian state's urban infrastructure – the architectural representations of nationhood. Among the institutions ransacked was the Kalil Aslakakimi cultural centre in Ramallah. Paintings were torn off the walls, poetry manuscripts scattered and stamped on. Other cultural buildings were vandalized, had equipment stolen or were used as latrines by occupying Israeli soldiers. The contempt for Palestinian culture and nationhood was expressed in the treatment of its buildings. Jeff Halper, coordinator of the Israeli Committee against House Demolitions, puts the fearsome D-9 armoured Caterpillar bulldozers at the centre of the Israeli war machine:

> The bulldozer certainly deserves to take its rightful place alongside the tank as a symbol of Israel's relationship with the Palestinians. The two deserve to be on the national flag. The tank as a symbol of an Israel fighting for its existence, and for its prowess in the battlefield. And the bulldozer for the struggle to displace Palestinians from the country.[42]

The message of the bulldozers, suggests Halper, is: 'You do not belong here. We uprooted you from your homes in 1948 and prevented your return, and now we will uproot you from all of the Land of Israel.'[43] Amid all this destruction, one building was conspicuous by the reticence with which it was handled by the Israeli Army – the Church of the Nativity in Bethlehem. This fortress-like complex of monasteries, churches and the original fourth-century Chapel of St Helena, built upon the reputed birthplace of Christ, was simply too conspicuous a Christian icon to be ravaged – even after Palestinian militants and civilians took refuge inside with the monks during the Israeli invasion of the town. The Vatican and the Anglican and Greek Orthodox churches put heavy pressure on the IDF not to storm the church. Both sides strenuously denied causing a fire in part of the basilica complex. Its symbolism and sanctity saved it from serious damage. Prolonged negotiations instead secured the end of the siege. The bulldozers were idle.

Palestinian heritage has been treated in a more expendable manner, however. The April 2002 incursion into the historic city of Nablus saw one of the largest single acts of destruction of Palestinian heritage since the aftermath of the creation of Israel. Nablus dates back to 71 BC and incorporates honey-coloured stone structures from Roman, Byzantine, Crusader, Mamluk and Ottoman times. It is a town of 150,000 people with a dense historic souk of winding alleys and minarets at its core. Before the IDF incursion, 2,500 historic structures were recorded, from Roman water cisterns to nineteenth-century mosques.[44] Despite being one of the most important towns in the West Bank, Nablus is not even identified on signs along the new Jewish settlers' roads (which are out of bounds to Palestinians). Instead signs point towards the archaeology of the millennia-old biblical town of Shechem, the ruins of which lie outside Nablus. The existence of the Palestinian city is not even acknowledged in the Israeli effort to carve out a continuity with their pre-Diaspora presence in the land. Like Jenin, it was the impenetrable urban core of Nablus that offered a physical barrier to Israeli military operations. Unlike the Church of the Nativity, the international importance of its heritage did not offer protection. On 3 April 2002 the IDF blasted its way in with bulldozers, Apache attack helicopters and F-16 jets. Throughout the centre historic stone buildings have been gouged, pocked or reduced to rubble. The damage was not as wholesale as in Jenin, but in some ways it has been worse – at least as far as Palestinian culture is concerned.

Diving below the dashboard seemed a reasonable response to the raking machine-gun fire from an Israeli tank that met my arrival in Nablus a few months later. A gaggle of stone-throwing Palestinian children may have been the ostensible draw but even though I was in a clearly marked 'Press' car, the

In April 2002 the IDF attacked the historic West Bank city of Nablus. An enormous amount of damage was caused to the city's architectural heritage. The al-Khadrah mosque (above, with shattered roof) – which has its origins 1,600 years ago as a Byzantine church – had its street frontage ripped off by an armoured bulldozer. The old section of the mosque has since been repaired but the newer wings have been levelled.

At the heart of Nablus's stone-built souk were an Ottoman caravanserai and 200-year-old traditional soap factories. They were wrecked by Israeli Apache helicopters and F-16 jets and then bulldozed. The IDF claims (without any disclosed evidence) that the buildings were being used as a bomb factory, claims disputed by the Palestinians, who say that the buildings were empty and in line for a European Union-funded restoration project.

tank swung its barrel at the windscreen and two armoured personnel carriers locked the car in a steel sandwich before we were allowed to bump over kerbstones and wasteland to a hotel above the souk. I was there to report on the damage as an eyewitness for *The Art Newspaper* and *The Independent on Sunday* in the face of earlier denials of damage by eminent Israelis, including Martin Weyl, the former director of the Israel Museum, who described the effect of the incursion on the historic fabric of Nablus as 'non-existent'.

Downtown Nablus was a ghost town under curfew. Entry to its centre was past hostile Israeli checkpoints, earth berms and shell-crumpled nineteenth-century and British Mandate-era buildings. The streets, chewed up by tank tracks, were almost empty but for rubble, rubbish and uprooted palm trees. Residents had been confined indoors for more than a hundred days and nights, the rubbish remained uncollected and the muezzin's call to prayer was unanswered. Only in the ancient souk, away from the patrolling IDF outside, was there any semblance of life: a few of its inhabitants buying vegetables from makeshift stalls, smoking in doorways or kicking a football around in a desultory way among the alleys and bomb-sites. In the middle of a crater, a little boy showed me the photograph of his brother, killed in the raids, which hangs on a string around his neck.

While some of the damage had been rapidly repaired, dozens of the rambling stone *hosh* (family courtyard houses) that make up the physical cement of the old city had been flattened while the breaking of stone bracing arches across the alleyways between them threatened further collapse of the interlocking three-dimensional jigsaw of structures. Another 200 houses were partially demolished. Twisted bedframes and tattered sofas poked out of the mounds of rubble. Eight people in one family were killed on 9 April when a bulldozer rammed their home, the al-Shu'bi *hosh*, and collapsed it onto its neighbour as the IDF drove a path for armoured cars into the souk. Two more people were pulled from the ruins a week later when the ongoing curfew was briefly lifted.[45] The rescue was shown on Israeli television. Further up the same street, two teacher sisters, Zoha and Soha Fretekh, were killed when a missile from an Apache helicopter smashed into the Okasha *hosh* next door. Among other buildings damaged or destroyed were the al-Khadrah mosque, converted from a Byzantine church in the eleventh century and since extended. Its historic frontage and part of its vaulted roof were smashed in by an armoured bulldozer and other, admittedly less historically valuable, parts of the complex were flattened. Two other historic mosques, which are around 1,600 years old (again built as early Christian churches), were also hit by heavy weaponry. An Ottoman hammam and a Greek Orthodox church were also damaged by shells. The World Heritage Committee of UNESCO condemned the damage to Palestinian heritage in Nablus, saying that it 'deplores the destruction and damage caused to the cultural heritage of Palestine'. It emphasized the 'exceptional universal value' of this heritage.[46]

In some ways the attacks, on the mosques at least, are surprising. Both sides in the conflict have avoided targeting each other's religious buildings, although there have been isolated incidents such as the Palestinian destruction of Joseph's Tomb, a sacred Jewish monument on the edge of Nablus, at the beginning of the intifada and an attack by Israeli extremists on a mosque in Tiberius, northern Israel. This is in marked contrast to the patterns of ethnic cleansing in other states such as the former Yugoslavia. Yasser Arafat ordered that Joseph's Tomb be rebuilt. It was, but was desecrated again after the Israeli attack on Nablus.

The most concentrated area of destruction in Nablus saw an F-16 jet bomb the very heart of the town's souk. Many *hosh*, a 200-year-old soap factory and an ancient caravanserai were devastated. Where there was once a dense quarter of historic stone buildings, it is now possible to drive through the area of rubble from one street to a road parallel on the other side of the crater. Only vestigial stone vaults, like a torn Escher painting, remain around the ragged edge of the site.

The IDF claimed, without evidence, that the historic soap-factory buildings were being used by militants and they cleared hundreds of local residents into nearby schools before bombing the area. It was a carefully planned strike. Local conservationist Naseer Arafat argues, however, that the buildings were totally and obviously empty. And why, he asks, did the army return two months later to flatten the rubble of the factory and the caravanserai? Arafat points out that the building had been earmarked for a £2.2 million European Union restoration project:[47] 'The question is', asks Arafat, 'why demolish [this and] two adjacent soap factories in addition to the seven connected houses only hours before the Israeli forces left [temporarily] in April?' It cannot be proved that, in Nablus, the IDF deliberately targeted Palestinian heritage – this is not Bosnia – but it has shown a blatant disregard for it, in contravention of the Hague Convention. This heritage is deemed, at the very least, expendable by the Israeli forces. A BBC documentary team subsequently visited Nablus and Jerusalem and confirmed my findings. It is hard to imagine Jewish heritage, or the patrimony of the major Christian churches, being bulldozed and shelled in the same way.

At the time of writing, Palestinian architects and conservationists are fighting a plan by the IDF (military order T/61/02) that calls for the demolition of the historic homes of 110 families in Hebron's old city so that a road can be widened and walled off to create a protected route between one of the most extreme of extremist Jewish settlements and the Haram el-Khalil, the ancient building in old Hebron that houses both the Tomb of the Patriarchs, sacred to Jews, and the Ibrahimi mosque, sacred to Muslims. It is, by tradition, the not very restful resting place of Abraham, Isaac and Jacob – prophets to both faiths. Nowhere, with the exception of Temple Mount/Haram al-Sharif, does the face-off between Muslim and Jew, Palestinian and Israeli, come so close – nose to nose under the same roof. Jews enter through one door, Palestinians through another.

The area and the building itself have long been sites of conflict. In 1929 a brutal Palestinian massacre killed 67 Jews and caused many other Jewish residents to flee the city. A revenge attack by a Jewish settler in 1994 killed 29 Muslims at prayer in the Ibrahimi mosque and the building was then shut by the Israelis for eight months. When it reopened it had been repartitioned, reducing the Muslim space from 90 per cent to 45 per cent, despite the illegal Jewish settlers being a tiny minority of a local population under foreign occupation.[48] Violence between the two groups has continued since, with routes in the city gated and an arson attack on the offices of Hebron's Waqf (Islamic Trust). It is a microcosm of the process of shifting borders and occupation. The buildings in Hebron's Jaber neighbourhood now scheduled for demolition range from the fifteenth century to the nineteenth. They form an intrinsic part of the historic setting of the Ibrahimi mosque and the southern gateway to the city.[49] The proposal comes after the Palestinian conservation group Riwaq's highly successful project to restore the old city, which was depopulated following its annexation by Israel. Plans to restore buildings in Jaber have been prevented by the Israeli military. Now settlers want to build a thousand-unit apartment block at one end of the contested road.[50] Set this disregard for Nablus and Hebron's architectural heritage in the context of the systematic destruction of contemporary Palestinian state and cultural infrastructure and it appears that Israel is not just indifferent but actively hostile to expressions of a competing right to the land. Nearly two millennia of cultural history is less important than undermining the Palestinian national cause.

Palestinian bomb attacks on Israelis within Israel, however, appear to be directed not at architectural representations of statehood or the military but at the everyday lives of its people; café quarters, nightclubs, hotels, markets and shops. Of course, these are softer, easier targets than heavily guarded institutions and allow maximum injury to vulnerable bodies, but it appears that the war by architectural proxy is very much one-sided; buildings are damaged incidentally by Palestinian terrorists in an attempt to kill and maim people. It is as if the suicide bombs are an attempt to discourage and reverse the influx of immigrants that have arrived since the creation of Israel. Certainly the ideology of the terror group Hamas is viciously anti-Semitic and goes way beyond the aim of promoting Palestinian statehood or even anti-Zionism in its attacks. Its rhetoric, with good reason, feeds Israeli fears that the Palestinians wish to drive them into the sea – notwithstanding Palestinian recognition of the Israeli state. Support for Hamas has, of course, been fed by Israeli actions in the Occupied Territories. Academic Robert Wistrich summed up the Israeli perspective:

> This has become a war of survival for every one of us – for the right to walk down a street, to go to a shopping mall, to take a bus, to sit in a bar, a cafeteria, a pizzeria, to go to the cinema, the theatre, a disco or a public space, to pray in a synagogue or to study on campus, without being blown to pieces by a homicidal bomber.[51]

In Jerusalem the attacks have been dubbed 'the war of the croissant' by some coffee-bar denizens because of the number of cafés attacked.[52] This may be a calculated policy on the part of the Islamic extremists: the ruination of everyday life and pleasures and so reducing the attraction for Diaspora Jews of making a life in Israel. Despite the security measures, the terrorists must have the reach to deliver a blow against the more obvious monumental symbols of a permanent Jewish presence but have rarely chosen to do so. Terrorists have traditionally been just that – creators of terror and fear – in an attempt to undermine resolve. Hamas and the al-Aqsa Martyrs Brigade are no exception. The mangled and bloody carcasses of bus after bus blown up in the shopping streets of Jerusalem's New City have certainly created uncertainty. Unlike the shells and gunfire of the West Bank, the threat here feels less predictable, more chancy, enervating everyday life. It is a familiar feeling to anybody who visited central London during the height of the IRA's bombing campaign. When buses pass down Jaffa Street it is tempting to pause behind the protection of the arcaded pavement's pillars.

Outside Israel, where Jews as individuals are less easily picked out, the opposite experience is true: in the absence of statehood, it is religious monuments that, in large part, stand out as a visible Jewish presence and as markers of identity. It is synagogues and Jewish cemeteries that have felt the fall-out from the Middle East crisis. Attacks in Europe and elsewhere by Islamic extremists, and by white neo-Nazis using the Middle East situation as a new excuse for their pre-existing violent anti-Semitism, have risen rapidly in recent years. Which of these groups is most to blame is a matter of some controversy but the escalation in anti-Jewish violence is clear. Arson attacks, for instance, have occurred in France, Belgium, the Netherlands, Germany and the UK. In 2002 there were 350 reported anti-Semitic incidents in Britain, including arson, assault and desecration of gravestones. This was a 13 per cent rise on the previous year. In France attacks rose six-fold in the same period.[53] Ariel Sharon responded by urging French Jews to take refuge in Israel. Some of these attacks on buildings have been of a different order of magnitude; an explosion at a Tunisian synagogue in April 2002 that killed ten tourists was followed by blasts at two Istanbul synagogues in November 2003. In the same year, ten neo-Nazis were arrested in Germany and accused of a plot to blow up the inauguration ceremony of a new Munich synagogue. The ceremony was scheduled for 9 November, the anniversary of Kristallnacht. Police found a hit list that also included several mosques and a Greek school.[54]

The porous, flexing border between Israel and the Occupied Territories has, in the past, worked in Israel's interest. Demolitions and settlement building have physically reshaped huge areas of land in an attempt to create a permanent Israeli presence that is impossible to unravel. International peace efforts have repeatedly, and unsuccessfully, pressured Israeli governments to put a halt to both. But with the suicide bombers making daily life somewhere between uncertain and terrifying for the Israeli public, this permeability has become as problematic as it is beneficial. Between September 2000 and September 2004, at least 2,778 Palestinians (557 under 18) had been killed by the Israeli security forces, and 632 Israeli citizens (110 under 18) murdered by Palestinian militants.[55] The solution, as in Berlin and

Cyprus, is a proposal for a permanent membrane: a 700 km security barrier to divide the two communities. The border shows every sign of becoming fixed. This in itself creates a problem, and not just for the ghettoized Palestinians on its eastern side. The decision to build the wall would appear to thwart ambitions by hardline Zionists who wish to claim the whole of Eretz Israel (with, preferably, the Palestinians 'encouraged' to go elsewhere). This Revisionist Zionism has its beginnings in the writings of Ze'ev Jabotinsky, the journalist and pioneer Zionist, who later became leader of the Irgun militia. Jabotinsky wanted no compromise to the ideal of creating an Israeli state in the whole of the former British Mandate of Palestine. His 'Iron Wall' doctrine (1923) was hugely influential and continues to be so on the Israeli right (including within Likud) among those who have never accepted UN partition: 'We must either suspend our settlement efforts or continue them without paying attention to the mood of the natives,' he wrote. 'Settlement can thus develop under the protection of a force that is not dependent on the local population, behind an iron wall which they will be powerless to break down.'[56] The gradualists of early Labour Zionism, such as David Ben-Gurion, were more willing to play it by ear: 'Erect a Jewish state at once, even if it is not the whole land,' he said. 'The rest will come in the course of time.'[57]

Jabotinsky's iron wall was a metaphorical one, of Israeli military muscle. A real wall might be an end to the vision. In November 2000, and in the face of opposition from the right, Labour Prime Minister Ehud Barak began the process of making the barrier physical with the decision to erect a length of security fencing at the northern end of the West Bank. Serious construction work on an extended barrier to fence the Palestinians (both in and out) began in April 2002. The barrier is being built on the 'seam area' – a strip of territory either side of the Green Line (the internationally recognized pre-1967 border). This barrier has been in place militarily if not physically for some years through the establishment of crossing points and the blocking of alternative routes. The Israelis claim that the new wall has radically reduced terrorist attacks within Israel itself. This may well be true, but with a concurrent campaign of assassinations of Hamas leaders it is difficult to tell which has had the greater effect. If this were the wall's sole purpose it would have some justification. However, while Barak's successor, Ariel Sharon, has pragmatically continued to implement Barak's proposals as part of his chimerical 'disengagement plan', he has also been keen to stress that the barrier is not permanent: 'The security line will not be the final border of the State of Israel', he has said, keeping the question of a Greater Israel ever open.[58]

The first 150 km northern stretch of the wall is now in place, together with additional short runs around Jerusalem. Its line makes significant departures from the Green Line to take in a number of illegal Jewish settlements in the West Bank, such as the 30,000-strong surburb of Maale

Adumim, and to reinforce the separation of East Jerusalem from outlying Palestinian towns and villages. A chunk of Bethlehem's territory (a largely Palestinian Christian town) will be encircled to incorporate Rachel's Tomb into the Jewish side of the divide. The result of this forced division is an annexation of territory by the Israelis and, in many areas, the erection of an impassable obstacle between Palestinian agricultural workers and their fields and between Palestinian villages and their hinterland. It is an 8 m high concrete monster set on a strip 30 m wide, that incorporates an anti-tank trench, 'killing strip', electric fence and a two-lane service road. It is a bristling statement of possession and a physical manifestation of a lack of faith in a peaceful settlement. It has also confiscated 40 per cent of the West Bank's best farm land, two-thirds of its wells and its major aquifers.[59] Palestinian property has already been requisitioned and demolitions begun to make way for the structure. In January 2003 the IDF bulldozed 62 shops in the Palestinian market village of Nazlat Issa; 108 of its 170 shops have since been ordered to evacuate. The IDF has justified the demolitions on the ground that they had been built illegally – but it was only necessary to build illegally after the army blocked access to the old market site. Nazlat Issa will find itself on the wrong side of the 'seam area', cut off from the rest of the West Bank. Subsidiary barriers reach out into the West Bank; the 40,000 inhabitants of Palestinian Qalqiliya are now surrounded by barbed wire and connected to the rest of the West Bank by just a single, policed gate.[60] As far as the Palestinians are concerned it is a new Berlin Wall. Only worse. The United Nations General Assembly and the International Court of Justice at The Hague agree; both have condemned the barrier, or the 'Terror Prevention Fence' as Sharon has taken to calling it.[61] In July 2004 The Hague ruled that the project was illegal and would 'destroy Palestinian hopes of self-determination in the territories seized by Israel since 1967'.[62] As prime minister, Ehud Barak has been fond of quoting the line 'Good fences make good neighbors', from Robert Frost's poem 'Mending Wall', in his support of the harmless-sounding seam barrier. Unfortunately Frost's doubts ('something there is that doesn't love a wall') are clearly not in Barak's mind. Nor in Sharon's. The bulldozers and builders are fighting Israel's fight again.

If borders are historic sites of impasse, beyond which neither side can impose its claim, their degree of porosity or impermeability is governed by feelings of security on one or both sides. Israelis, according to historian Meron Benvenisti, relate to the Green Line in a way that reflects 'the basic need to see it as a psychological boundary line, with "home" lying on one side, and chaos and barbarity on the other'. The Israeli barrier is now intended to be permeable in one direction only; outwards from Israel.[63] Berlin's green line – the Wall – was impermeable almost from the start and soon became a symbol at global level of the Cold War impasse between Stalinism and

The 'Iron Wall' policy of early radical Zionists is now finding its expression in the concrete 'Separation Barrier' between Israel and the West Bank. In justifying its construction, the Israeli government has stressed its contribution to security from suicide bombers within Israel but its construction (and the demolitions it has entailed) has also been an opportunity for further land-grabs and a means of controlling the Palestinian 'other' on the opposite side of the wall.

capitalism, between totalitarianism and freedom, West and East, between the two dominant ideologies of the twentieth century. Physically it was, together with its metaphoric twin, the Iron Curtain, the embodiment of a divided Europe. Building it entailed the destruction and wrenching apart of large areas of the city of Berlin and, later, its own fall recharged issues of monumentality and memory on both sides of its line. Yet today less than two fragmented kilometres survive in short crumbling stretches. Most of its course in the inner city had been obliterated little more than a decade after it fell. Its beginnings were even more rapid: on 13 August 1961 the GDR began to fence its citizens in. Although it was West Berlin that was surrounded – and was for some years under siege – it was this small island of capital that was extra-mural. The wall was built to prevent East Germans escaping from the Soviet sector to liberal democracy in the West. It was an impassable barrier to people in both directions, except for unthreatening groups of east-bound, hard-currency-carrying tourists.

The Berlin Wall began with a temporary fence, but after various incarnations it became a formidable barrier. The GDR described the structure as the 'Anti-Fascist Protection Rampart', designed to secure peace. The reality is that it was part of a frontier designed to stop the further loss of people, nearly 2.5 million of whom had fled from the GDR since 1949, mainly into West Berlin. Economically and in terms of morale, it was a disaster for the East. As the wall went up, U-Bahn and railway lines were cut; rivers and canals divided. Crossing points were reduced from 81 to seven within a month. A system of fortifications 155 km long, between 3.5 and 4.2 m high and 50 m wide, had evolved by the 1980s. Around 106 km of this length was the concrete wall of popular imagination.[64] The idea of the Wall as a protective guard for East Berliners was easily recognizable as a farce; its physical form made this obvious. The orientation of its defences and footings demonstrated that it was not built to withstand attack from the West but to prevent escape. More than 100 people died in attempting to flee across it. Apartment blocks on the line of the Wall first had their west-facing doors and lower windows blocked (recalling the creation of Venetian ghettos) and were later demolished. At Bernauer Strasser in central Berlin, the divide between the East and West was the building frontage line itself on the south side of the street. The front doors and windows were quickly sealed after people escaped and the buildings eventually demolished. Sometimes the façades were retained *in situ* and incorporated into the Wall itself. Other ruins were also incorporated, including gravestones from the Hedwig Cemetery, which were used for paving the road in the Wall's 'death strip'. In areas where it was important to turn a presentable face to capitalism, west-facing façades of buildings were renovated, even where their rear and side wings had been demolished. Only vital structures, such as a railway yard and the VEB Bergmann-Borsig factory, were allowed to stay in the vicinity of the Wall's eastern side.[65]

It was a terrible achievement in such a dense urban location. The demolitions ripped a brutal tract 50 m wide through the heart of a major city, sundering it entirely in two. On either side of the Wall many acres of war damage lay derelict for decades. It is the power of this sundering that fascinated and repelled Cold War tourists to the city for 30 years.

If the destruction carried out to secure the Wall was, in large part, pragmatic, the 1985 demolition of the, as it turns out, poorly named Church of Reconciliation on Bernauer Strasse most definitely was not. It was a final and highly symbolic act of destruction by the GDR that made news around the world. The late nineteenth-century Gothic Revival mission church was built in an area of deep poverty. From the turn of the century it was heavily involved in supporting the homeless and the unemployed of what was to become the revolutionary 'Red Wedding' district. Its proletarian credentials did not save it from the determinedly atheistic state. When the Wall was built the church found itself cut off, not just from its parish but marooned in the Wall's death strip, which also tore through the Sophien Cemetery next door. The church survived for 24 years after partition before first the body of the church and then its spire were blown up. The reason given was security –

Built in the 19th century as a mission church in the working-class Wedding district of Berlin, the Church of the Reconciliation became a casualty of the Berlin Wall. The Gothic Revival structure, which had survived for 24 years marooned in the Wall's death-strip, was destroyed by the GDR in January 1985. Security reasons were given (improving the line of fire), but it was widely seen as a statement of political will by the crumbling regime. Since the fall of the Wall, a chapel has been built on the site.

creating a clear line of fire – but its destruction can be seen as a statement of permanency for the Wall and a political system at a time when the GDR was, in reality, crumbling from within. The high profile of Christian opposition groups in East Germany cannot have helped secure its future either. West Germany's chancellor Helmut Kohl referred to the church in a state of the nation address the following month: 'This event is a symbol,' he said. 'The demolition of the church shows us how long, how difficult and how uncertain the path is before us in order to overcome the division of Europe and the division of Germany.'[66] Manfred Fischer, the parish's minister, noted that every church building is theologically symbolic but, in addition to this, 'something significant occurred when the tower collapsed in on itself. Was it defeat or being forced to bid farewell to something familiar?'[67] The church in the death strip was, he says, 'less a symbol of reconciliation than the impossibility of reconciliation.' Its demolition by the GDR removed an image of hope, one that clashed with the message of the Wall. Fischer points out that the very act of erasing this image actually presented another image to an international audience; film footage of the spire toppling again and again, he argues, demonstrated the true nature of the GDR regime.[68]

With equal counter-symbolism, it was this same stretch of wall that was chosen for the start of its official demolition on 13 June 1990. Already the wall was fragmenting. Since the jubilant opening of the checkpoints on 9 November 1989, Berliners had climbed all over the Wall, dancing on its parapet, chipping and hammering away at it. The fall represented freedom and signalled the end of physical division. Accompanied by the toppling of statues to oppressors across the region, it also symbolized the fall of Stalinist Eastern Europe to the wider world. There was an eagerness among people to be part of its destruction using their own hands. 'Wall-peckers' armed with hammers stripped the wall back to its reinforcement bars. The fabric of the Wall and its ancillary structures, such as watchtowers, disappeared at an astonishing rate. By the spring of 1990 the Deutsches Historisches Museum was proposing that a segment of the Wall be made a national monument. Former Federal Chancellor Willy Brandt argued that: 'a piece of that hideous construction be left standing . . . in remembrance of an historical monstrosity'.[69] Bernauer Strasse's stretch of wall was identified as especially loaded with meaning, but even this section fell victim to the chaotic demolitions along the Wall's length, with stretches tumbling before protection resolutions could be passed. Only a 200-m run was left to become the official monument site, and not without a bad-tempered debate over the conflicting desires of those who wanted to obliterate the city's divisions and those wishing to preserve a record of a significant element of Berlin's twentieth-century history. Elsewhere, remaining stretches of wall are sparse. Large sections have been taken away, pulverized and sold as road-fill. In a few places its line has been marked by stone or metal strips set in the ground, for example

East and West German border guards join in the demolition of the Berlin Wall following its fall on 9 November 1989. The fabric of the Wall vanished at a rapid rate, leading for calls to conserve a section of it. Today it is a difficult task to trace its former course through the city, and its fragments have been commodified, recalling the fate of rubble from the fall of the Bastille in the French Revolution.

behind the Reichstag. In others, the desire to reunite the city physically and mentally, and in so doing forget the past, has assured its utter obliteration. Its oblivion. Map in hand, it is now no easy task to follow the course of the wall on foot. It is astonishing that something that felt so omnipresent in old West Berlin has vanished. The Wall would loom at the end of streets closing the vista, or it would suddenly turn a sharp angle, blocking your route through areas like Kreuzberg – an area near the heart of the city before the Wall, then very much at its margins during the Wall's existence. The massive Potsdamer Platz development nearby, designed by teams of international architects including Renzo Piano and Richard Rogers, is an attempt to re-create a commercial city hub on a site alongside the Wall that had remained a wasteland and no-man's land throughout the post-war period. Over the years West Berlin had removed even tramlines, lampposts, pavements and the U-Bahn station entrances. A *tabula rasa* had been created on which to impose a new international identity for the city centre that made little or no reference to the site's past identity. Nearby Niederkirchnerstrasse, formerly Prinz-Albrecht-Strasse and notorious as the Gestapo's headquarters, con-tains the only other substantial stretch of wall surviving in the city centre. This too has been raddled by 'wall-peckers', leaving the ribbons of rusting reinforcement bars exposed.

Outside the city centre, the largest section of remaining wall has become
known as the East Side Gallery, forming a stretch of graffiti and artwork
more than a kilometre long that became the site for an international art competition in 1990. Like the informal graffiti through the West Berlin section of
the Wall during its life, its transformation into a huge canvas did not seek to
deny the Wall's presence but to comment on it. This was a freedom not
allowed on the Wall's east side.

In contrast to the West Berlin approach, the erection of a security wall
near Jerusalem separating the Jewish settlement of Gilo from the neighbouring Palestinian village of Beit Jala has been characterized by a refusal to recognize its own presence. Here, the settlers' side of the wall has been carefully
painted with a view, now in actuality blocked, of the Palestinian landscape
beyond. It is a depiction that carefully excludes any real or represented
Palestinian residents and is a denial of the wall's, and in some way the
conflict's, very existence.[70] Similarly traces of the fifteen-year long civil war in
the Lebanon are being denied in the rebuilding of Beirut a few hundred miles
to the north. During the course of the war the 'Green Line' between what had
become segregated Muslim West and Christian East Beirut physically divided
the city in two, an abandoned no-man's land in which vegetation flourished.
Its line is now vanishing beneath a rapid rebuilding programme undertaken
by the government in conjunction with the private, but government-
influenced, Solidere company. The architectural evidence of the historically
heterogeneous city centre is vanishing at the same time. The 180 ha project
stresses an abstract unity that harks back to a shared Phoenician or Levantine
heritage rather than the pluralist reality of the still politically shaky country.[71]

In the process of the Berlin Wall's own destruction, a curious process of
commodification unfolded. Informal souvenir hunters were discouraged
and the marketing of fragments of the Wall was handed in December 1989
to a former GDR state-owned firm Limex-Ban. It is a strange echo of the
granulated fate of the Bastille and has been followed by the incorporation of
fragments of Dresden's bombed Frauenkirche into souvenirs such as watches
to coincide with its reconstruction by the post-communist regime. This commodification is examined in a fine book by Polly Feversham and Leo
Schmidt, *The Berlin Wall Today*, in which a ready parallel is made with the
fragments of the True Cross. These relics of a demolished ideology now sell
for substantial sums, especially large pieces with quality graffiti, which have
fetched up to US$300,000: 'The Wall's disappearance is partly due to the
public's continuing desire to take home these little lumps of demystified evil
as souvenirs,' explain Feversham and Schmidt. 'The fragments, like pieces of
the True Cross, assumed a potency which was the antithesis of the symbolic
totality of the structure while it stood.'[72] Fragments of the Wall, argue the
authors (and it is also true of the Bastille and Dresden's fragments), represent both an attempt to capture an historic monument and the privatization

of a public structure. Walter Benjamin's description of the souvenir as a container of 'extinguished experience' is also cited. The process, it seems, is an attempt not so much to conjure up the massive physicality of a structure but to humble it and grasp it. To erode its fearfulness.

In this struggle between memory and forgetting it is the latter that appears to be winning, but in souvenirs memory clings on in an individualized, fragmentary way rather than as a collective experience. The communal reality is lost to an ersatz version; a nostalgia pricked by harmless concrete trinkets. Commerce and ideological revisionism, as well as individual attacks on an icon of death and division, have ensured that *in situ* memories, with all their intrinsic power of place, have largely been lost. Capital has indeed triumphed.

At the same time there has, in contrast to the *Mauerkrankheit* ('Wall-sickness') suffered by some depressed, even suicidal East Berliners in their city prison, been some sense of loss in the absence of the Wall. A void remains filled by 'Ostalgia' for the old East and for the youthful anarchy of life in divided West Berlin. An opinion poll conducted in May 1990 found that 25 per cent of West Berliners and 20 per cent of East Berliners had some nostalgia for the Wall and the pre-homogenized city.[73]

A similar phenomenon of wall-sickness has been observed among Turkish Cypriot soldiers patrolling the barrier dividing Nicosia. The Cypriot capital was initially divided in 1963 to reduce intercommunal strife between Greek and Turkish Cypriots, then emphatically partitioned in 1974 following the Turkish invasion of the island. Here, too, calls for reunification have been mounting, especially on the Turkish side of the border, which has wound down into economic stagnation since division in comparison to the Greek side. The difference is likely to intensify now the Greek half of the island has won EU membership.

Conflict between Turks and Greeks on the island grew more violent after Cyprus became independent of the UK in 1960. It was here that the British army drew the original Green Line (with a green pen) through the centre of the historic walled city. An Athens-backed coup aimed at assimilating Cyprus into Greece (*enosis*) led to the Turkish invasion, the occupation of 37 per cent of the island by Turkey and the extension of Nicosia's Green Line 180 km from coast to coast. Severe ethnic cleansing and population exchanges immediately followed, and cultural cleansing with it. The Turks ethnically cleansed the north of the island, village by village, at the same time as the Greeks tried to prevent Turkish Cypriots fleeing north (and so reinforcing an ethnic divide). Later, thousands of Turks were allowed north in return for an end to the expulsion of Greeks to the south of the Green Line. Thousands of Turkish peasants were brought in from mainland Turkey to the new Turkish Republic of North Cyprus to take the place of the displaced Greeks. Attacks on Greek material culture in the North were an early signal of Turkey's intention to remain in Cyprus permanently rather than, as they claimed, a temporary intervention to protect the Turkish minority on the island. The destruction of Greek heritage was an insurance against future *enosis*; the northern zone was soon no longer identifiably Greek. In the Greek zone, by contrast, Islamic monuments have been safeguarded and even repaired – the Greek Cypriots have nothing to prove territorially by their destruction. In the months and years following partition, all but a handful of northern Cyprus's 502 Greek Orthodox churches, some of Byzantine origin, were vandalized, looted, demolished or put to new uses including as mosques, stables, latrines, stores and a cinema. Armenian churches on the island have suffered a similar end, as they did on the Turkish mainland. Virtually all Greek place names have been replaced with Turkish. The destruction was methodical with secular Greek monuments, archaeological sites and graveyards also targeted. Icons, mosaics and other artefacts dating back to the sixth century have found their way onto the world art markets in large numbers.

Investigations in 1976 by *The Times* and *The Guardian* in London were both clear that the damage caused was not just casual vandalism and neglect – it was systematic. As *The Times* wrote:

> It is important to distinguish between random damage that might have been caused by drunks after a night out, and the demolition of crosses, tombstones and heavy marble slabs which weigh several hundredweight and would need men with sledgehammers to destroy them. We found nothing to fit the first category . . . the process of obliterating everything Greek has been carried out methodically.[74]

The Guardian in its report, 'The Rape of Northern Cyprus', concurred:

> The vandalism and desecration is so methodical and so widespread that they amount to the institutionalised obliteration of everything sacred to a Greek . . . In some instances, an entire graveyard of 50 or more tombs had been reduced to pieces of rubble no larger than a matchbox . . . we found the Chapel of Ayios Demetrios at Ardhana empty but for the remains of the altar plinth and that was fouled by human excrement . . . At Syngrasis, the broken crucifix was drenched with urine. Tombs gaped open wherever we went . . . crosses bearing the pictures of those buried beneath . . . had been flattened and destroyed.[75]

The damage and destruction can also be seen, in part, as an act of revenge as well as Turkification. The pre-partition conflict had meant deaths and atrocities in communities, both Turkish and Greek Cypriot, who had once lived sided by side. The erosion of Greek architectural heritage in the Turkish

The 1974 invasion of Cyprus by Turkish forces led to the full partition of the island and the
wholesale destruction of Greek heritage in the Turkish republic established in the north. The
12th-century St Mamas church in the village of Mórphou (renamed Güzelyurt) is a rare survivor.
It was damaged and housed sheep following the flight of Mórphou's Greek inhabitants, but
its artistic importance later led to its reopening as an icon museum. However, in 2004 it was
damaged by a bomb laid by suspected Turkish Cypriot nationalists ahead of the first Orthodox
service in the church for 30 years, which was attended by Greek Cypriot refugees from the village.

The vandalized Greek Orthodox church of St George in the Turkish Cypriot village of Koma Tou Yialou. The Greek population was brutally ethnically cleansed between 1974 and 1976 and the village resettled by Anatolian Turks.

zone has continued in the decades since. A later *Times* report of 1980 found more evidence of desecration: a church near Famagusta being used as a latrine with the remains of a Bible being used as toilet paper.[76] In 1990 *Frankfurter Allgemeine Magazin* found the Armenian monastery of Sourp Magar, which dates back to AD 1000, in ruins with graffiti celebrating the 'victorious executioners' who caused the damage.[77] As recently as 2001 the Council of Europe intervened to stop plans to turn Sourp Magar into a hotel.[78]

In a reversal of this trend, the island's heritage, in Nicosia at least, has featured strongly in recent moves towards unification. The Nicosia Masterplan being promoted by the Greek side in tandem with the Turkish half of the city has sought to regenerate areas of its historic core. Since division, the south side of the city has bulged outward and upwards with tower blocks and new residential areas, while the area around the Green Line itself and most of the historic areas of Nicosia's northern sector has remained little changed since 1974. Houses with washing up still in the sink and empty shops advertising long defunct brands still attest to the speed of flight and the zombie state of the no-man's land. UN soldiers still protect a fleet of imported 1974 Toyota Corollas that never left the showroom. Elsewhere, a rusting yellow Morris Minor buried in weeds on the Green Line has become a landmark mentioned in the UN cease-fire agreement. The Turkish government has claimed that the line starts at the rear bumper, the UN argues that it's the front one. A Catholic church in the zone enjoys indeterminate status, having entrances on both sides of the line. The whole area of eighteenth-century houses and ancient churches and mosques is crumbling. Progress on restoration has been much faster on the richer Greek side but the impetus is now there on the north side too, hindered by a decades-long international embargo that has only just ended. The UN and the European Commission are backing the regeneration plan as a move towards physical reintegration and re-unification. Two symbolic projects are being funded, the restoration of an

Ottoman hamman on the Greek side and of a market in the north. Expertise from both sides of the divide is involved in the bi-communal scheme.

Discussions on reunification have recently broken down again to the consternation of the mass of Turkish Cypriot people who had voted 'yes' in a 2004 reunification referendum and threatened a 'Berlin Wall' style assault on the divide if the impasse continued.[79] In the week after the Greek Cypriots were accepted into the EU the northern government responded to its own people's threats by opening border crossings for the first time since partition. Around 20,000 Turkish Cypriots have now applied for Cypriot passports, which would allow them to live and work in the EU; the petty divisions of the island have become much less meaningful in an internation-alized Europe. Turkish hardliners opposed to an agreement are still making their feelings known, though: in August 2004 a bomb blast shattered the windows of the Greek Orthodox church of St Mamas in the northern town of Güzelyurt (as the Turks renamed Mórphou), just days before the first planned service in the building for 30 years. Guards were immediately placed around mosques in the Greek south.[80] Memories of a unified island are continually stoked on the Greek side with the phrase *dhen xehno* ('I don't forget') flashed up before the nightly TV news over images of formerly Greek villages and churches now in the occupied north. However, Greek Cypriots recently voted a heavy 'no' to the reunification terms in the same referendum. It proposed a loose federation of two states but did little to assuage long-standing Greek Cypriot grievances.[81]

Nicosia, the Cypriot capital, was initially divided in 1963 to reduce inter-communal violence before being emphatically divided along with the rest of the island following the 1974 Turkish invasion. The original 'Green Line', drawn with a green pen, is patrolled by UN soldiers and has only recently had its checkpoints reopened to the islanders on either side. Buildings on its northern side have been empty and decaying for three decades.

Barriers are often self-imposed, of course, from the revolutionary barricade to Ahmedabad's *pols*: defence serving the purposes of the community within. That is not to say that the divisions are freely chosen – just necessary. Northern Ireland, notably Belfast, is a case in point. Although partition of the island of Ireland is a colonial imposition, the divisions within the province have often been erected in the first instance by the antagonistic communities themselves (in large part by Catholic Nationalists), but the desire to maintain and strengthen them comes from both communities (Protestant/Loyalist as well as Catholic) and from the state. And, as in Israel and the Occupied Territories, it is ordinary houses rather than monuments that have taken the brunt of physical destruction within the city.

Although it has origins in the twelfth century, in the early nineteenth century Belfast was still the Protestant plantation town established in 1603 by the British government for English and Scots immigrants, who would alter the demographic make up of the rebellious colony. Catholics from the countryside then moved into the city to work in the cotton and flax mills of the roiling Industrial Revolution and later to escape the Great Famine. By 1830 a third of the workforce was Catholic. Other industries such as ship-building remain closed to them on a sectarian basis. Patterns of Catholic settlement within Belfast followed the lines of employment. Even in the late nineteenth century the boundaries between Catholic and Protestant areas of the city were marked by barricades at times of sectarian tension. There was ethnic rioting in every decade between the 1870s and the 1930s. Today's Cuper Street peace wall follows almost the same line as an 1880s barricade.[82]

By the end of the twentieth century a growing number of the walls, fences and 'interface' zones between communities had become permanent, a trend that had accelerated massively with the outbreak of The Troubles in the 1960s.[83] Though not contiguous, like Berlin's or Nicosia's long, impermeable barriers, the length and height of these walls is still growing. The segregation endemic to the city has intensified over the past 30 years to the point where it is virtually complete (98 per cent) in the working-class inner city.[84] Segregation in the initial post-war period was still around the 50 per cent level. West Belfast has long been a majority Catholic area and East Belfast a Protestant stronghold with a jigsaw of mixed and contending enclaves on the north side. The violence and destruction pre-partition, however, was minimal compared to what was seen following partition.

Post-ceasefire, the city remains a strange place, trembling like a dog with anticipation as sectarian violence continues at a low, grumbling level. On previous visits to Belfast I had stayed in the suburbs beyond Queen's University. Lecturer and social-worker territory, it is a leafy, non-sectarian, middle-class enclave of the sort found not far from any of the UK's red-brick universities. In inner Belfast it is exceptional. On my last visit, though, I stayed in the terraced heart of Loyalist East Belfast among the machine-gun murals and goons in shell-suits pretending not to listen to your accent when you buy something in a shop. The atmosphere is closer to the wary suspicion of West Mostar than the excitability of the West Bank. Discussing 'The Troubles' in the kitchen of the friend I was staying with, I was shushed as she stood up to close the kitchen window before we could continue in lowered voices. Walls have ears here and it is easy to imagine how your own home can rapidly feel unsafe.

The Troubles – the war for the reunification of Ireland waged by the IRA against Loyalist paramilitary groups and the British state, and later against Protestant civilians – began in the era of civil rights protests across the Western world. Deep-seated Nationalist resentment, nurtured in an environment of long-standing discrimination against the Catholic minority in the north, led to protests for equality, a violent Loyalist backlash and the intervention of the British army. These forces ostensibly came to protect the Catholic enclaves from attack but arrived after, not before, the besieged residents of Derry's Bogside had successfully barricaded and defended their enclave. In the communal riots that flared then and have continued since, houses have been bombed, stoned and burnt out on a vast scale. Housing had long been a contentious issue; Catholics had the worst of it but both sides in the province still suffer disgracefully low housing standards. Catholics, though, were systematically discriminated against in public housing by the Loyalist-led Stormont Parliament before its replacement by direct rule from Whitehall and the appointment of an independent Housing Executive in 1971.[85] The housing issue once had heightened significance given that entitlement to vote in local elections was limited to ratepayers. The first civil rights march in August 1968 was a protest march over housing allocation.

The destruction of housing in Belfast has not been imposed in the interests of the state (although there are some arguable incidents to the contrary) but by the paramilitaries and the hostile communities themselves. In 1969 the earliest large-scale clashes in Derry's Bogside and Belfast's Falls and Ardoyne areas saw hundreds of houses set on fire. Almost 60,000 fled their homes between 1969 and 1973 as sectarian violence between adjacent communities erupted. Arson, physical attacks, bombs, murders and threats left thousands of homes vandalized, empty or burnt out. Around 5 per cent of Belfast's Catholic population was forced to move and 80 per cent of the damaged property belonged to Catholics.[86] The introduction of internment without trial in August 1971 also saw widespread damage and the evacuation of more than 2,000 homes. The following year saw more than 14,000 houses damaged in violent exchanges and many were subsequently demolished. Improvised self-protection barriers solidified into permanent 'peace' lines. Later, conspiracy theories regarding the British government's intentions were heightened after army maps appeared to show the city divided into a Catholic West, marked in green, and a Protestant East, marked in orange, either side of Belfast's River Lagan. Such fears may not always have been far-fetched in the light of Margaret Thatcher's proposal, in the wake of the IRA's bombing of the Grand Hotel in Brighton during the 1984 Conservative Party Conference, to undertake the wholesale relocation of Catholics from Ulster to the Republic, partitioning Belfast and redrawing the border with the South. She was quickly dissuaded from her Cromwellian vision and it remained secret for almost two decades.[87]

As in Israel, the targeting of each community's religious buildings has been surprisingly limited. Orange halls and Catholic churches and schools have been damaged, but both sides, despite the ample evidence of sectarian, faith-based killings, are keen to present the struggle as political. The wave of Loyalist attacks on pubs in the 1970s (landlords in both communities were traditionally Catholic) is just one example, however, of how the sectarian and the territorial are entwined. Large-scale IRA bomb attacks on physical structures within Northern Ireland have, in the main, been directed at military, police and economic targets rather than the architectural symbols of the opposing community *per se*. The consequences of IRA bomb attacks on the commercial centre of Belfast were profound. The city centre was not architecturally neutral, given the imperial pedigree of public buildings such as Belfast City Hall, but what had been one of the few shared spaces in the wider city was made treacherous for everybody. More than 300 shops were destroyed, a quarter of all retail space. Even after the cease-fire, with the removal of the ring of steel and checkpoints around the city centre, many are not comfortable there. Different entrances to the Castle Court shopping centre, for instance, can be a good indicator of which direction home is, and hence your religion.

And, more than ten years after the 1994 cease-fire, pipe-bombs, petrol bombs and other missiles remain a daily threat in Belfast where communities rub up against each other. Peace walls three or more metres high continue to be built to keep them apart. Routes from one enclave to the other have been reduced in number or gated so that they can be closed in times of high tension. Ulster academic Tony Hepburn has described the resulting seg-regation process as a 'ratchet effect'; the separating out accelerates in times of severe conflict but does not reverse in more peaceful periods.[88] The situa-tion is at its worst in public housing and much less marked in middle-class areas, suggesting that fear and competition for resources between two very poor communities has a significant part to play. The outcome is a series of mono-faith enclaves rubbing up at conflict-riven interfaces. Some 27 of these have generated permanent barriers, ranging from Cuper Street's massive concrete fortifications to aestheticized decorative brick 'environmental bar-riers' and an enormous fence dividing Alexandra Park into two sectarian areas. Large road schemes have also been used as community dividers. In the isolated Catholic Short Strand enclave in East Belfast, huge barriers divide

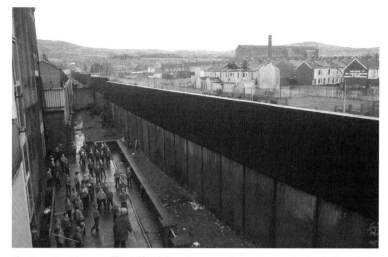

The Cuper Street 'peace wall' in Belfast follows the course of an earlier sectarian barricade erected in the 1880s. The inner city is now riven with these divides, of various materials and heights, and their number has grown in recent years even as the peace process unfolds. Inner Belfast is now almost entirely segregated into mono-religious enclaves.

Catholic back gardens from the rear yards of Protestant families that back on to them. The area appears in a permanent state of siege. You don't have to belong to the opposite faith group to be vulnerable in East Belfast, just an outsider – two Australian tourists were brutally beaten on the street weeks before my last visit for no apparent reason.

More often though, the peace walls do not run between back gardens but are marked by a swath of dereliction and vacant ground where houses and businesses have been destroyed and it is not safe to build anew. A recent study estimates that this vacant territory, void of buildings, amounts to 7 per cent of the city. Some areas have vacant strips between 400 and 600 m wide.[89] Vast areas of the city are now physically fragmented and attempts at building integrated housing estates have largely failed. Physically, culturally and mentally, the city is in pieces. Housing development is beginning to creep back towards the peace walls on the Catholic side, forced there by a burgeoning population that wants to live within the safe areas of their own community. By contrast, those Protestants who have the option to move away from the city altogether to the Protestant hinterland take it in large numbers. Getting the necessary agreement from both sides of a peace wall for development close by is extremely difficult – especially where housing is proposed. Both sides are also suspicious of new housing layouts they regard as being led by security considerations – an incipient Haussmannization. Although buffer zones have been built in the form of industrial estates and business parks, most land remains derelict. Other British cities, such as

Liverpool, Newcastle or Glasgow, still have their share of dereliction but nothing on the scale of Belfast, where business investment remains tightly circumscribed within the city centre. The poor and dispossessed have been left to fight each other. Every house, whether neatly painted or semi-ruinous, has slatted venetian blinds at every window – protection against a bomb-blast or a device for allowing the surveillance of the unsafe streets without being seen? What has been built tends to be introverted, fortress architecture fighting off the hostile environment.

The Catholic expansionism demonstrated by the new housing is seen as aggressive by the adjoining Loyalist communities and the process is often met with violence. It adds to Protestant fears of being overwhelmed; a fear already in their mind given statistics showing that Catholics could form a majority of Northern Ireland's population by the middle of this century. The fear is expressed in the Loyalist rallying cries 'Not an Inch' and 'What we have we hold'. Conflict is consequently intensifying along community boundaries despite the official cease-fires. The decanting of Loyalist residents from failing and largely derelict public housing estates, such as the Torrens Estate and the Manor Estate in North Belfast, has led to accusations of ethnic cleansing, amid anger that the redeveloped estates may become home to Catholics from across the nearby peace-line. While Protestants move or are moved away, Catholics make up 83 per cent on the housing waiting list (in 2004) in the north of the city. Northern Ireland commentator David McKitterick has described North Belfast as a 'permanent low-level battlefield, with advances and defeats measured in terms of streets and sometimes individual homes'.[90] Even where peace walls are absent, lines of demarcation are known by locals. The flags, political murals and painted flagstones effectively state territorial claims and mark the transitions between nationalist and loyalist areas. Hence the Palestinian and Israeli flag-waving of 2002. These are, literally, warning signs. The fear of encroachment was made horribly visible recently with the Loyalist intimidation of primary schoolchildren walking to the Holy Cross Catholic school in Ardoyne, an area Catholics are expanding into. A further peace wall, the fourth since the 1994 cease-fires, along the length of the Ardoyne Road is the depressing solution proposed (in addition, Loyalists would argue, to the reallocation of their failing estate enclaves to Catholics).

Belfast's barriers have allowed ground to be held on both sides for more than three decades, but around them micro-transfers have resulted in the almost total segregation of the inner city. The stage of mass attacks on housing as a weapon of war may be over, at least, despite the ongoing small-scale attrition. The demolition and segregation have, however, achieved nothing for the Loyalists in terms of securing their grip on the city. They are losing their demographic and political primacy. The need for further peace walls can be seen as a last-ditch effort to defend their presence at least spatially.

Catholics may in the past have welcomed the walls for their own protection but the same structures may soon be an obstacle to their expansion. These days, conflict in the interface zones is indicative of this changing balance. But a changing balance does not mean victory or peace. With an enemy always near to hand, but with whom there is no shared space, there can be neither communication nor understanding. A recent survey in Belfast found that almost 70 per cent of young people had never had a 'meaningful conversation' with those of the other religion (education in the province is faith-based). Over 60 per cent of people thought that communications had worsened since the ceasefire. The impasse remains.[91]

Division combined with the proximity of the 'other' also promotes heightened cultural self-definition and the exaggeration of distinctions that are objectively slight – the narcissism of minor differences. The parades, flags and liberal use of gable-end emblems in Belfast actually point to the minor cultural differences between Protestants and Catholics in the city. Their two cultures are, at root, little different – especially architecturally. There is nothing to divide them environmentally, so the differences are literally brushed on to create threatening but superficial architectural war paint. This is not a dispute between minarets and spires. Churches are not especially useful either as symbols or as targets in this environment.

Israel (as opposed to Judaism) is, like Northern Ireland, a relative neophyte in terms of having a national culture, and here too there is a desire to emphasize their differences from those with a competing claim to the land. The creation of an Israeli identity has been at the expense of Palestinian desires for the same, just as Catholic expansionism is a threat to the Loyalist sense of collective selfhood. Rival claims to memories that are located in place are in conflict. In and across Israel's 'seam area', the possibility of a new Palestinian state emerging is deeply threatening. While Palestinian memories of a cultural identity connected with the land are long, unlike Israelis they have enjoyed no recent history as an independent state; no collective memories of themselves *as a nation* despite obvious memories *as a people* rooted in the land of Palestine. Israeli attacks on Palestinian housing, heritage and infrastructure can, therefore, be seen as not just asserting 'facts on the ground' but as an attempt to pre-empt the possibility of a Palestinian national identity, with its associated powerful collective memories, its history as state, from emerging. Porous borders may create security issues for Israelis but the alternative is fixing their own identity within set parameters and allowing the Palestinians to do the same.

Israel may be hedging its bets on its borders but internally it has a record of demolishing the non-Jewish architectural record. Like the demolition of the Church of the Reconciliation in Berlin, or the vandalism and desecration of churches in Northern Cyprus, it is a state's way of saying 'no turning back'.

Ironically, the Jewish settlements in the West Bank are imposing an alien architectural tradition onto the land in terms of their hilltop locations and their use of European housing typologies, both of which are at odds with the climate and the vernacular. In their attempt to reclaim a biblical inheritance, they are in danger of obliterating the characteristic architecture and urban morphology of the land. And, in fixing a new Israeli identity, a genuine history of shared inhabitance (if not hegemony) on the land alongside the Arabs, and going back thousands of years, is being lost. The emphasis on maintaining a difference between two Semitic peoples is the greater imperative.

The longevity of Israel's security fence is difficult to determine but its most effective role, for the foreseeable future, is the measure of control it offers over Palestinian lives. This is not just about keeping Palestinians out of Israel but about keeping them in their cage. In many ways, it is a more audacious undertaking than that seen in Cyprus, Belfast or Berlin. Continuing damage to architecture in Cyprus, Israel and Ireland is, however, indicative of continuing insecurity, which, as in India, can be ruthlessly exploited by those with an interest in promoting division between groups. Although Ayodhya began as a religious issue, as in Northern Ireland the struggle is primarily political: a will to power and territory whipped up by politicians and played out among the powerless and those owning little or nothing. The division of the subcontinent into Pakistan and India has created an enemy on each other's doorstep and, consequently, an enemy within. Bilateral threats of war are reflected in murderous riots where, as well as people, their symbolic and everyday architecture suffers. Attempts at further segregation could lead India down the Bosnian path or follow Belfast's route to an uneasy separate but parallel existence with their 'intimate enemies'. Or perhaps Belfast is learning from Ahmedabad's *pols* and its peace wall-lined enclaves will be with us for centuries?

Were divisions to be overcome, would the physical reminders of separation in Belfast, Cyprus and Israel be sacrificed as in Berlin – an enforced forgetting in the interests of a new unity or neighbourliness? It is better than war at least, although the lack of visible lessons of past failures encourages the lessons to be lost too. Whatever the case, partition is an unnatural and inherently unstable state and the more emphatic the barrier the greater the indication of an unfinished process. The lines of division result in an ugly civic scarification, a scar to be scratched at by repeated campaigns waged on the physical environment along its line and which spreads contagion well beyond the wound itself. Good fences do not make good neighbours; they foster defensiveness, fear and otherness. In these circumstances, attack can be seen as the best form of defence.

6 Remember and Warn I: Rebuilding and Commemoration

History repeats itself, but the special call of an art which has passed
away is never reproduced. It is as utterly gone out of the world as the
song of a destroyed wild bird.

JOSEPH CONRAD, *THE MIRROR OF THE SEA* (1906)

It was the songs of the nationalist Serbs being played in the bars with renewed
vigour that provided the first clue to the anger being stoked in Serbian Banja
Luka. Muslims who had been ethnically cleansed from the town were back
in the summer of 2001 to lay a foundation stone ceremonially for the rebuilding of a mosque on its bulldozed site – a symbolic act that the Serbs
were determined to prevent. The songs helped fuel a riot that saw elderly
Muslims pelted with stones, bottles and eggs, and a pig let loose to defile the
site. The British ambassador was among those forced to take refuge from the
mob in a nearby community centre. On the other side of the square, outside
the city hall, the largest Orthodox church in Bosnia is being built.

Attempts to rebuild mosques have been resisted by hostile crowds and
by bureaucracies all over Bosnia since the 1995 Dayton Accords officially
brought an end to the fighting. In Stolac, the now Croat-controlled municipality was suddenly and repeatedly inquorate when meetings were
scheduled with Muslim rebuilding proposals on the agenda. Bosnia, post-
Dayton, is still divided into the autonomous Republika Srpska and Bosnia-
Herzegovina proper, and divided again into ethnically based cantons. It seems
a vain hope to try to achieve reintegration through monuments. Such hostility has repeatedly thwarted efforts by the outside community to return
refugees to towns and villages from which they had been ethnically cleansed.
Many do not want to return to a place where they would be surrounded by
their former torturers and the killers of their families, to no home and no

job: to where the familiar physical reminders of their presence and their culture had been erased. Others, like the Muslims of Banja Luka, have been determined to reassert their presence and their visibility with the rebuilding of their monuments. But without the presence of a local community to inhabit and use these buildings such gestures can appear hopelessly fragile. Not to try, though, would be an admission of defeat, of no longer having a right to be there, of no longer belonging. So mosques and Muslims are returning to many hostile areas of the country, including hardline Croat Stolac.

In Kozarac, a village once home to a Muslim majority community of some 25,000 souls (all of whom were brutally ethnically cleansed and their houses burnt), there are now just 6,000 Muslim returnees. They have rebuilt their mosque, the minarets of which were blasted by the Serbs. The uneasy peace is regularly broken by violence between the returnees and their still-resident Serb persecutors. A bomb has been thrown at a new Bosniak bar but its owner is defiant: 'This café is my finger stuck up to the Serbs who did not want us here. In fact, that is what those minarets are, on the mosques that no one goes to: fingers stuck up at the Serbs.'[1]

Rebuilding can be as symbolic as the destruction that necessitates it. Construction can be used to cement a violent sundering of the built environment or to weave the fabric of a former life back together. Doing so creates new touchstones for collective memory. What were once unintentional monuments – the places of worship, libraries and fountains of everyday life – by their rebuilding can become new, intentional monuments to the events that caused their destruction. History moves forward while looking over its shoulder; how much to commemorate and remember, how much needs to be forgiven then forgotten in the interests of peace within and without? There is a danger in life becoming reified in permanent honour to memories of suffering. Rebuilding, whether carried out by perpetrators or their victims, can also serve to mask the past; to erase the gaps, the voids, the ruinations that bear witness to history. And whoever rebuilds does so in a situation of power relations reflecting the post-destruction context.[2] Memory and forgetting are roped together for ever; tensions between the two do not loosen this bind. Forgetting is normal; most of our lives are consigned to oblivion. What is remembered, both individually and collectively, is partial and not necessarily accurate in an attempt to create a meaningful, coherent narrative and identity. The pitfalls of reconstruction in circumstances where there has been an attempt at forced forgetting by the destruction of material culture are particularly treacherous. Not to rebuild, though, would be a counsel of despair. In addition to pragmatic reconstruction necessary for the resumption of life there remains a need to remember, a need to call to account, and a need to prevent destruction from being repeated. Above all, there is a need for truth to be expressed in the raising of buildings. But whose truths are being constructed? Are false memories being erected?

Saravejo is now a very different city to what it was before the Bosnian war. Its repaired physical fabric is not so different but its population is now 80 per cent Muslim, twice its pre-war percentage. And the sight of veiled women trailing their robed husbands is disturbing to the secular Muslim girls, all crop-tops and belly-button piercings, as they take part in a dawdling dusk *passeggiata* down Titova Street. It is a post-war phenomenon. Much of the city's multi-ethnic architecture has been restored but it belies a reality where neighbourhoods now tend to be ethnically based and hostile to other communities across the street. Bosnia's national identity continues to be predicated on the notion of cosmopolitan tolerance. Government efforts to reinforce this ideal include banknotes and stamps depicting archaeological artefacts from a safely distant medieval Bosnian past and a reopened National Museum that stresses the long roots of all communities in the country. Yet, Cyrillic street-signs have vanished from the city. There are new complexities and contradictions to replace those of old.

Mostar remains divided into a Catholic Croat West Mostar and a Muslim East. The rebuilding of the old bridge was completed in 2004 with international help and a great deal of fanfare, but its new connecting arch, however graceful and faithful to the original design, is, similarly, a statement of hope in a less divided future rather than a sign of a present reality. Aleske Santica Street on the front line remains in ruins while competing interests fight over

The 1866 Franciscan church of SS Peter and Paul in Mostar, shown here before the Bosnian War, was shelled and burned out by the Serb-led JNA in April 1992, but the adjoining monastery survived. The city was initially attacked by Serbian forces, who targeted Catholic and Muslim monuments. The Croats later besieged the Muslims in East Mostar, attacking mainly Muslim but also some Orthodox architectural targets.

Following the Bosnian war the modest Franciscan church was replaced, with the support of the Catholic Church, by a gargantuan new concrete structure. Its steroidal campanile is as much a one-fingered gesture to the Muslims remaining in the city as the 33 m high crosses placed on top of Hum Hill. The crosses and the campanile dominate the minarets of the Ottoman quarter.

its future. Attempts to remove the dangerous ruins of one apartment block were stopped after gun-wielding former residents turned up, fearing that their last hope of returning would be lost. A nearby school is judged a major step forward because Catholic and Muslim children are studying under the same roof. But the school is physically split down the middle: staircases are divided in two, some classrooms are Muslim, others Croat. There are two separate playgrounds, two head teachers, two curricula, two bells.[3] On the Catholic side of Mostar, the historic Franciscan church of St Peter and St Paul, destroyed by the Serbs, has been replaced by a concrete basilica complete with an outsized steroidal campanile rearing up to dominate the townscape. Like the giant white crosses erected on the hills ringing Mostar, it is another architectural one-fingered gesture – this time directed at the Muslims. To the latter's satisfaction, the bell-tower is apparently not sturdy enough to support the intended carillon of bells – partly, so the rumours go, because of a vast bomb shelter excavated below the church.

There are signs of hope. In 2004, Bosnia's governor, Paddy Ashdown, ordered Mostar's competing ethnically based councils to unite to form a single municipality for the city with a single budget and merged emergency medical services. Ambulances and city buses may soon cross the divide between East and West Mostar once again. On the Muslim side of Mostar the historic Ottoman quarter is steadily being restored, often with great care. But Muslims now make up only a third rather than two-thirds of the city's population and are in a permanent minority. There are no mosques left in West Mostar.

Near the old front line an open-air unity concert for youth organized by the EU went off without incident. A Bosnian singer sang his famous song about the old bridge and the mixed Croat/Muslim crowd sang along with him. But it is still not safe for some Muslim Mostarians, especially the men, to visit the undamaged west of the city, where some of the cafés are owned by warlords who benefited from the carnage of the conflict. On Saturday nights young East Mostarians party wildly among the derelict palazzos and pulverized shops of its main street, but many Mostarians, East and West, are still leaving the city for good, unhappy with the reactionary attitudes of the

It was hit, repeatedly, by Serb shells during the siege of Sarajevo, but the Gazi Husrev Beg mosque in the city, one of the most important mosque complexes in the Balkans, survived the Bosnian war. The mosque, seen here in the 1980s, was built in 1530 by the architect Ajem Esir Ali, and had a highly ornate interior typical of Balkan Ottoman religious architecture. Along with the mosque was built a han, a madrasa, public baths and a bazaar. It is situated in the historic heart of the city near the Orthodox and Catholic cathedrals and the synagogue.

The 1996 restoration of the Gazi Husrev mosque (which continued a programme of works agreed on the eve of the war) damaged the building still further. Funded by the Wahhabist Saudi government, the interior was stripped of its internal surface decoration as far as possible. Saudi funding has similarly compromised the restoration of buildings in Mostar and Kosovo. The mosque has since been restored once again by local conservationists to something approaching its earlier appearance.

incoming peasants who have taken the place of their more cosmopolitan former neighbours. Other young secular Muslims have turned to religion for answers.

Elsewhere in Bosnia and in Kosovo, the restoration of monuments has not been as meticulous in re-creating the country's distinctive pre-war Islamic heritage as it has in Mostar. Some mosques are being rebuilt at a price. When the funding has come from Saudi sources there are usually strings attached. The richly decorated interiors characteristic of Balkan Islamic architecture have given way to the austere whitewash demanded by the Wahabi Islam of their Saudi funders. The Gazi Husrev Beg central mosque in Sarajevo has been one casualty of this sectarian programme. The damage caused by its rebuilding, by its whitewashing and the removal of applied decoration, was in some ways more thorough than that caused by Serbian shelling. A subsequent, more historically faithful interior has since replaced the whitewash but Islamic extremism now has a toehold in society.

Even if a new and unpleasant truth is being expressed in this architecture, modern critiques are likely to find it more acceptable than the uncritical rebuilding in replica of damaged or destroyed historic buildings. History, with its claim to truth, is too often being replaced by heritage, as historian David Lowenthal has argued, and heritage, he says, is a 'declaration of faith in the past – a prejudiced pride in the past is not the sorry upshot of heritage but its essential aim'. Heritage, according to Lowenthal, is warped history.[4] It is an important warning of the uses and abuses of a rebuilt architectural record.

Was history being replaced by heritage when Warsaw's citizens chose to rebuild the historic core of their capital as an exact copy of what was lost? Purists may decry the decision as fakery and as Disneyfication, but to Varsovians it was (as it is for Bosnia's Muslims) a matter of pride and defiance to demonstrate that their culture had not been decapitated along with its statues, as Himmler intended when he identified the capital with the 'brain' of the country.

Poland had been repeatedly conquered and divided up over the centuries and had won its independence again only in 1918. In the inter-war years Polish interest in identifying and preserving its built heritage had reached new heights with conservation schemes and laws designed to protect what was left of its historic architecture. Under the noses of the German occupiers, Polish architects and art historians were busy recording its architecture ready for rebuilding. Around 10,000 remnants of Warsaw Castle's interior – doors, fireplaces, columns and panelling – were secreted away after nocturnal forages to recover the fragments. Voluminous records of the city's buildings were hidden in the Technical University's architecture department and among the monks' tombs at the Piotrków monastery. Although nearly 800,000 Varsovians were dead and 85 per cent of the city had been destroyed in the Uprising (along with many of the carefully collated architectural records), rebuilding began almost immediately in the wake of the Soviet capture of the city in 1945. Despite enormous privations, hunger and homelessness, by April 1945 reconstruction work had begun on three houses in the Old Town Square, at the Tin-roofed Palace, the Prymasowski Palace and a church on Leszno Street. King Sigismund's statue had been rescued from the rubble and in July the statue of Copernicus was unveiled once more (it had been reinscribed 'the Great German' by the Nazis, then destroyed in the Uprising).[5] Over the following decades the city centre with its castle, churches, palaces and streets was faithfully restored to its pre-war appearance – give or take the odd Stalinist pile and dubious monuments to Polish–Soviet brotherhood. The single-mindedness of the re-creation astonished the world.

It is hard not to see here a legitimate decision by the Poles to rescue their history from oblivion, but there is no doubt either that the new Old City is a fantasy made fact. It certainly obliterates a phase in its history and the rebuilding process itself was not unproblematic; some of the material for

The Church of St Alexander, Warsaw, was razed by the Nazis in 1944 along with the majority of the city following the failure of the Warsaw Uprising. The Neo-classical rotunda was built in 1818–26 by the architect Piotr Aigner. Like much of the historic city centre, it was rebuilt in close facsimile in the post-war period but it lacks the finesse of the original. The reconstructed city has been described as a 'Disney operation'.

The Old Town Market Square was at the heart of medieval Warsaw and lined with merchants' houses. It was destroyed by the Nazis in 1944 and it too was painstakingly rebuilt in the post-war period. Poles prepared for the rebuilding of their city by documenting the buildings and salvaging architectural elements – even while under Nazi occupation.

rebuilding came from the Silesian town of Breslau (now Polish Wrocław), which, after Poland was liberated, was ethnically cleansed of its long-standing German population and had many of its Germanic monuments taken down. This was part of a vengeful campaign of expulsion, by the Poles and other liberated nations, of millions of ethnic Germans from their territories.[6] Many millions were killed across Eastern Europe (the exact figures are disputed). Tens of thousands alone died in the forced marches and many of the Germanic refugees who made it to Dresden then lost their lives in the British carpet-bombing of the city. Fredric Jameson, who has described Warsaw's rebuilding as 'Disney related operations', has a point when he argues that in such situations there needs to be a 'careful disassociation between the categories of historicity and authenticity'.[7] The deaths of millions of Germans and Poland's own Germanic heritage have been lost in the narrative of Warsaw's celebrated rebuilding.

Nor was the whole of Warsaw's wartime experience expressed in its rebuilding; the story of the Warsaw Uprising was suppressed, under the direction of

Moscow, because of the less than noble involvement of the Soviets in this episode. Under communism and in the interests of ideology, the sufferings of Warsaw's Jews were also diminished by eliding them with a wider commemoration in monuments to all victims of fascism. For the Poles, there was a desperate desire to reinforce an identity that had been in grave danger of disappearing. The fear of having been almost erased from history created a will to reassert that history even at great cost. Memories of what had existed were, by themselves, insufficient: the rebuilding of Warsaw was to make memories manifest through a re-creation of the corporeal experience of the city, even if it is an artifice. There is a faith that rebuilding can achieve a new certainty even if the destruction itself has already demonstrated the fragility of such comforts.

Post-Soviet Russia has also seen an attempt to set the clock back to pre-revolutionary times in order to find a new national identity that has Russian Orthodoxy as a component. The re-creation of the Cathedral of Christ the Saviour, demolished by Stalin, and of other lost monuments, such as the Resurrection Gate in Red Square and the early seventeenth-century Kazan Cathedral, is evidence of this. Yet the re-creation of these politically useful icons from scratch has taken place at a time when the genuine historic Moscow is vanishing at an alarming rate. Rich developers allied with the city's powerful mayor, Yuri Luzhkov, are tearing down old buildings to make way for flats for a wealthy elite. Alex Komech, director of the State Fine Art

Stalin's creation of a new atheistic order in the Soviet Union demanded the banishment of religious structures. The vast Tsarist Cathedral of Christ the Saviour in Moscow (completed 1883) was one of thousands of churches closed, converted to new uses or demolished. It was dynamited in December 1931 and rebuilt in the post-Soviet era, being consecrated in 2000.

The destruction of the Cathedral of Christ the Saviour in Moscow, 1931.

Institute, said: 'The rate at which the historical centre is disappearing is comparable with Stalin's rebuilding of Moscow. Since the 1990s at least 500 historic buildings have been pulled down, 50 of them historic monuments.'[8] By promoting shiny new relics, wider truths about the built environment are consigned to these giants' shade.

In Ukraine, too, independence has been marked by a coordinated plan for the rebuilding of many significant monuments destroyed during the Soviet era. The 'Programme and Procedures for the Re-creation of Prominent Monuments of the History and Culture of Ukraine' identifies 56 suitable buildings.[9] The cathedral of St Michael of the Golden Domes was the first to raise its gilded Cossack helmet domes above the Kiev skyline once again, followed by the cathedral of the Dormition. Many of the religious, secular and military monuments on the list are included with the intention of reviving Ukraine's Cossack heritage. Some nineteenth-century additions to St Michael's were not included in the replica but faked twelfth-century brickwork was, giving the visitor an impression of a continuous historical presence for the Ukrainian nation. Pilasters high on the building are faked in paint rather than being genuinely rebuilt. There is an undoubted quality of kitsch and falsification. Other re-creations include a Cossack hetman's palace and the burial chapel of the Cossack hetman Pavlo Doroshenko.

In a study investigating this rebuilding of Ukraine's medieval past, Olenka Pevny notes that these monuments, together with flags, portraits of historic Cossack heroes, displays of military might and a new Independence monument in Kiev's Independence Square (formerly Red Square and occupied by a colossal statue of Lenin) have created a new locus for shared experiences and for stimulating collective memories – new and old: 'It is the familiarity and ubiquity of their forms as much as the very act of their creation and then intended incorporation into the rituals of daily life that bridges the gap between past and present, perceived as having been created by the untimely destruction of their predecessors.'[10] As in Warsaw, this is the reinvention of tradition and a reassertion of identity through architecture, but one that looks to a certain past rather than an uncertain future.

Newly forged national identities are also too often exclusory and intolerant of plurality in their rush to create a coherent unity that is justified historically but selectively. This is a pattern evident throughout the republics of the former Soviet Union and in the Eastern Bloc countries beyond. The Ukrainian government has at least made a gesture in the direction of plurality with their rebuilding programme set to include the Selim mosque in Feodosia and the Golden Rose synagogue in L'viv, although no construction dates have been set. There is a danger in these rescue missions of implanting false memories that accord to the post-destruction mores and an official version of history. Rebuilt history may be read as an authentic document of the past when it is a forgery. This is especially true for architecture, which is an expensive business and the shape of which is generally moulded by the hands of the wealthy and powerful. Architecture's apparent permanence makes it especially useful for such purposes.

While a desire for continuity, however manufactured, can be a primary motive in terms of rebuilding, the legacy of the Second World War and the Holocaust to Germany is a discontinuity with its past. The country is still struggling between opposing desires to remember and forget. Stemming from this there remains in Germany a profound ambivalence towards its architectural record. The struggle began almost as soon as the Allied bombs stopped falling.

W. G. Sebald's 1997 Zürich Lecture 'Air War and Literature' notes the continued silence in German literature regarding the pounding of its cities into heaps of bricks by Allied carpet-bombing.[11] Around 600,000 German civilians were killed and 3.5 million homes were destroyed, yet a national amnesia prevails regarding the horrors inflicted on non-combatants and upon Germany's cultural heritage. To some, the carnage of Dresden and Hamburg may have appeared due retribution for the atrocities of the death camps; for others, Sebald suggests, the experience may have been simply too overwhelming to comprehend and register. Post-war Germany, he argues, simply got on with the task of rebuilding and looking single-mindedly to the future: 'A reconstruction tantamount to a second liquidation in successive phases of the nation's own past history prohibited any looking backwards.' He tells the story of a young Swedish journalist travelling by train in 1946 through the 'lunar landscape' of urban Germany: 'The train was crammed full, but no one looked out the windows and he was identified as a foreigner himself *because* he looked out.' Is this the shame of a defeated people or the self-imposed collective guilt of a people whose countrymen had inflicted such terrible suffering on others? Sebald's argument was pre-empted by Hannah Arendt's 1950 observations:

> Nowhere is this nightmare of destruction . . . less felt and less talked about than in Germany itself . . . Amid the ruins, Germans mail each other picture postcards still showing the cathedrals and market places, the public buildings that no longer exist . . . In France and Great Britain people feel greater sadness about the relatively few land-marks destroyed in the war than the Germans do for all their lost treasures together.[12]

Sebald and Arendt may have been correct in identifying the dominant psychological response to destruction in the immediate aftermath, but there was also a profound critique developing within Germany of its city rebuilding programme. There was much discussion and the rebuilding was by no means an uncontested process of simply looking forward. *Vergangenheits-bewältigung*, the concept of coming to terms with or 'mastering' the past, emerged in the 1950s particularly in relation to the legacy of the Third Reich. In *Munich and Memory: Architecture, Monuments and the Legacy of the Third Reich*, Gavriel Rosenfeld examines in painstaking detail how this process was played out in the rebuilding of one city.[13] Munich was the birthplace of the Nazi party, the Capital of German Art and the Capital of the Movement. It was the subject of a radical redesign proposal to create the Führerstadt, a plan realized only in fragments but one that left a legacy of Nazi architecture and spaces unparalleled outside Berlin.

Rosenfeld identifies three competing groups arguing over the future of the post-war city: Modernists, who desired a complete break with the anti-modern past of the Third Reich; traditionalists, who saw the Third Reich as a product of rootless modernity and so yearned for the resurrection of the pre-Hitlerian historic city; and critical-preservationists who maintained that rebuilding had to incorporate the memory of both the Nazi period and the Allied bombing that destroyed 60 per cent of the Altstadt. For the latter, acceptance of loss and the integration of damage into the city's collective identity was a central criterion of mourning. In large part it was the traditionalists who prevailed, especially in the earlier phases. Blaming 'Hitler's war' for the destruction of Munich and in so doing casting themselves as victims, they distanced themselves from the recent past. Nazi buildings could be condemned and historic buildings restored *in toto*.

'We once again have the tower of St Peter. Its trusted silhouette . . . soars in the sky as if nothing happened,' recorded one observer about the restoration of the rebuilding of a church that dated back to the twelfth century.[14] A priest at Munich's Frauenkirche compared, with stunning insensitivity, the need to rebuild his church with the rebuilding of the temple at Jerusalem after the Babylonian exile.[15] In this desire to draw a veil over the Nazi era, the citizens of Munich were aided and abetted by the occupying US forces and their denazification process. In June 1945 the Control Council of the Allied forces issued Directive No. 30, 'The Liquidation of German Military and Nazi Memorials and Museums'. All relevant buildings had to be 'completely destroyed and liquidated' by 1 January 1947.

In actuality, although many Nazi buildings damaged in the air raids were subsequently levelled, the pattern in Munich and elsewhere tended towards a superficial denazification by the removal of swastikas, eagles and other insignia. Among the few intact buildings that were demolished to their foundations as a result of this order were the two Ehrentempels, classical temples to Nazi martyrs built on the historic Königsplatz, a square that had been turned into the granite Plattensee parade ground and the ceremonial heart of Nazism. After the war, the square itself was turned into a determinedly utilitarian car park before its paving was eventually ripped up and replaced with the grass lawns that existed prior to its Nazification. Rather than being rebuilt, other Nazi buildings were retained with minor modifications and normalized, including the Führerbau and the Haus der Deutschen Kunst (a centrepiece of Nazi cultural policy opened in 1937). The Parteibauten was simply screened by the planting of a row of linden trees in front of it. Street lamps personally designed by Hitler were, however, removed. The post-war Munich that emerged from the rubble looked remarkably similar to its pre-war incarnation with little or no obvious visible memories or critical interpretation of the Nazi period. As late as 1979 the Bürgerbräukeller, site of Hitler's beer-hall putsch, vanished without protest under the new Gasteig cultural complex. One of the few buildings that determinedly resisted this willed forgetfulness is the Alte Pinakothek, the grand nineteenth-century Renaissance Revival art gallery, the south façade of which was rebuilt 'incorporating scars' from the war and using a simple brick infill to patch the shattered stonework and leaving the pockmarks of bullet holes visible. In the late 1960s this exemplar of critical preservation, which in its repaired frontage provoked memories of the reality of war, narrowly missed being rebuilt in decorous facsimile.[16] In short, even though there have been fierce debates in the city about what to preserve, rebuild or demolish – which continue today – Munich's self-identity as a city of culture has triumphed, conveniently leapfrogging its darker, Nazi period and establishing a false continuity with its peaceful nineteenth-century past.

There is little in the way of authenticity in the rebuilding of 'historic' Munich, Warsaw, Moscow and Kiev. As destruction in outright wars and ongoing low-intensity conflicts continues across the world, this issue is of increasing concern to the international conservation community. The need for authenticity in the restoration of historic buildings has been incorporated in the conservationist Charter of Venice since 1964, but it was reaffirmed vigorously in the 1994 Nara Document on Authenticity at an international gathering of conservation experts held in the midst of the Bosnian war. It notes that:

> In a world that is increasingly subject to the forces of globalization and homogenization, and in a world in which the search for cultural identity is sometimes pursued through aggressive nationalism and the suppression of the cultures of minorities, the essential contribution made by the consideration of authenticity in conservation practice is to clarify and illuminate the collective memory of humanity.

It is a call for truth in architecture.

Because of this principled approach UNESCO has declared that any attempt to rebuild Bamiyan's Buddhas will result in the site being removed from the list of World Heritage sites forthwith. It is, however, spending money stabilizing the blast-damaged niches. Attitudes within Afghanistan to the idea of rebuilding the statues vary. The provincial government is in favour but the country's leading archaeologist decried the idea as a 'Disney re-creation'.[17] It is a view echoed by the director of the Bamiyan Buddhas site: 'There will be no historical value in what we rebuild. And it's part of our history that the Taliban destroyed them; to rebuild would be to cleanse that history.'[18] The people of Bamiyan itself are equally aware of the nuances of meaning that rebuilding the statues (even if technically feasible) would bring. A local Muslim religious leader, Haji Abdhulla, will not be drawn but concedes that 'they were symbols of tolerance'. His son wants the Buddhas back: 'If they remain destroyed we will suffer from the emptiness of the niches . . . Rebuild and maybe we will forget the misery of the Taliban who burnt down our village.' Zahir Mohamedi, one of the Bamiyan prisoners forced to place the explosives around the statues, agrees: 'Maybe if we did [rebuild] we might get our honour back. We our proud of our history.'[19] Should sentiment outweigh scientific rationality and sound conservation practice? This is a religious monument after all, even if to a faith long-vanished from the region. One solution offered by a local is to rebuild just one statue: 'That would give us a sense of what we had lost,' says Haji Feda, 'but we would still have an empty niche to tell the world of this attack on our cultural history.'[20] If not critical preservation, this would be critical restoration of a sort; even if a sort unlikely to meet with the approval of UNESCO. The idea has the merit at least of both mourning a loss and restoring an icon of tolerance – in a land that surely needs one – without utterly masking the past. Yet it would remain a falsification.

And in Bosnia, how many of its shattered mosques should be rebuilt from their foundations to match their previous incarnations? How many should be repaired, with and without the scars of war incorporated? It would be hard to decry totally Bosnian wishes to be as defiant as the Varsovians in rebuilding a history slated for erasure, even if historical truth is obscured in the restored architecture. There are no easy answers but, where possible, critical preservation and reconstruction remains the most honest course, with the cracks and fissures and layers of experience incorporated as reminders of the experience of the stones and of the people who lived among them and continue to do so.

Elsewhere, countries and peoples who, perhaps, have never come close to annihilation can live more safely with redevelopment rather than facsimile rebuilding – and even with continued ruination as a symbol of a struggle overcome. The built historical record may have been damaged but was nowhere near erased. The rebuilding of English cities after the Second World War displayed remarkably little sentiment in relation to the past. Wholesale renewal (already the goal of pre-war Modernists and progressives) was taken up with vigour after victory in much the same way as 'homes fit for heroes' was a rallying point for societal renewal after the First World War, even in the absence of a significant war from the air. Some key monuments were rebuilt in replica after 1945 (the House of Commons and Buckingham Palace, for instance), but certain war-damaged buildings have been retained as ruins – namely churches. A number of the City churches in London are now memorial gardens incorporating fragments of wall and often a repaired tower. At other sites it is just the tower that remains. Kenneth Clark, T. S. Eliot and John Maynard Keynes were among the signatories of an August 1944 letter to *The Times* calling for some ruins to be preserved.[21] A book, *Bombed Churches as War Memorials*, was produced to promote the project.[22] St Luke's, Liverpool, is a provincial example of this trend. There is obviously a long tradition of positive regard for ruins in the Romantic English land-scape tradition, which has in some cases extended to urban locations. This drew initially on classical era ruins as witnessed on the Grand Tour, but came to incorporate the ruinous wake of Henry VIII's dissolution of the monasteries and the building of new ruins – follies – in the eighteenth and nineteenth centuries. The architect antiquarian Sir John Soane had his Bank of England scheme illustrated as a ruin even before it was built. Coventry Cathedral is the greatest post-war example of this Picturesque tendency. The city's original cathedral, part of a Benedictine priory, was left to decay after the dissolution of the monasteries in 1539. The nearby thirteenth-century parish church of St Michael was eventually raised to cathedral status in 1918. Its destruction in the bombing raid of 14 November 1940 was followed by a decision the following day to rebuild, but the new cathedral was built entwined and in dialogue with the ruins of the old. The rebuilding was regarded as an opportunity to remember suffering and promote forgiveness rather than as a statement of defiance. The cathedral has established a min-istry of 'peace and reconciliation' that intervenes in wars, and a cross of nails, recovered from the ruins, is its symbol. The image of the phoenix – of resurrection and of rebirth through fire – is also closely associated with the building. The maintenance of ruins as records of terrible events is not confined to England. The French village of Oradour-sur-Glane remains as a ruin, frozen in time with a burnt-out Citroën still crumpled in its main street. It is a shrine to the 643 villagers massacred by the Nazi 'Das Reich' army division on 10 June 1944. Hundreds of women and children were among those locked into the church and then burned alive. The motive for the attack remains unclear. Hiroshima (perhaps one of the few instances where bombing into submission succeeded) had no choice but to rebuild; here too, however, a ruined exhibition hall dome remains at the heart of the city – the ground zero of nuclear destruction. To have left no physical trace of the devastation would have been to abnegate the trauma. There needs to be evidence of lessons learned – even if that lesson was learned by the victims rather than the perpetrators. And, of course, the victims need to be remembered too. Sites of horror seem to demand physical manifestations of the events if a sense of place is to be maintained. Resisting the push to architectural amnesia has resulted in attempts at commemoration that seek to mark and explain the past rather than avoid it. Out of sight can become out of mind.

As at Coventry Cathedral and other church ruins in England, Berlin decided to incorporate the ruins of the war-damaged Kaiser-Wilhelm-Gedächtniskirche (memorial church) into a new church building by architect Egon Eiermann. Together with the Mercedes-Benz logo on top of the Europa-Center, the church became the focus and symbol of West Berlin's new centre: faith and capitalism – in contrast to the atheistic and planned economy of the East. More recently, a new Church of Reconciliation has been rebuilt in contemporary form at the Bernauer Strasse Berlin Wall memorial with the old church bells incorporated into the design. But Berlin has, otherwise, been rather late in coming to terms with its past; for a long time such questions were elbowed aside by the presence of the Wall. While many buildings 'infected' with Nazism, by reason of their design or their history, were destroyed in the capture of Berlin, some were actively targeted after occupation: the Soviet forces demolished Speer's Neue Reichskanzlei (chancellory), for example. Other monuments, including the Reichstag, burnt out on the accession of Hitler to power and the ultimate Soviet objective in their drive into Berlin, remained in ruins for many years. Later, other buildings, such as Spandau Prison, were demolished for fear that they might become shrines for neo-Nazis. Physical reminders of Nazi crimes have been preserved in few places. The open-air Topography of Terror exhibition established within the ruins of the Gestapo and ss headquarters building is one. It was only direct action by a group of young activists that prevented the site being cleared for a road scheme. On 8 May 1985 the group arrived at the long-abandoned mound of overgrown rubble and started digging, gradually unearthing the basement cells at the heart of the 'brown terror'. The site is now a museum to the victims of fascism and a 'site of contemplation'. Plans for a permanent museum building designed by Peter Zumthor were abandoned in 2004. The work completed since 1993 is to be razed while another architectural competition is considered.

It was the fall of the Berlin Wall and the decision to move the reunited Germany's capital back to Berlin from insipid Bonn that revived the tensions between memory and forgetting. The new capital had to decide what to do with the legacy of the repressive East as well as the Nazi remnants of the war era. Germany's politicians were extremely sensitive to their new capital being tainted by association – especially as the power of the reunified country was threatening to some of its more anxious neighbours. Pragmatism won out over the initial desire to flatten the likes of Hitler's vast Reichsbank and Aviation Ministry. They are both now used by the Federal Government. The Aviation Ministry has been rehabilitated as the Federal Finance Ministry, with a senior official defending the decision by arguing, rather hopefully, that the building was where Luftwaffe conspirators planned to assassinate Hitler and, as such, was a 'building of the resistance during the Third Reich'.[23] The new buildings of the capital's government precinct otherwise determinedly avoid the old. They are built on an east–west axis crossing the River Spree rather than gathering along Unter den Linden or aligning themselves with Hitler's planned north–south triumphal avenue – the spine of Germania. Critical preservation has reached Berlin too, with Sir Norman Foster's remodelling of the ruined outcrops of the Reichstag as the new home of the Bundestag. The scrawls of Soviet soldiers remain on the walls of the otherwise avowedly contemporary and neutral interiors. The gutted dome of the building has been replaced with a glass dome, inside which people can climb ramps that spiral up to a roof terrace while peering down at their representatives in the debating chamber below. The symbolism of openness and democracy is obvious in the new work and the burden of history remains present in the old.

East Berliners, meanwhile, have not always been happy to see their own recent architectural history bulldozed. The reunification was an ending of division by conquest rather than a coming together of different traditions. An exception to this wariness was the unloved GDR Foreign Ministry demolished in 1995, although the new authorities, as Michael Wise in his book *Capital Dilemma* points out, were still guarded in their approach to the matter: 'Mindful that Communists have been accused of sweeping history out of view with similar actions, the government took care to use a bizarre linguistic contortion, "*Rückbau*" . . . meaning "reverse building" rather than "*Abriss*" (demolition).'[24] Less welcome, to many East Germans at least, was the Bundestag decision taken in 2002 to demolish the Palast der Republik (part East German parliament, part fun palace for the people) and rebuild the Stadtschloss (or at least its façades) in its place.[25] It looks like an attempt to erase more than 60 years of Berlin's recent history. The 1,200-room, seventeenth-century Hohenzollern palace, the Stadtschloss, which had dominated central Berlin, was badly damaged in the Second World War. Demolition of the ruins of the Baroque building, which had been the home of the Prussian royal family, began in 1950 in an attempt to remove this reminder of Prussian militarism and 'an inglorious past'. The Garrison Church and the city palace of nearby Potsdam were levelled for similar reasons. East German leader Walter Ulbricht said: 'The centre of our capital city . . . and the area of the present Palace ruins, must become a great square for demonstrations in which the fighting spirit and will to rebuild of our people can be expressed.'[26] There was opposition even within East Germany to the plan, but the demolition went ahead with the help of hundreds of FDJ (Free German Youth) 'volunteer building cadres'. The Schlossplatz on which it stood was renamed Marx-Engels Platz and was indeed used for the GDR's own military parades.[27] One balcony section from the Schloss was preserved in the façade of the new East German Council of State building – the balcony from which Karl Liebknecht declared a socialist republic on 9 November 1918. Today, the Stadtschloss project's private backers point out the importance of the castle to the urban design of the historic precinct. They have gathered together powerful supporters, including German Chancellor Gerhard Schröder and architects I. M. Pei and the late Philip Johnson, for rebuilding at least three of the castle's façades.[28] As yet the money is not in place. Even its purpose is unclear; there is talk of using one wing of the new building for an upmarket hotel and other areas for shops, museums and 'special event' rooms. By any standards the Palast der Republik is an ugly piece of architecture, but it is an extraordinary decision for a republic to re-create a royal castle, half a century after it was destroyed and little of which remains, and to do so with no firm purpose other than sentimentality. As in Munich, it is for reminders of a pre-Hitlerian Germany that conservatives yearn, not the built evidence of Nazism or Communism. The supporters of rebuilding also point to apparent precedents for the entire rebuilding of destroyed monuments following conflicts, Mostar Bridge and Warsaw among them, but none of these examples involved the removal of subsequently built structures in a bid to rebuild the past. Local architects are resisting the push towards comprehensive demolition of the Palast der Republik. Cornelius Hertling, as president of the Berlin Chamber of Architects, made the case against the ongoing destruction of memory: 'We find it unacceptable that buildings that have become part of urban history are being erased from memory precisely because they are historically burdened. History and identity are therefore being eradicated.'[29]

New reminders have also been created in Berlin where there were none before, of which Daniel Libeskind's Jewish Museum is the most powerful. He has described his work as a search for 'a new and responsive urbanism [that] navigates between the Scylla of nostalgic historicism and the Charybdis of totalitarian *tabula rasa*'.[30] Berlin's Holocaust memorial, the Monument to the Murdered Jews of Europe completed in 2005, has proved more controversial. On a site near the Brandenburg Gate, it takes the form of a vast undulating field of 2,700 stone monoliths designed by architect Peter Eisenman and sculptor Richard Serra. Questions have been asked about when enough commemoration is enough.

Former Berlin mayor Eberhard Diepgen campaigned against the 'grandiose' scale of the memorial and forced a reduction in its size. It was argued, improbably, that central Berlin had no historical connections with the Holocaust.[31] In supporting the rebuilding of the Stadtschloss, Annette Ahme, the head of the Berlin Historical Society, complained:

> It is very important for the history of National Socialism to be taught and remembered in museums, concentration camps, memorials and so on. But it makes no sense to overload the city with these pedagogical things and have every building and empty lot proclaim forever, 'You evil Germans'. The city must be beautiful so that people will be happy and they will not repeat these mistakes.[32]

It is a curious argument to suggest that a beautiful city will prevent ugly actions. It is the builders and destroyers who make policy and war not the buildings themselves. Ahme's comments also suggest a vain wish to confine commemoration to certain contained points within a neutral built environment overall.

Has a commemorative *Schlussstrich* (bottom line) been reached, as some would argue, less than 30 years after Germany properly began its process of self-examination in the 1960s? Munich has more than 100 monuments recording aspects of the war but, as Gavriel Rosenfeld points out, 'an enormous disparity persists between monuments commemorating victims and those documenting the deeds of the perpetrators'.[33] Nine out of ten of Munich's monuments have been erected to German victims – around half of the total are to the German resistance. Only one (the site of the former Gestapo headquarters), says Rosenfeld, truly commemorates a site of perpetrator criminality. And when is enough enough, when there are still attacks on Jewish patrimony in Germany by neo-Nazis? Even so, contemporary Germany remains unique in being a country prepared to commemorate its own historical crimes and to make architectural decisions to record them, however imperfectly. Memorials in Germany, argues the German-Irish novelist Hugo Hamilton, 'have become religious sites that provide a new kind of holiness and guide us towards a fair and racially tolerant society. If there is such a thing as absolution, it is only by remembering and revisiting these sites.'[34]

Absolution. Hamilton's choice of word, suggesting, as it does, repentance, renewal and a wiping away of sins, is revealing. It is an aspect of *Vergangenheitsbewältigung* that Theodor Adorno addressed in 1959. Does mastering the past mean working through the memories in a psychological sense in order to turn the page, then wipe out the memory?[35] Clearly not for Hamilton, who urges sites to be revisited, but recent critics of the traditional monument have argued that they embody precisely this danger. A monument becomes a full stop to remembering with actual memories fading after the erection of a fixed object. It becomes just another artefact in the cityscape.

It is a notion that has, in the past few decades, provoked artists to propose 'anti-monuments'. In the 1980s the German artist Horst Hoheisel famously created a 'negative form' in his memorial in Kassel to the deported Jews of the city. He used the site of a fountain destroyed by the Nazis (it was built with Jewish money) to create a funnel deep into the ground, down which water flowed into the darkness. It was a mirror image of the previous fountain. Explained Hoheisel: 'The sunken fountain is not a memorial at all, it is only history turned into a pedestal, an invitation to passers-by who stand upon it to search for the memorial in their own heads.'[36] A Holocaust monument unveiled in Hamburg-Harburg in 1986 by fellow German Jochen Gerz consisted of a 12 m high lead-sheathed block that was slowly lowered into the ground over seven years, burying its entire length and the graffiti

Dresden's Frauen-kirche before and after its destruction in February 1945 and following its reconstruction. The church, designed by George Bähr, was built between 1726 and 1743. It survived shelling by the Prussian army in 1760 when the shells simply bounced of its stone dome. The fire-storm created by Allied bombing that destroyed 15 sq km of the city, baked its structure and it disintegrated on 15 February. The rubble remained as a war memorial under the GDR government until its reconstruction following German reunification. The new exterior was completed in 2004.

scratched into the lead until just its top remained visible. These are intriguing and poignant responses to commemoration, yet they also use materiality
to create the desired 'recognition' effect – even if the material is buried.

It is true, though, that it is not only the 'presence' of a building that can
have this power, either whole or as a ruin, because, as Hoheisel recognized,
an absence, a void, can be an equally powerful prompt. To maximize their
power, however, voids need to be contained, whether within a building such
as Libeskind's Jewish Museum or between structures. Absence is most readily measured against something present. Dresden's Frauenkirche, left as a
pile of rubble after the Second World War, was a powerful statement – a void
in the city – retained as a reminder of 'capitalist warmongering'. It also
became a site for anti-GDR protests. The rebuilding of the church after the
fall of the regime has been described as itself an attempt to erase the memory
of the GDR and exclude memories of the Second World War.[37] In this case, it
is not the destruction of a building but the filling of a void that may encourage forgetting.

The future of the huge void in Manhattan left after 11 September has provoked much soul-searching. Rebuilding may be an act of resistance to some,
but to others disturbing a site where such a massive loss of life has occurred
is a sacrilege. Whilst the US government rapidly rebuilt the Pentagon within
a year in a very conscious message to terrorists, reminding them of
America's military capabilities, the future of the World Trade Center site has
seen conflict between rebuilders and memorializers. Thousands of people
died on a very valuable piece of real estate. Initial responses to the site
ranged from rebuilding the twin towers in replica through to leaving the site
permanently ruined as a tangible reminder of the devastation and as a mass
grave. Unlike the Pentagon, an executive decision could not be taken without
consulting New Yorkers themselves. An immediately popular idea was to
maintain the fifteen-storey fragment of the south tower that remained standing as a twisted ruin surrounded by a memorial garden. This, in itself, was
not without risk. As the American journalist Eric Fredericksen argued: 'It ele-
vates architecture above human lives and makes a showpiece of something
that was turned into an instrument of death. It collectivises deaths in a time and
a place where the individual is paramount. And it flirts with aestheticising
murder.'[38] There is a ready case to make against these arguments – people
are familiar with ruins as memorials to death, as the truncated columns in
any nineteenth-century necropolis show. But the danger of aestheticizing
murder was a real one; the Metropolitan Museum of Art's Director is quoted
as saying the ruin was a 'masterpiece'. New York architecture critic Herbert
Muschamp said the perforated metallic ruin recalled Frank Gehry and Issey
Miyake's work.[39] Manhattan, though, had lost 1.25 million square metres of
prime office space and part of its skyline, not to mention billions of dollars

for the site's owners. The compromise was to rebuild on part of the site ('bigger and better', demanded architect Bernard Tschumi; 'even more beautiful', demanded Mayor Giuliani) and devote the remaining space to a memorial. An exhaustive competition process produced a winning design team led by Daniel Libeskind.

There is something deeply troubling about Libeskind's original winning design – now horribly compromised – for the World Trade Center. It was not the spire and sunken memorial garden (all that will remain of the void); surprisingly for Libeskind, these are firmly in the traditional monumental canon. It was not, necessarily, the forms; they would have sung in harmony with the composition of the Manhattan skyline (which the Twin Towers never did) and greatly improve the urban design of this part of the city at ground level – much better than the windswept plaza of old. What appeared to be the surface fractures or dizzying diagonals are familiar Libeskind devices and there may well have been a case for them to be as present here as in his Denver Art Museum extension and a prosaic building for London Metropolitan University. What is worrying is the messages it is sending. Libeskind is the commensurate architect of memory and the symbolism of memory. His fractured Star of David at the Berlin Jewish Museum and shattered globe for Salford's Imperial War Museum could easily have been one-liners in the hands of a less skilled architect, but instead they work. In the case of the Jewish Museum, it works wonderfully: the yawning chamber that is the climactic element of the museum is a haunting evocation of imprisonment, totalitarianism, fear and loss. However, despite the creepy ravings of marginal Holocaust deniers, the meaning of the Nazi horrors has entered the collective consciousness. The meaning of Ground Zero is, by contrast, much more contested. Or at least it should be. Libeskind, coming back to New York from Berlin after two decades, appears not to have questioned the American establishment's hegemony in interpreting the meaning of the events of 11 September. The result is remarkably lacking in complexity and has become less so as the developers have asserted their financial demands as the scheme evolved.

In explaining the scheme Libeskind pointed to the retention of the exposed slurry wall that holds back the Hudson and forms a container for the memorial site itself: he says this 'engineering wonder' is a 'symbol of the strength and endurance of American democracy'. He recalls his arrival in New York by ship as a teenager and seeing the Statue of Liberty and Manhattan's towers, adding that the World Trade Center foundations are as 'eloquent as the Constitution itself, asserting the durability of Democracy and the value of individual life'. The proposed spire is, he said, 'reasserting the pre-eminence of freedom and beauty'. It also echoes Liberty's torch.[40] Setting aside the element of hyperbole about the resonance of the foundations, the narrative Libeskind is now intending to construct in New York is the triumph of hope, of American democracy and freedom. While it is perfectly understandable and necessary to commemorate this horror and hope for its resolution, without understanding why it happened and how to prevent similar atrocities in the future, the scheme becomes an unproblematic memorial to US propaganda and false memory rather than the monument the dead deserve. Freedom and democracy are values that are well worth commemorating even if the US has been a miserable failure in encouraging such values worldwide. New York critic Herbert Muschamp attacked Libeskind's design as 'emotionally manipulative', but surely that is what commemorative monuments are meant to be?[41] It is the manipulation of history rather than emotion through architecture that is troubling. When history is not understood it is more likely to be repeated.

'Never again' is understandably an important component of contemporary Jewish identity. A determination never to see a repeat of the Holocaust explains, in part, the single-mindedness of Jewish architectural historians in their efforts to identify former synagogues and (especially) Jewish graveyards of the Diaspora – often in the face of continuing anti-Semitism, including the ongoing vandalism of Jewish patrimony. This is especially true in Eastern Europe where, under a post-war communism hostile both to religion and to any potential opposition grouping, the region's Jewish architectural heritage continued to be neglected long after the war. Jewish suffering under the Nazis was also conflated into memorials to those who died in the struggle against fascism and the specifics of their experience downplayed and forgotten. Synagogues that had been burnt down or turned over to new uses and desecrated cemeteries were largely state-owned and often remained out of reach to the much diminished Jewish community. Those structures remaining have become monuments that are both a testimony and a warning.

The race to save what is left of this Jewish heritage has gathered pace with the fall of the Eastern Bloc's Communist regimes. The situation offers both the opportunity for access and restoration but also threats from resurgent chauvinistic nationalisms and a commensurate rise in *active* racism and anti-Semitism. Jewish Heritage Council activist Samuel Gruber argues that, like the few Jews who emerged alive after the Holocaust, 'these buildings are survivors. They are an important link in the fragile chain of memory – all that remains of the once great civilization of Jewish Eastern Europe.'[42] There is also a Talmudic responsibility to tend graveyards continually: 'the Jewish tombstones are fairer than Royal Palaces'. At the same time as a number of synagogues and graveyards are slowly being repaired, others are the subject of fresh attacks. The spring/summer 1998 edition of the quarterly report of the JHC, for instance, lists bomb attacks in the previous year on synagogues in Riga and Moscow; synagogues vandalized or set ablaze in Romania and Estonia; cemeteries desecrated in Irkutsk, Moscow and Warsaw.[43] This situation is also true of Germany, where old synagogues and Jewish cultural centres have been built and rebuilt across Germany in recent years. A project at Darmstadt Technical University is steadily rebuilding all the synagogues destroyed on Kristallnacht – but in virtual reality using computer-aided design. The project was begun after a neo-Nazi arson attack on Lübeck's synagogue in 1994.[44] In Berlin itself, the magnificent golden-domed Neue Synagogue on Oranienburger Strasse has been restored as a Jewish museum after decades languishing as a ruin in East Berlin. It is a jolt, however, to walk down the street and see that the building still needs an armed guard.

It is this continuing fragility of Diaspora monuments, the broken temples across the world, that makes the staying of Israel's hand with regard to Temple Mount all the more pointed and poignant. At the heart of a state created as a refuge for a people whose heritage and lives have ruthlessly and endlessly faced destruction sits a ruined temple. The Wailing Wall, a fragment from past destruction, is surely a more potent and consistent architectural symbol of the Jewish experience than any Third Temple could be. Restoring architecture can never resolve conflicts but how can the recognition of guilt or the expiation upon which reconciliation depends emerge if there is no memory of the crime? The Bosnians, meanwhile, have with help from other European countries embarked on plans to rebuild Sarajevo's National Library at the centre of their capital. This is matched by an international programme to support an in-gathering of manuscripts to make good, if only in a limited way, some of the incalculable losses to the historic record. It remains to be seen how much ruination the Bosnians can tolerate as a reminder of what has been lost, but the restoration of the library building must take this into account in a critical way. In the meantime, the inscription on the plaque attached to the ruined walls of the library remains: 'Remember and Warn'.

7 Remember and Warn II: Protection and Prosecution

... This is how one pictures the angel of history. His face is turned
toward the past. Where we perceive a chain of events, he sees one
single catastrophe which keeps piling wreckage and hurls it in front
of his feet. The angel would like to stay, awaken the dead, and make
whole what has been smashed. But a storm is blowing in from
Paradise; it has got caught in his wings with such a violence that the
angel can no longer close them. The storm irresistibly propels him into
the future to which his back is turned, while the pile of debris before
him grows skyward.

WALTER BENJAMIN, 'THESES ON THE PHILOSOPHY OF HISTORY, IX'

'I have been all the way through this desert from Basra to here', said Sgt
Sprague, on duty a few kilometres north of the 8,000-year-old remains of
the city of Ur, 'and I ain't seen one shopping mall, or fast food restaurant.
These people got nothing.'[1] Sgt Sprague of White Sulphur Springs, West
Virginia, may be especially ignorant of the material heritage of Iraq, but the
cultural myopia reflected in his comments is hardly surprising in the army
of a country that has for half a century refused to ratify the 1954 Hague
Convention for the Protection of Cultural Property in the Event of Armed
Conflict. Along with the United Kingdom, the United States is one the few
nations across the world that have failed to do so. It is the Convention's pro-
hibition on attacking culturally important locations except where 'military
necessity imperatively requires such a waiver' that worries these two permanent members of the UN Security Council; freedom of action in war takes
priority over world heritage.

If the United States had signed up to the Hague Conventions they would,
in addition to a requirement to avoid such targets, have had a clear legal duty

of care to the monuments and cultural artefacts of occupied Iraq (they have a duty under international customary law in any case). Whether they would have implemented them and guarded Baghdad's priceless museums and the Koranic library rather than the Oil Ministry is another matter. On the eve of the US invasion of Iraq in February 2003, an article in the US Air Force Association's *Airforce* magazine, 'In Search of Lawful Targets', made no mention of either the 1954 Convention or the 1977 Additional Protocols to the Geneva Conventions, which do not include the 'military necessity' waiver and prohibit all hostilities against historic monuments, works of art or places of worship 'which constitute the cultural or spiritual heritage of people'. Also under these additional protocols, attacks on any site in pursuit of anything other than a military objective became a war crime. The US has not signed this crucial piece of international humanitarian law either.[2]

It can easily be argued that this matters little, given the conspicuous failure of international law protecting cultural property to deliver any real protection. The chapters of this book have outlined the myriad ways in which the world's built cultures have been destroyed by violent acts and continues to be so from Nigeria to Indonesia, Russia to Sudan (all of whom are signed up to the Convention). The 1954 Hague Convention, which emerged from the cultural devastation from the air during the Second World War, appears predicated on the idea, at least in part, that the duties its protocols impose on countries to make provision for cultural protection and to educate their armed forces would create a moral pressure on countries that would serve to diminish damage. In this they have failed. The Hague Convention measures are part of the military manuals of many signatory countries' armies, but even this has been no guarantee of meaningful implementation. That the legal provisions will be understood by front-line troops is, perhaps, a vainer hope.

Instead, it was the active selection of specific built targets, houses and palaces, shrines and cathedrals, first seen in Turkey, which increasingly came to characterize twentieth-century conflicts. The point is that the destruction is often the result of political imperatives rather than simply military necessity. The jockeying of the imperial powers in and around both World Wars, the Cold War and the collapse of the Eastern Bloc has, each time, created and re-created nationalisms, shifting and redirecting ethnic and religious identities along the way, and launched repeated struggles to retain or destroy the architectural markers of the past or to compete over their future meaning; to rebuild or replace them. The Convention also assumes that it is nation states who will make up the combatants rather than the ordinary citizens, irregulars, militias or terrorist groups who have often been at the forefront of attacks, especially in the nationalist and sub-nationalist wars after the Second World War. The terror threats to, and bombing of, ideologically significant buildings tear large holes in the Hague

Convention safety net, even with the application of the Geneva Convention to non-international conflicts as well.

Despite these failures, and with the lessons of the Bosnian war at hand, the diplomatic community and conservationists have been active in trying to strengthen cultural protection. In 1999 a diplomatic conference was held at The Hague to update the Convention by the agreement on a Second Protocol to the 1954 Convention, which, among other measures, incorporates the 1977 Geneva Convention (restricting attacks solely to military objectives) more directly into the Hague Convention and establishes, more directly, individual criminal responsibility for damage to cultural sites. Relatively few countries have, so far, signed up.[3] On the ground, the United Nations has responded to the damage and looting following the invasion of Iraq by announcing the creation of a rapid reaction force, 'cultural blue berets', using (for the moment) Italian troops to be deployed where culture is at threat from war or national disasters.[4] It is an admirable initiative but it remains to be seen whether such a flying squad would be effective; the record of the 40,000 international peace-keepers whose duties include the protection of the monuments of Kosovo has been abysmal. Serbian claims of the destruction of their monuments by Kosovars and NATO bombing during the

The destruction of monuments in the former Yugoslavia continues. In March 2004 a mob of young Serbs set fire to the historic Islam-aga mosque in Nis, Serbia. The attack, and one on the Bayrakli mosque in Belgrade, were a response to the destruction of dozens of Orthodox churches and monasteries in Kosovo by Kosovar nationalists the day before. They were the last two Ottoman mosques in Serbia.

Kosovan war may have been wildly exaggerated propaganda at the time, but there has been widespread damage to Serbian heritage in the UN Protectorate since. In 2004 this culminated in ethnic riots in Kosovo that saw Orthodox churches and monasteries in Prizren and elsewhere damaged or destroyed. The violence spread to the recently renamed republic of Serbia and Montenegro, where Belgrade's only remaining mosque burned in retaliation.[5] UNESCO Director General Koïchiro Matsuura said of this latest wave of ethnic-cleansing: 'Beyond monuments and heritage, it is a memory and cultural identity that is being destroyed.'[6]

This is exactly right. But for international condemnation and international law to mean anything more than pious intentions it must be enforced. Crucial to this is the prosecution of those guilty of destruction in breach of the law. Until recently, such action has been all too rare.

Early twentieth-century attempts at dealing with the destruction of monuments took the form of war reparations. The 1919 Treaty of Versailles specifically stipulated the return to the cathedral of St Bavo in Ghent of six side panels from the Van Eyck altarpiece that had been bought by the royal museum in Berlin in 1821. Germany was also required to restock the University Library at Leuven, following accusations that German troops deliberately destroyed one of Europe's most important library collections in 1914.[7] The German destruction and American-funded rebuilding was recorded in a plaque on the new library building, but this building too was severely damaged in the Second World War. The Germans once again got the blame when they attacked in 1940, although some damage should perhaps be ascribed to British bombing in 1944. The accusations of barbarian German attacks on civilized values stuck on both occasions.[8]

German war criminals at the Nuremberg Trials, led by Goering, Rosenberg and Ribbentrop, were the first to face prosecution for crimes against culture as set out in the 1907 version of the Hague Convention. The plunder and destruction across the Eastern front by Rosenberg's men were, the Soviet prosecutor General Rudenko told the court:

> Crimes against culture, occupying a definite place of their own. These crimes epitomized all the abomination and vandalism of German fascism . . . The destruction of national monuments, schools, literature, and the compulsory Germanization of the population followed the German occupation everywhere, in obedience to the same criminal principle which governed the ensuing pillage, rape, arson and mass murders.[9]

The Soviets said that in the Moscow province alone the Nazis had destroyed 112 libraries, 4 museums, 54 theatres and cinemas. They looted and destroyed the Peterhof palace outside Leningrad and numerous other monuments around the city. Across Soviet territory, the State Library at Odessa was, according to the prosecution, one of 43,000 public libraries destroyed – along with 84,000 schools and university buildings, 1,670 Orthodox churches, 237 Catholic churches, 69 chapels, 532 synagogues and 258 other religious buildings. Also among these losses were the twelfth-century Borisoglebsky Cathedral at Chernihiv, the cathedral in the monastery of St Euphrosyne at Polatsk and, around Novgorod, the Antoniev, Khutynsky, Zverin and Derevyanitzky monasteries. In total, the Germans were indicted with the destruction, in full or in part, of 1,710 towns and cities and 70,000 villages – 6 million buildings in all.[10]

Goering got off lightly from this line of questioning, Although he was accused of targeting cultural sites during the Luftwaffe's bombing campaign, the issue was not dwelt on; after all, Bomber Harris could just as easily have been in the dock, and the Allies knew it. The aerial bombers of Dresden, Hamburg, Hiroshima and Tokyo, of Vietnam and Cambodia, have never been sent for trial.

The degradation and murder of almost six million Jews did of course form a central component of the Nuremberg Trials and the destruction of synagogues during the war years was mentioned in this context; however, any connection between the destruction of material culture and what came to be called the genocide of the Jews, Poles and Soviet citizens was only hinted at ('the same criminal principle') during the trials.

After Nuremberg, attacks on architecture, and their links to war crimes and crimes against humanity, were barely noted, let alone prosecuted. That was until the war in the former Yugoslavia, when the connection could hardly be missed. The statutes establishing the International Criminal Tribunal for the former Yugoslavia (ICTY) being held at The Hague include, in addition to the ability to bring charges of genocide and other crimes against human-ity, the remit to bring charges under the 1954 Hague Convention and the later additional Geneva protocols for violations of the laws or customs of war, including:

- Wanton destruction of cities, towns or villages, or devastation not justified by military necessity.
- Attack, or bombardment, by whatever means, of undefended towns, villages, dwellings or buildings.
- Seizure of, destruction or wilful damage done to institutions dedicated to religion, charity and education, the arts and sciences, historic monuments and works of art and science.
- Plunder of public and private property.[11]

A number of Croats, Serbs and Muslims have been indicted for such cul-tural attacks. These include Ratko Mladić and Radovan Karadžić, who have had charges brought against them for various crimes including the destruction of sacred sites. The Croat who ordered the destruction of Mostar's bridge, General Slobodan Praljak, is also facing prosecution for his deeds. Usually these indictments for crimes against culture and property have formed part of wider accusations of persecution, deportation, rape, torture, mutilation, mass-murder and, ultimately, genocide rather than culture being central to the cases before the court. The shelling of Dubrovnik's Old Town and the surrounding area, however, appears to have been used as something of a test case and forms counts 10–12 in the ongoing (at the time of writing) trial of Struger, Jokić, Zec and Kovacević – the Serbian army and naval commanders in charge of the shelling.[12] The prosecution case makes specific mention of Dubrovnik's UNESCO World Heritage site designation, the Croats' deliberate demilitarization of the area and the display of the (supposedly protective) Hague Convention emblem on buildings denoting their cultural status. The destroyers of Stolac's mosques have also been charged.

The key defendant, Slobodan Milošević, is himself before the court at The Hague on indictments for crimes committed from Vukovar to Kosovo, including genocide, grave breaches of the Geneva Convention and other crimes against humanity that include religious persecution and the violation of the laws or customs of war, specifically: 'The intentional and wanton destruction of religious and cultural buildings of the Bosnian Muslim and Bosnian Croat communities including, but not limited to, mosques, churches, libraries, educational buildings and cultural centres.'[13] The counts of genocide do not specifically refer to the destruction of Bosnian and cultural heritage, but evidence of their fate has been debated at the trial. Harvard librarian András Riedlmayer, who has done much to bring the systematic levelling of Bosnia's mosques and libraries to the world's attention, has undertaken research at the court's request. With dozens of photographs of buildings before and after they were attacked and the evidence of witnesses, his research sets out in relentless detail the pattern of attacks on monuments from Sarajevo's National Library to country mosques and fountains.

Milošević's cross-examination of the witness is revealing. In what appears to be a desire to distance himself from the charges of genocide, Milošević draws a distinction between cultural heritage and religious heritage and recasts the destruction as part of a civil war, emphasizing the destruction of Serbian monuments in the conflict: 'I consider this matter important,' he argued, 'because you certainly know that the reciprocal destruction of religious structures is the religious component of a civil war, whereas destruction of monuments of culture would be tantamount to genocide.' Riedlmayer, in his answers, resists the suggestion of equivalence in the destruction of each community's heritage, pointing out the 'nearly complete eradication of non-Serb religious structures' in Bosnian Serb-held areas and the survival of many Serb monuments in Bosnian government-held lands.[14]

The fate of architecture was also part of the evidence in the trial of General Radislav Krstić for the genocide at Srebrenica, where it was considered a marker proving that there was genocidal intent in the mass murder that took place. In the appeal hearing against the guilty verdict, the partially dissenting opinion of Judge Shahabuddeen (which was dissenting on the degree of criminal responsibility, not the sentence) stated:

> Standing alone, forcible transfer is not genocide. But in this case the transfer did not stand alone . . . It was part – an integral part – of one single scheme to commit genocide, involving killings, forcible transfer and the destruction of homes . . . It is established that the mere destruction of a culture of a group is not genocide . . . But there is a need for care. The destruction of culture may serve evidentially to confirm an intent, to be gathered from other circumstances, to destroy the group as such. In this case the razing of the principal mosque confirms an intent to destroy the Srebrenica part of the Bosnian Muslim group.[15]

At last the connections between the destruction of culture and of the people who created it are being fully articulated in a court of law – and, in part, by Milošević himself.

The ravaging of Tibet's architectural heritage by China should also be seen as evidence of such intent. Estimates suggest that around 1.2 million Tibetans have been killed by the Chinese since 1950. This has never been officially recognized as genocide under international law, despite the killings, torture, religious persecution, imprisonment and the Tibetans' displacement by ethnic Chinese; the intent to destroy a people physically has not been proven. However, according importance to the cultural destruction that has taken place shifts the picture; the Tibetans, as a group, may remain in body, but their cultural distinctiveness *as a group* is in danger of vanishing – a people shorn of their culture and identity. This is the erasure of a people as a people – the annihilation of their historic conditions of life. I would argue that incorporating the erasure of Tibetan architecture and culture into the argument strengthens the case for a charge of genocide.

The ITCY trials have also demonstrated the importance of gathering detailed evidence on the pattern and methods of destruction in wars if the true nature of the conflict is to be revealed and if alarms are to be sounded. The ruined synagogues of Kristallnacht and the ruined castle of Warsaw were, without doubt, a warning of what was to come; not simply architectural destruction but a sign of impending ethnic cleansing and genocide. The destruction of Ayodhya's Babri mosque and those of Gujarat that followed are, similarly, instances of cultural cleansing accompanying ethnic cleansing, a situation that could easily degenerate into genocide. The international community should be on its guard for the mass destruction of a people when it sees the destruction of their cultural artefacts.

Judge Shahabuddeen made it clear that his opinion was 'not an argument for the recognition of cultural genocide' as a specific and separate crime against humanity. But should it be? Madeleine Albright, on a visit to Israel in September 1997 as US Secretary of State, described the demolition of Palestinian houses by the Israelis as 'provocative', but, she added, referring to Islamic militant attacks on Israeli civilians: 'There is no moral equivalence between killing people and building houses.'[16] She is right, of course, even if her phrase is amended to the 'destruction of houses'. (My critique of Israel, incidentally, is not saying that the IDF's actions are worse than those of the Palestinian bombers – just more relevant to the process under discussion in their misuse of built environment in the service of war and nationalist aims.) Albright's comments miss the point, however. Safeguarding a built heritage or even the simple homes of civilians against bombing, burning or dynamiting is not an issue separate from conflict and justice; it is an intrinsic part of the process as the bombers, arsonists, the drivers of armoured bulldozers and their political and military directors know.

Without wanting to dilute the unique nature of genocide as 'the gravest and greatest of crimes against humanity', characterized by a 'single-minded intent behind the barbaric actions',[17] or to set 'cultural genocide' on a par with systematic mass murder, it is evident, judging by the actions of would-be eliminators, that the task of destroying a group extends beyond the corporeal body to the community body and its collective life and identity as expressed through language, customs, art and, in this case, architecture. Raphael Lemkin, the lawyer who successfully persuaded the United Nations to adopt the 1948 Genocide Convention, mentions culture in his 1944 paper *Axis Rule in Occupied Europe*. Here, Lemkin coined the word genocide and framed its parameters. He argued that the term was intended to

> signify a coordinated plan of different actions aimed at the destruction of the essential foundations of life of national groups, with the aim of annihilating the groups themselves, the first phase of which is 'the destruction of the national pattern of the oppressed group' . . . The objective of such a plan would be the disintegration of the political and social institutions of culture, language, national health, dignity, and even the lives of the individuals belonging to such groups. Genocide is directed against the national group as an entity, and the actions involved are directed against individuals, not in their individual capacity, but as members of the national group.[18]

The destruction of monuments and Jewish patrimony in his native Poland were offered in evidence.

Eleven years earlier, with the mass murder of the Armenians in mind, Lemkin had submitted a paper to a Madrid conference on international law that rehearsed the arguments in favour of protecting *both* the bodily and the cultural integrity of groups.[19] He directly linked 'barbarity', conceived as 'the premeditated destruction of national, racial, religious and social collectivities', with 'vandalism', the 'destruction of works of art and culture, being the expression of the particular genius of these collectivities'.[20] Lemkin understood that a group could be annihilated if their group identity had been erased. 'It takes centuries and sometimes thousands of years to create a natural culture, but Genocide can destroy a culture instantly,' he observed, 'like fire can destroy a building in an hour.'[21] These arguments extend the concept of genocide well beyond the individual human body and make the link to the fate of material culture explicit, but they failed to make it into the UN Genocide Convention. The destruction of the essential foundations of life, a group's national pattern, the expression of their particular genius, is more than just an evidential marker, it is cultural genocide. It is the danger facing the Tibetans – genocide by other means.

Lemkin should be revisited and the 1948 Genocide Convention should be amended, or accompanied by a new, specific crime of 'cultural genocide' – at least in circumstances where it is intrinsically linked to mass murder (even if this murder falls short of genocide in and of itself). Such a crime should fall under the jurisdiction of the proposed permanent International Criminal Court. There may even be an argument for criminalizing cultural genocide where there have been no large-scale killings but population transfers accompanied by the eradication of the exiled group's built record – the experience of Northern Cyprus, for instance – but this risks undermining the unique concept of genocide. A separate crime of 'cultural cleansing' is, perhaps, appropriate. Urbicide, with its specific intent to eradicate a city and the associated conditions of heterogeneity that make a shared life possible, should also be examined as a phenomenon worthy of legal redress – although it is a significantly more difficult case to prove.[22]

Architecture in the twentieth century became, more and more, a weapon of war rather than something that gets in the way of its smooth conduct. Architecture is not just maimed in the crossfire; it is targeted for assassination or mass murder. This language is purposeful: it is not about establishing a moral equivalence but creating an awareness of the forces at work that govern the fate of architecture in conflicts and the interrelationship between its fate and the fate of people, individually and collectively. The artefacts of a culture are part and parcel of the collective identity of their producers; their history – how they understand themselves, where they came from and where they are going.

It has become something of a commonplace to refer to George Orwell's work to support a writer's position, yet in the matter of creating false pasts

Orwell, as ever, offers useful insights. In his novel *1984* it is an engraving of the church of St Clement Danes in London on the wall of a junkshop that causes Winston Smith to muse on the Party's use of architecture to manipulate memory:

> It was always difficult to determine the age of a London building. Anything large and impressive, if it was reasonably new in appearance, was automatically claimed as having been built since the Revolution, while anything that was obviously of an earlier date was ascribed to some dim period called the Middle Ages. The centuries of capitalism were held to have produced nothing of any value. One could not learn history from architecture any more than one could learn it from books. Statues, inscriptions, memorial stones, the names of streets – anything that might throw light on the past has been systematically altered.[23]

Enforced forgetting indeed. And it is this very same church that forms the backdrop to a statue of Bomber Harris, the terrorizer and destroyer of cities, unveiled in 1992. Placing him on a pedestal understandably provoked an outcry (not least from the mayor of Dresden). The raising of the statue and the reaction to it embodies the continued power struggle between memory and forgetfulness, truth and propaganda. If we accept Freud's position that nothing is truly forgotten, only repressed, then the coerced repression of memories through the manipulation of the built record needs to be fought if we are to have the freedom to remember or discard our memories voluntarily. This book is not an urging to live in the past surrounded entirely by the architectural relics of earlier times, but with reminders that are freely chosen and with a plurality of these reminders in order positively to reflect heterogeneity within societies. Difference need not be otherness. Memories of past wrongs also need to be kept alive without chauvinism poisoning the hope of a shared future.

Even in the absence of its builders, a dead building, like a dead language, can be sadly eloquent. It can speak for the sufferings of the Armenians, the Jews and for the Bosnian Muslims whose bones lie in the mass graves of Foča interlocked with fragments of carved stone screens and turned wood. Enlightenment values of equality, justice, reason and aspirations for a history that is objective are at stake, not to mention the notion of a collective world patrimony that evolved from the legacy of the French Revolution. The next few years will see whether the commitments to protection so easily swept aside during the conflicts of the twentieth century will mean anything at all in the twenty-first. The outcome of the ITCY trials and the deterrent effect of severe sentences for those found guilty of crimes on the basis of the destruction of a community's built heritage are vital if a climate is to be created where the unacceptability of such actions is understood. It is important to hope but it is hard to be optimistic. Prior to the 2003 war on Iraq, the UN Security Council press conferences were held in front of the backdrop of a tapestry reproduction of Picasso's *Guernica* hanging in the UN building in New York. When US Secretary of State Colin Powell made his case for war in February 2003, however, the horror of *Guernica* was literally, and metaphorically, covered up.

References

1 Introduction: The Enemies of Architecture and Memory

1 George Orwell, 'Looking back at the Spanish Civil War', *New Road* (London, 1943).
2 *New York Times*, 21 August 1992.
3 See, for example, M. Christine Boyer, *The City of Collective Memory: Its Historic Imagery and Architectural Entertainments* (Cambridge, MA, 1994) and Dolores Hayden, *The Power of Place: Urban Landscape as Public History* (Cambridge, MA, 1995).
4 Eric Hobsbawm, 'The New Threat to History', *New York Times Review of Books*, 16 December 1993.
5 Eric Hobsbawm and Terence Ranger, *The Invention of Tradition* (Cambridge, 1983).
6 Hannah Arendt, *The Human Condition: A Study of the Central Dilemma Facing Modern Man* (Chicago, IL, 1958).
7 Henri Lefebvre, *La production de l'éspace* (Paris, 1974); Eng. trans. Donald Nicholson-Smith (Oxford, 1991).
8 See, for example, Monica Spiridon, *Spaces of Memory: The City-Text*, European Thematic Network, online publication, www.lingue.unibo.it (undated). See also Rudy J. Koshar, 'Building Pasts: Historic Preservation and Identity in 20th Century Germany', in *Commemorations: The Politics of National Identity*, ed. John Gillis (Princeton, NJ, 1994).
9 Alois Riegl, *Der moderne Denkmalkultus* (Vienna, 1903); part Eng. trans. as 'The Modern Cult of Monuments: Its Character and its Origin', *Oppositions*, 25 (Fall 1982), pp. 21–51.
10 Dario Gamboni, *The Destruction of Art: Iconoclasm and Vandalism since the French Revolution* (London, 1997).
11 Donald L. Horowitz, *The Deadly Ethnic Riot* (Berkeley, CA, 2002), p. 436.
12 Kevin Lynch, *The Image of the City* (Cambridge, MA, 1960).
13 Adrian Forty and Susanne Kuchler, eds, *The Art of Forgetting*, Materializing Culture

(Oxford, 2001).

14 Aldo Rossi, *L'architettura della città* (Padua, 1966; Eng. trans, Cambridge, MA, 1982).

15 Joël Candau, *Mémoire et identité* (Paris, 1998), pp. 21–5.

16 Paul Ricoeur, *Memory, History, Forgetting*, trans. Kathleen Blamey and David Pellauer (Chicago, IL, and London, 2004), pp. 96–120.

17 Maurice Halbwachs, *La mémoire collective* (Paris, 1950), chap. 1.

18 Pierre Nora, 'From Lieux de mémoire to Realms of Memory', preface to Pierre Nora and Lawrence D. Kritzman, eds, *Realms of Memory: Rethinking the French Past*, I (New York, 1996).

19 Pierre Nora, 'The Reasons for the Current Upsurge in Memory', www.eurozine. com, 19 April 2002.

20 David Lowenthal, *The Past is a Foreign Country* (Cambridge, 1985).

21 Milan Kundera, *The Book of Laughter and Forgetting* (London, 1988).

22 Ronald Wright, *Stolen Continents: The Indian Story* (London, 1993).

23 Ibid.

24 Georges Bataille, 'Architecture', *La dictionnaire critique* (Paris, 1992).

25 Gamboni, *The Destruction of Art*, p. 33, caption 6.

26 Christopher Hibbert, *The French Revolution* (London, 1980).

27 Emmerich de Vattel, *Le droit des gens: ou Principes de la loi naturelle appliqués à la conduite et aux affaires des nations et des souverains* (Neuchâtel, 1758), III, chapter 9; quoted in Jiří Toman, *The Protection of Cultural Property in the Event of Armed Conflict* (Aldershot and Paris, 1996).

28 Jiří Toman, *The Protection of Cultural Property*.

29 Adolf Hitler, meeting at Obersalzburg, 22 August 1939.

2 Cultural Cleansing: Who Remembers the Armenians?

1 Chuck Sudetic, New York Times News Service, 9 November 1993.

2 Slavenka Drakulić, *The Observer*, 14 November 1993.

3 A. Read and D. Fisher, *Kristallnacht: Unleashing the Holocaust* (London, 1989), pp. 73–4, 134–5.

4 The discovery of the structure was reported in *British Archaeology*, 12 (March 1996), but its history is disputed.

5 Martin Luther, *Against the Jews and their Lies* [1543], trans. Martin H. Bertram. Available at: www.humanitas-international.org.

6 Elizabeth Domansky, '"Kristallnacht", the Holocaust and German Unity', *History and Memory*, IV/1 (1992).

7 Darmstadt University of Technology, Department of CAD in Architecture, and others, eds, *Synagogues in Germany: A Virtual Reconstruction* (Basel, 2004), p. 131.

8 Read and Fisher, *Kristallnacht*, p. 65.

9 International Military Tribunal Nuremberg, Transcripts and Documents in

Evidence, Trials of Major War Criminals 374–PS, 3063–PS.

10 L. Scott Lerner, 'The Narrating Architecture of Emancipation', *Jewish Social Studies*, VI/3 (spring/summer 2000), p. 1.

11 Darmstadt, *Synagogues in Germany*, pp. 24–7.

12 Read and Fisher, *Kristallnacht*, p. 75.

13 Ibid., p. 99.

14 Ibid., pp. 118–19.

15 Arthur Flehinger, *Jewish Chronicle*, 9 November 1979.

16 Alfons Heck, *The Burden of Hitler's Legacy* (Frederick, CO, 1988), p. 61.

17 Read and Fisher, *Kristallnacht*, p. 106.

18 *The Sources of the Serb Hegemonistic Aggression: Documents*, ed. Bože Ćović (Zagreb, 1991), pp. 106–24.

19 Noel Malcolm, *Bosnia: A Short History* (London, rev. 1996), p. 55.

20 L. Silber and A. Little, *The Death of Yugoslavia* (London, 1995), pp. 29–35.

21 Attributed to Vladika Nikanor, a senior figure in the Serbian Orthodox Church; quoted in Mirko Djordjevic, *War Cross of the Serbian Church: Facing Democracy*, Helsinki Committee for Human Rights in Serbia (Belgrade, 2002), p. 79.

22 M. Povrzanovi, 'Ethnography of a War: Croatia 1991–92', *Anthropology of East Europe Review*, XI/1–2 (1993), pp. 117–25.

23 Council of Europe, *War Damage to the Cultural Heritage in Croatia and Bosnia Herzegovina*, January 1994, and *Spiritual Genocide: A Survey of Destroyed, Damaged and Desecrated Churches, Monasteries and other Church Building [sic] during the War 1991–1993*, Museum of the Serbian Orthodox Church, Belgrade, 1994; cited in Council of Europe, *War Damage to the Cultural Heritage*, and UN Security Council, *Destruction of Cultural Property* report, UN Commission of Experts, Annex XI, 28 December 1994.

24 *The Independent*, 20 June 1994.

25 Ibid.

26 Kemal Bakaršić, 'The Libraries of Sarajevo and the Book that Saved our Lives', *The New Combat: A Journal of Reason and Resistance*, 3 (Autumn 1994), pp. 13–15.

27 Ibid.; see also the testimony of András Riedlmayer in the ongoing trial of Slobodan Milošević at the ICTY. Transcript for 8 July 2003, www.un.org/icty.

28 *Report on the Devastation of Cultural, Historical and Natural Heritage of the Republic/Federation of Bosnia and Herzegovina: from 5 April 1992 until 5 September 1995*, Institute for the Protection of the Cultural, Historical and Natural Heritage of Bosnia-Herzegovina (Sarajevo, 1995).

29 Author's interview, July 2001. See also Riedlmayer testimony, 8 July 2003.

30 Cited in report to the US Commission on Security and Cooperation in Europe, Washington DC, Hearing on Genocide in Bosnia-Herzegovina, 4 April 1995.

31 Author's interviews with Ferhad Mulabegović and Dr Sabrina Husedzinović, July 2001.

32 Ibid.

33 Ibid.

34 Ibid.

35 Ibid.

36 *Devastation of Cultural, Historical and Natural Heritage* (1995).

37 Ibid.

38 Ibid.

39 Testimony of András Riedlmayer, transcript for 8 July 2003.

40 BBC Worldwide Monitoring, BH Radio, Sarajevo, 2 September 2004.

41 Riedlmayer testimony. See also *Crimes in Stolac Municipality, 1992–1994* (Sarajevo, *c.* 1996). For full text see the Community of Bosnia home page, http://www.haverford.edu/relg/sells/cobhome3.html.

42 See above. Information from author's interviews, including with Sue Ellis, return and reconstuction taskforce officer at the Office of the High Representative, Mostar, July 2001.

43 *Crimes in Stolac Municipality, 1992–1994.*

44 Figures cited by the Radical Statistics Group, including International Red Cross counts. www.radstats.org.uk.

45 Riedlmayer testimony, transcript for 8 July 2003.

46 Ibid. Map prepared by Bekir Besić, a refugee from Banja Luka.

47 *New York Times*, 21 August 1992.

48 *Los Angeles Times*, 28 March 1993; cited in A. Riedlmayer, 'From the Ashes: The Past and Future of Bosnia's Cultural Heritage', in *Islam and Bosnia: Conflict Resolution and Foreign Policy in Multi-Ethnic States*, ed. Maya Shatzmiller (Montreal, 2002).

49 David Dawidowicz, *Synagogues in Poland and their Destruction* (Jerusalem, 1960).

50 Richard Sennett, *Flesh and Stone: The Body and the City in Western Civilization* (New York, 1996), pp. 212–51.

51 Ibid., p. 216.

52 Quoted in Daniel Jonah Goldhagen, *Hitler's Willing Executioners: Ordinary Germans and the Holocaust* (New York, 1997), p. 141.

53 Read and Fisher, *Kristallnacht*, pp. 164–5.

54 J. Noakes and G. Pridham, *Nazism 1919–1945*, III: *Foreign Policy, War and Racial Extermination: A Documentary Reader* (Exeter, 1988), p. 1053.

55 Ibid., pp. 1061–7.

56 Dawidowicz, *Synagogues in Poland and their Destruction.*

57 Ibid.

58 *Jewish Heritage Report*, II/1–2 (Spring/Summer 1998).

59 Samuel Gruber, 'Jewish Monuments of Eastern Europe', *The Legacy of the Holocaust and Preservation Today*, College Art Association Annual Meeting, Chicago, IL, 1992.

60 Warsaw District general directive, 2 October 1940; see Noakes and Pridham, *Nazism 1919–1945*, p. 1065.

61 Noakes and Pridham, *Nazism 1919–1945*, p. 1069.

62 Ibid.

63 *The Independent*, 27 November 2000.

64 Testimony of Reverend Vartan Hartunian. Ellis Island Oral History Program Archive, 1986.

65 Raymond Kévorkian and Paul B. Paboudjian, *Les Armeniéns dans l'Empire Ottoman à la veille du genocide* (Paris, 1992).

66 T. A. Sinclair, *Eastern Turkey: An Architectural and Archaeological Survey* (London, 1987).

67 William Dalrymple, *From the Holy Mountain* (London, 1997).

68 Ibid., citing J. M. Thierry and Patrick Donabedian, *Les arts Arméniens* (Paris, 1988), pp. 87–8.

69 Ibid.

70 Accompanying notes for the exhibition *Armenian Churches in Eastern Turkey: A Legacy for Humanity*, Oakland, CA, March 2003.

71 *Armenian Weekly*, 15 March 2003, and Samvel Karapetian, 'The Armenian Cemetery of Jugha has been Annihilated', online report by the NGO Research on Armenian Architecture (RAA), www.raa.am/Articles/Juga.

72 Alexis Alexandas, *The Greek Minority of Istanbul and Greek–Turkish Relations 1918–1974*, Centre for Asia Minor Studies (Athens, 1992), pp. 252–89.

73 Ibid.

74 European Parliament resolution, 'On a Political Solution to the Armenian Questions', Doc. A2–33/87.

75 Dalrymple, *From the Holy Mountain*, p. 88.

3 Terror: Morale, Messages and Propaganda

1 Michael Scott Doran, 'Somebody else's Civil War', *How did this Happen? Terrorism and the New War*, ed. James F. Hoge jr and Gideon Rose (New York, 2001), pp. 31–52.

2 Broadcast 21 May 2003; reported in *Sydney Morning Herald*, 22 May 2003.

3 *Sydney Morning Herald*, 29 March 2004.

4 Quoted in Jason Burke, *Al-Qaeda: The True Story of Radical Islam* (London, 2004), p. 175–6.

5 See, for instance, Karen Armstrong, *Jerusalem: One City, Three Faiths* (New York, 1997).

6 Burke, *Al-Qaeda: The True Story of Radical Islam*, p. 240.

7 Statements to the 1998 Congressional Hearings on Intelligence and Security, Senate Judicial Committee, 24 February 1998.

8 Burke, *Al-Qaeda: The True Story of Radical Islam.*

9 *Sunday Times*, 6 January 2002.

10 Joseph Conrad, *The Secret Agent: A Simple Tale* (London, 1907), chapter 2.

11 H. G. Wells, *The War in the Air* (London, 1908, repr. Harmondsworth, 1941).

12 *The Independent*, 12 September 2002.

13 *Patterns of Global Terrorism*, United States Department of State, 1995.

14   Kathryn Lucchese, doctorate paper, College of Geosciences, Texas A&M University, 2001.

15   Khachig Tololyan, 'Cultural Narrative and the Motivation of the Terrorist', in *Inside Terrorist Organizations*, ed. David C. Rapoport (London, 2001), p. 220.

16   Reported in a paper by Giovanni De Gennaro, Deputy Chief of the State Police Force, at the first European meeting of 'Falcon One' on organized crime, Rome, 26–28 April 1995.

17   Patrick Cooney, 'The Raj in the Rain', *The Guardian*, 10 November 2001.

18   Mark Bence-Jones, *A Guide to Irish Country Houses* (London, revd 1988), p. xxiii.

19   Ibid., p xxi.

20   Kevin Kearns, 'Preservation and Transformation in Georgian Dublin', *Geographical Review*, LXXII/3 (July 1982), pp. 270–90.

21   Tom Garvin, *Irish Times*, 18 May 2000.

22   See for instance, Tomas MacCurtain, *Burning of Cork City by British Forces, December 1920: A Tale of Arson, Loot and Murder* (Hereford, 1978).

23   Ibid., pp. 30–36.

24   Sven Lindqvist, *A History of Bombing* (Eng. trans., London, 2001), p. 113 [unpaginated].

25   Robert Fisk, *Pity the Nation: Lebanon at War* (Oxford, 1990; 3rd edn, 2001), p. 186.

26   Nicola Lambourne, *War Damage in Western Europe: The Destruction of Historic Monuments during the Second World War* (Edinburgh, 2001), p. 50.

27   Max Hastings, *Bomber Command* (London, 1979). See also Robin Neillands, *The Bomber War* (London, 2001), p. 147.

28   Lambourne, *War Damage in Western Europe*, p. 53.

29   Niall Rothnie, *The Baedeker Blitz: Hitler's Attack on Britain's Historic Cities* (London, 1992).

30   Ibid., pp. 61 and 85.

31   Ibid., p. 69.

32   Ibid., p. 131.

33   Louis P. Lochner, trans., *The Goebbels Diaries 1942–43* (London, 1948), pp. 189–90.

34   Lambourne, *War Damage in Western Europe*, pp. 92–3.

35   Ibid., p. 98.

36   Ibid., p. 140.

37   Hastings, *Bomber Command*, p. 128.

38   Ibid.

39   Angus Calder, *The Myth of the Blitz* (London, 1991), p. 250.

40   Hastings, *Bomber Command*, p. 132.

41   Ibid., pp. 174–5.

42   Anthony Trythall, *'Boney' Fuller* (London, 1977), p. 226.

43   *Frankfurter Zeitung*, 1 July 1943.

44   Hastings, *Bomber Command*, p. 208.

45   A Review of the Work of Int 1, Bomber Command Internal Report, 1945.

46   Ibid.

47 Hastings, *Bomber Command*, pp. 341–4.

48 Frederick Taylor, *Dresden* (New York, 2004).

49 Tami Davis Biddle, 'Why Bomber Command Attacked Cities during the Second World War', online essay, BBC History Online, July 2001.

50 BBC *Timewatch*, 'Bombing Germany', broadcast 23 August 2001, and *The Guardian*, 23 August 2001.

51 Ibid. See also Hermann Knell, *To Destroy a City: Strategic Bombing and its Human Consequences in World War II* (Cambridge, MA, 2003).

52 Withdrawn memorandum from Churchill to Chiefs of Staff Committee and the Chief of Air Staff, 28 March 1945; cited in Hastings, *Bomber Command*, pp. 343–4.

53 Hastings, *Bomber Command*, p. 344.

54 Council of Europe, *War Damage to the Cultural Heritage in Croatia and Bosnia-Herzegovina*, January 1994.

55 *Spiritual Genocide: A Survey of Destroyed, Damaged and Desecrated Churches, Monasteries and other Church Building [sic] during the War 1991–1993*, Museum of the Serbian Orthodox Church, Belgrade, 1994; cited in Council of Europe, *War Damage to the Cultural Heritage*.

56 *A Report on the Devastation of Cultural, Historical and Natural Heritage of the Republic/Federation of Bosnia and Herzegovina: from 5 April 1992 until 5 September 1995*, Institute for the Protection of the Cultural, Historical and Natural Heritage of Bosnia-Herzegovina (Sarajevo, 1995).

57 Andrew Herscher and András Riedlmayer, 'Architectural Heritage in Kosovo: A Post-War Report', *US/ICOMOS Newsletter*, 4 (July–August 2000).

58 Ibid.

59 Ibid.

60 Author's interview with Marija Koyakovitch, August 2001.

61 *Daily Telegraph*, 13 November 1991.

62 Author's interview with Marija Koyakovitch, August 2001.

63 UN Security Council, *Destruction of Cultural Property* report, UN Commission of Experts, Annex XI, 28 December 1994.

64 Miljenko Foretic, ed., *Dubrovnik in War* (Dubrovnik, 1993).

65 Ibid., pp. 19, 52 and 62.

66 Dario Gamboni, *The Destruction of Art: Iconoclasm and Vandalism since the French Revolution* (London, 1997), p. 42.

67 Lynn H. Nicholas, *The Rape of Europa* (London, 1994), pp. 229–72.

68 Ibid., p. 237.

69 Order number OKW/WFST/OP (H) No772989/44; cited in Larry Collins and Dominique Lapierre, *Is Paris Burning?* (London, 1965), p. 7.

70 Files of the First US Army (FUSA) report 2055, 26 August 1944; 4th Div. G2 Periodic Report 2000, 26 August 1944; FUSA After Action Report, August, cited in Collins and Lapierre, *Is Paris Burning?*

71 See, for instance, Fox News report 'Iraqis, Marines, Pull Down Saddam Statue', 9 April 2003.

72 *Washington Post*, 14 April 2003, and *New York Times*, 16 April 2003.

73 *The Independent*, 15 April 2003.

74 Micah Garen, 'The War within the War', *Archaeology* (July/August 2004), pp. 28– 31, and *The Guardian*, 2 April 2003.

75 *The Guardian*, 31 August 2004.

76 *The Guardian*, 15 January 2005.

77 *The Art Newspaper*, 6 April 2005.

78 See, for instance, *The Guardian*, 25 August 2004.

79 Kamil Mahdi, 'A Cultural Genocide', *Al Ahram Online*, 14 October 2004.

4 Conquest and Revolution

1 Heinrich Himmler, *Some Thoughts on the Treatment of the Alien Population in the East*, memorandum, 15 May 1940; cited in J. Noakes and G. Pridham, *Nazism 1919–1945*, III: *Foreign Policy, War and Racial Extermination: A Documentary Reader* (Exeter, 1988).

2 Lynn H. Nicholas, *The Rape of Europa* (London, 1994), p. 70.

3 Ibid., pp, 57–80; see also Adolf Ciborowski, *Warsaw: A City Destroyed and Rebuilt* (Warsaw, 1968), pp. 44–57.

4 Noakes and Pridham, *Nazism 1919–1945*, pp. 922–96.

5 Ibid., pp. 988–9.

6 Documents and Plans of Warsaw's Destruction and Restoration (Pabst's Plan, Bureau for the Restoration of the Capital Archives), 1942–50, State Archives of the City of Warsaw.

7 Noakes and Pridham, *Nazism 1919–1945*.

8 Ibid., p. 996.

9 Ciborowski, *Warsaw: A City Destroyed and Rebuilt*, pp. 44–57.

10 Noakes and Pridham, *Nazism 1919–1945*, p. 996.

11 See, for instance, *The Final Demolition of Lhasa*, Kyicho Kuntun pressure group (1993); Knud Larsen and Amund Sinding-Larsen, *The Lhasa Atlas: Traditional Tibetan Architecture and Townscape* (Chicago, 2001); and *The Independent*, 10 October 2000.

12 Reuters, 9 October 2003.

13 *The Economist*, 23 December 2000.

14 *The Final Demolition of Lhasa*.

15 Ibid.

16 *The Times*, 18 August 2001.

17 *The Final Demolition of Lhasa*, pp. 151–64.

18 Reuters, 19 August 2000.

19 Larsen and Sinding-Larsen, *The Lhasa Atlas*.

20 *Tibetan News Update*, December 2001.

21 *Tibet News*, v/2 (March–June 2001).

22 *The Economist*, 30 March 2002.

23 *South China Morning Post*, 14 March 2005.

24 See, for instance, Bernard Wasserstein, *Divided Jerusalem: The Struggle for the Holy City* (London, 2001), pp. 4–5.

25 Avi Shlaim, *The Iron Wall* (New York, 2000), p. 10.

26 See, for instance, Benny Morris, *The Birth of the Palestinian Refugee Problem* (Tel Aviv, 1991).

27 Erna Paris, *Long Shadows: Truth, Lies and History* (Toronto, 2000), p. 252.

28 Meron Benvenisti, *Sacred Landscape* (Berkeley and Los Angeles, CA, 2000), pp. 11–54.

29 Walid Khalidi, ed., *All that Remains: The Palestinian Villages Occupied and Depopulated by Israel in 1948* (Washington, DC, 1992), p. xxxiv.

30 Benvenisti, *Sacred Landscape*.

31 Ibid., p. 169.

32 Avi Shlaim, *The Iron Wall*, p. 245; and *Ha'aretz*, 31 December 1997.

33 *The Guardian*, 3 February 2001.

34 Karen Armstrong, *Jerusalem: One City, Three Faiths* (New York, 1996).

35 See ibid., p. 168, for an alternative expression of the ten degrees of holiness in the 'Jewish map of the world'.

36 Con Coughlin, *A Golden Basin Full of Scorpions: The Quest for Modern Jerusalem* (London, 1997), p. 51.

37 Armstrong, *Jerusalem: One City, Three Faiths*, p. 352.

38 Coughlin, *A Golden Basin Full of Scorpions*, p. 135.

39 Ibid., pp. 106–8.

40 Wasserstein, *Divided Jerusalem*; Armstrong, *Jerusalem: One City, Three Faiths*, pp. 402–3.

41 Meron Benvenisti, *City of Stone: The Hidden History of Jerusalem* (Berkeley and Los Angeles, CA, 1996), p. 83.

42 Wasserstein, *Divided Jerusalem*, pp. 334–7; Benvenisti, *City of Stone*, p. 74.

43 Coughlin, *A Golden Basin Full of Scorpions*, p. 234.

44 *Australian Financial Review*, 26 September 2003.

45 Coughlin, *A Golden Basin Full of Scorpions*, pp. 241–2.

46 Gallup Israel poll, The Loyalists of Temple Mount, February 1996.

47 Benvenisti, *Sacred Landscape*, pp. 274–6.

48 Ibid., p. 280.

49 See, for instance, *The Art Newspaper* (October 2001).

50 *The Guardian*, 4 October 2002.

51 Reuters, 17 February 2004.

52 Coughlin, *A Golden Basin Full of Scorpions*, pp. 230–31.

53 UNESCO Report, 'Jerusalem and the Implementation of 29c/Resolution 22', 5 October 1999.

54 Ibid.

55 *A Policy of Discrimination: Land Expropriation, Planning and Building in East*

Jerusalem, B'Tselem, the Israeli Information Center for Human Rights in the Occupied Territories (May 1995).

56 Wasserstein, *Divided Jerusalem*, pp. 99–100, and Armstrong, *Jerusalem: One City, Three Faiths*, pp. 347–9.

57 William Dalrymple. *From the Holy Mountain* (London, 1997), pp. 332–59.

58 Ibid.

59 Ibid., p. 333.

60 *A Policy of Discrimination*, B'Tselem.

61 Ibid.

62 Ibid.

63 Karen Armstrong, paper delivered to the Talloires Symposium on Jerusalem, May 2002, Tufts University Center, Talloires, France.

64 Leon Trotsky, 'What is Proletarian Culture and is it Possible?' [1923], in *Leon Trotsky on Literature and Art*, ed. Paul N. Siegel (New York, 1970), p. 43.

65 Ibid., p. 45.

66 See, for instance, Catherine Cook, 'Sources of a Radical Mission in the Early Soviet Profession', in *Architecture and Revolution*, ed. Neil Leach (London, 1999), pp. 13–37.

67 Natasha Chibireva, 'Airbrushed Moscow: The Cathedral of Christ the Saviour', in *The Hieroglyphics of Space*, ed. Neil Leach (London, 2002), pp. 70–79.

68 Ryszard Kapuścinski, *Imperium* (London 1994), pp. 103–5.

69 Ibid., pp. 173–4.

70 See, for instance, Alex de Jonge, *Stalin and the Shaping of the Soviet Union* (London, 1986).

71 Olenka Pevny, 'Rebuilding a Monumental Past', in *East European Perspectives*, J. B. Rudnyckyi Lecture Series, University of Manitoba (Winnipeg, 2001).

72 Nicholas, *The Rape of Europa*, pp. 193–4.

73 Simon Leys, *Chinese Shadows* (New York, 1977), pp. 54–5.

74 See, for instance, Stanley Karnow, *Mao and China: Inside China's Cultural Revolution* (New York, 1972).

75 Philip Bridgham, 'Mao's Cultural Revolution: Origin and Development', *China Quarterly*, 29 (January–March 1967), pp. 1–35.

76 Leys, *Chinese Shadows*, pp. 57–8.

77 Gordon Bennett and Ronal Motaperto, *Red Guard* (New York, 1971), p. 81.

78 Wang Chao-tien, *A Red Guard Tells His Own Story* (Taipei, 1967), pp. 34–5.

79 Leys, *Chinese Shadows*.

80 Ibid., pp. 91–103.

81 Ibid.

82 Ibid., p. 58.

83 Samantha Power, *A Problem from Hell: America in the Age of Genocide* (London, 2003), pp. 87–90.

84 Ibid.

85 Gregory Stanton, 'Blue Scarves and Yellow Stars: Classification and Symbolism in

the Cambodian Genocide', paper delivered at the Montreal Institute of Genocide Studies, April 1989.

86   Ben Kiernan, ed., *How Pol Pot Came to Power: A History of Communism in Kampuchea, 1930–1975* (London, 1985).

87   Cited in David Chandler, Ben Kiernan and Chantou Boua, ed. and trans., *Pol Pot Plans the Future: Confidential Leadership Documents from Democratic Kampuchea, 1976–1977*, Yale University Southeast Asian Studies Monograph Series 33 (New Haven, CT, 1988), p. 113.

88   Stanton, 'Blue Scarves and Yellow Stars'.

89   Cited in Anthony Daniels, 'In Pol Pot Land: Ruins of Varying Types – Cambodia', *National Review*, 29 September 2003, p. 27.

90   Stanton, 'Blue Scarves and Yellow Stars'.

91   Bogdan Bogdanović, 'Murder of the City', *New York Review of Books*, XL/10 (27 May 1993).

92   Ibid.

93   'Mostar92 – Urbicide', in *Space and Society*, XVI/62 (1993), pp. 8–25.

94   Ivo Andric, *The Bridge over the Drina*, trans. Lovette F. Edwards (London, 1995).

95   Martin Coward, 'Community as Heterogeneous Ensemble: Mostar and Multi-culturalism', paper for the ISA Annual Convention, Chicago, February 2001.

96   *The Independent*, 1 September 2002.

97   *The Independent*, 14 November 2001 and 10 December 2001.

98   Ibid.

99   *Sydney Morning Herald*, 20 November 2004.

100   *The Times*, 24 November 2001.

101   Finbarr Barry Flood, 'Between Cult and Culture: Bamiyan, Islamic Iconoclasm, and the Museum', *Art Bulletin*, LXXXIV/4 (December 2002), pp. 641–59.

102   *Sydney Morning Herald*, 20 November 2004.

103   *The Independent*, 12 October 2001.

104   Bogdanović, 'Murder of the City'.

105   Martin Heidegger, *Discourse on Thinking* (Eng. trans., New York, 1966).

106   Le Corbusier, *Vers une architecture* [Paris, 1923]; Eng. trans. as *Towards a New Architecture* (London, 1927).

107   Robert Bevan, *The Specificity of the Aesthetic: A Critique of Janet Wolf's Aesthetics and the Sociology of Art* [1983], unpublished Postgraduate Paper, Oxford Brookes University, 1990.

108   Dinu Giurescu, *The Razing of Romania's Past* (Washington, DC, 1989), p. 2–11.

109   Doina Petrescu, 'The People's House, or the Voluptuous Violence of an Architectural Paradox', in *Architecture and Revolution*, ed. Neil Leach (London, 1999), pp. 188–95.

110   Lucian Boia, *Romania* (London, 2001), p. 288.

111   Giurescu, *The Razing of Romania's Past*, p. 49.

112   Ibid, p. 51.

113   Petrescu, 'The People's House', p. 194.

5 Fences and Neighbours: The Destructive Consequences of Partition

1   Author's visit to Belfast, July 2002.
2   Cited in Scott Bollens, 'City and Soul', *City: Analysis of Urban Trends, Culture, Theory, Policy, Action*, V/2 (2001), pp. 169–87.
3   *The Independent*, 16 March 2002.
4   Pankaj Mishra, 'Holy Lies', *The Guardian*, 6 April 2002.
5   Richard M. Eaton, 'Temple Desecration in Pre-Modern India', *Frontline*, XVII/25 (9 December 2000) and XVII/26 (23 December 2000). See also Kristin Romey, 'Flashpoint Ayodhya', *Archaeology* (July–August 2004).
6   Ibid.
7   See, for instance, *The Economist*, 27 July 2002.
8   *The Independent*, 4 April 2002.
9   Concerned Citizens Tribunal, 'An Inquiry into the Carnage in Gujarat', 2002, www.sabrang.com.
10 *The Guardian*, 2 March 2002.
11 Romey, 'Flashpoint Ayodhya', pp. 49–55.
12 *Sydney Morning Herald*, 28 June 2004.
13 Figures from Israeli Committee Against House Demolitions (ICAHD), 2004, and B'Tselem, the Israeli Information Center for Human Rights in the Occupied Territories, *Demolishing Peace: Israel's Policy of Mass Demolition of Palestinian Houses in the West Bank* (1997).
14 Amnesty International, *Under the Rubble: House Demolition and the Destruction of Land and Property*, 18 May 2004.
15 *The Guardian*, 25 August 2004, quoting calculations in the Israeli newspaper *Yedioth Ahronoth*.
16 Jeff Halper, 'The Key to Peace: Dismantling the Matrix of Control', ICAHD, 2001, www.icahd.org.
17 Reports by B'Tselem, *Demolishing Peace* (1997) and *LandGrab: Israel's Settlement Policy in the West Bank* (May 2002).
18 See, for instance, Zvi Efrat, ed., *Borderlinedisorder*, catalogue accompanying the Israeli Pavilion exhibition at the 8th International Architecture Biennale, Venice, 2002; and B'Tselem report, *LandGrab* (May 2002).
19 B'Tselem, *A Policy of Discrimination: Land Expropriation, Planning and Building in East Jerusalem* (May 1995).
20 Ibid.
21 Ibid.
22 See, for instance, Amnesty International, *Israel and the Occupied Territories, Shielded from Scrutiny: IDF violations in Jenin and Nablus*, 4 November 2002.
23 *The Guardian Weekly*, 24 September 2004.
24 B'Tselem, *Demolishing Peace* (1997) and *LandGrab* (May 2002).
25 Stephen Graham, 'Clean Territory: Urbicide in the West Bank', *Open Democracy* (August 2002).

26 B'Tselem, *LandGrab* (May 2002).

27 BBC report, *Israel Settlement Building Grows*, 2 March 2004.

28 *The Guardian*, 24 August 2004.

29 Ibid.

30 BBC news report, 17 March 2005.

31 *Sydney Morning Herald*, 20 July 2002.

32 Amnesty International, *Israel and the Occupied Territories, Shielded from Scrutiny*.

33 Ibid.

34 *Sydney Morning Herald*, 7 January 2003.

35 Amnesty International, statement on Rafah demolitions, 14 January 2002.

36 Amnesty International, *Under the Rubble: House Demolition and the Destruction of Land and Property*, 18 May 2004.

37 Ibid.

38 Graham, 'Clean Territory: Urbicide in the West Bank'.

39 Edward Said, *Reflections on Exile and Other Essays* (Cambridge, MA, 2000), p. 173.

40 Report of the Secretary-General prepared pursuant to General Assembly resolution ES-10/10 (Report on Jenin), 2002.

41 Ibid.

42 Jeff Halper, 'The Message of the Bulldozers', ICAHD, 9 August 2002, www.icahd.org.

43 Ibid.

44 Robert Bevan, 'The Silent Casualty', *Independent on Sunday*, 1 December 2002, and the author's visit to Nablus, October 2002. See also ICOMOS Heritage at Risk report, April 2002, submitted by the Palestinian National Committee of ICOMOS.

45 Amnesty International, *Israel and the Occupied Territories, Shielded from Scrutiny*.

46 UNESCO World Heritage Committee, 26th Session, June 2002.

47 Author's interview, October 2002.

48 See, for instance, *The Independent*, 11 April 2001.

49 Diana Digges, 'The Politics of Preservation', *Christian Science Monitor,* 29 July 1999.

50 *Ha'aretz*, 2 December 2002.

51 *The Independent*, 12 August 2002.

52 *Sunday Telegraph*, 17 March 2002.

53 *The Guardian Weekly*, 8 April 2004, reporting the findings of the European Monitoring Centre on Racism and Xenophobia.

54 *The Guardian Weekly*, 18 September 2003.

55 See www.btselem.org for latest figures.

56 Ze'ev Jabotinsky, *Writings: On the Road To Statehood* (Jerusalem, 1959); quoted in Avi Shlaim, *The Iron Wall* (New York, 2000), p. 13.

57 David Ben Gurion, *Letters to Paula* (London, 1971); cited in Avi Shlaim, *The Iron Wall*, p. 21.

58 *The Australian*, 20 December 2003.

59 *Le Monde Diplomatique*, July 2003.

60 Ibid.

61 Associated Press, 17 January 2004.

62 *Sydney Morning Herald*, 12 July 2004.

63 Efrat, ed., *Borderlinedisorder*, p. 34.

64 Polly Feversham and Leo Schmidt, *The Berlin Wall Today* (Berlin, 1999), pp. 28–40.

65 Ibid.

66 Manfred Fischer, 'The History of the Chapel of Reconciliation', in *Berlin Wall: Memorial Site, Exhibition Center and the Chapel of Reconciliation on Bernauer Strasse* (Berlin, 1999), p. 34.

67 Ibid., pp. 34–5.

68 Ibid.

69 Ibid., p. 11.

70 *The Independent on Sunday*, 23 June 2002.

71 C. Nagel, 'Reconstructing Space, Recreating Memory: Sectarian Politics and Urban Development in Post-War Beirut', *Political Geography*, XXI/5 (2002), pp. 717–25.

72 Feversham and Schmidt, *The Berlin Wall Today*, p. 126.

73 Ibid., p. 122.

74 *The Times*, 27 May 1976.

75 *The Guardian*, 6 May 1976; see also Michael Jansen, 'Cyprus: The Loss of a Cultural Heritage', in *Modern Greek Studies Yearbook*, II (1986), pp. 314–23.

76 *The Times*, 19 August 1980.

77 *Frankfurter Allgemeine Magazin*, 30 March 1990.

78 *Cyprus Mail*, 19 June 2001.

79 *The Guardian Weekly*, 2 January 2003.

80 *Londra Gazete*, 2 September 2004.

81 *The Guardian Weekly*, 29 April 2004.

82 Ciaran Mackell, 'The Shankhill/Falls Interface: A Design Approach', PhD thesis, University College, Dublin, 1999 [unpublished].

83 Frederick Boal, 'Segregation and Mixing: Space and Residence in Belfast', in *Integration and Division: Geographical Perspective on the Northern Ireland Problem*, ed. F. Boal and J. Douglas (London, 1982), pp. 249–80.

84 *The Independent*, 6 April 2004.

85 David McKittrick and David McVea, *Making Sense of The Troubles* (London, 2001), p. 251; Michael Poole and Paul Doherty, *Ethnic Residential Segregation in Belfast* (Coleraine, 1995).

86 Ibid., p. 59.

87 *The Guardian*, 16 June 2002.

88 A. Hepburn, 'Long Division and Ethnic Conflict: The Experience of Belfast', in *Managing Divided Cities*, ed. S. Dunn (Keele, 1994); see also Brendan Murtagh, ed., *Planning and Ethnic Space in Belfast*, (Coleraine, 1993).

89 Mackell, 'The Shankhill/Falls Interface'.

90 *The Independent*, 24 August 2004. See also Neil Jarman and Chris O'Halloran, *Peacelines or Battlefields: Responding to Violence in Interface Areas* (Belfast, October 2000), www.conflictresearch.org.uk/publications/porppubs.

91 Research by Peter Shirlow, University of Ulster; cited in BBC news report, 4 January 2002.

6 Remember and Warn I: Rebuilding and Commemoration

1 *The Guardian*, 1 September 2004.
2 Brian Osborne, 'Landscapes, Memory, Monuments and Commemoration: Putting Identity in its Place', draft paper for the Ethno-cultural, Racial, Religious and Linguistic Diversity and Identity Seminar, Nova Scotia, November 2001.
3 Author's interview.
4 David Lowenthal, 'Fabricating Heritage', *History & Memory*, X/1 (1998), pp. 5–24.
5 Adolf Ciborowski, *Warsaw: A City Destroyed and Rebuilt* (Warsaw, 1968), p. 44.
6 Norman Davies and Roger Moorhouse, *Microcosm: Portrait of a Central European City* (London, 2002).
7 Fredric Jameson, 'History Lessons', in *Architecture and Revolution*, ed. Neil Leach (London, 1999), p. 80.
8 *Daily Telegraph*, 19 October 2004.
9 Cited in Olenka Pevny, 'Rebuilding a Monumental Past', in *East European Perspectives*, J. B. Rudnyckyi Lecture Series, University of Manitoba (Winnipeg, 2001).
10 Ibid.
11 W. G. Sebald, 'Air War and Literature' [1997], collected in his *On the History of Natural Destruction* (New York, 2003).
12 Hannah Arendt, 'The Aftermath of Nazi Rule: Report from Germany', in *Commentary* (October 1950), p. 342.
13 Gavriel Rosenfeld, *Munich and Memory: Architecture, Monuments, and the Legacy of the Third Reich* (Berkeley and Los Angeles, 2000).
14 *Münchener Katholische Kirchenzeitung* (1953), cited ibid.
15 Rosenfeld, *Munich and Memory*, p.36.
16 Ibid., pp. 76–106.
17 *Sydney Morning Herald*, 20 November 2004, pp. 186–7.
18 Ibid.
19 Ibid.
20 Ibid.
21 Christopher Woodward, *In Ruins* (London, 2001), p. 212.
22 Ibid.
23 Michael Z. Wise, *Capital Dilemma: Germany's Search for a New Architecture of Democracy* (New York, 1998), p. 93.
24 Ibid., p. 113.
25 See Andreas Huyssen, 'After the War: Berlin as Palimpsest', *Harvard Design Magazine*, 10 (winter/spring 2000); and *New York Times*, 27 October 2004.
26 See Förderverein Berliner Schloss website at www.berliner-schloss.de.

27   Ibid.; see also Wise, *Capital Dilemma*, and Brian Ladd, *Ghosts of Berlin: Confronting History in the German Landscape* (Chicago, 1997).

28   www.berliner-schloss.de.

29   Wise, *Capital Dilemma*, p. 111.

30   Daniel Libeskind, 'Traces of the Unborn', in *Architecture and Revolution*, ed. Neil Leach (London, 1999), p. 128.

31   Toby Axelrod, *Jewish World Review*, 25 September 1998.

32   Wise, *Capital Dilemma*, p. 115.

33   Rosenfeld, *Munich and Memory*, pp. 280–305.

34   Hugo Hamilton, 'The Loneliness of Being German', *The Guardian*, 7 September 2004.

35   Cited in Rosenfeld, *Munich and Memory*, p. 2.

36   James E. Young, 'The End of the Monument in Germany', *Harvard Design Magazine*, 9 (Fall 1999).

37   Adrian Forty and Susanne Kuchler, eds, *The Art of Forgetting, Materializing Culture* (Oxford, 2001), p. 9.

38   *Architectural Record* (January 2002).

39   Cited ibid.

40   Daniel Libeskind, World Trade Center Design Study, February 2003.

41   *Architectural Record* (January 2002).

42   Samuel Gruber, *Jewish Monuments in Eastern Europe: The Legacy of the Holocaust and Preservation Today*, paper delivered at the College Art Association Annual Meeting, Chicago, February 1992.

43   *Jewish Heritage Report* (spring/summer 1998).

44   Darmstadt University of Technology, Department of CAD in Architecture, and others, eds, *Synagogues in Germany: A Virtual Reconstruction* (Basel, 2004).

7   Remember and Warn II: Protection and Prosecution

1   *The Guardian Weekly*, 27 March 2003.

2   Rebecca Grant, 'In Search of Lawful Targets', *Airforce*, LXXXVI/2 (February 2003).

3   Second Protocol to the Hague Convention of 1954 for the Protection of Cultural Property in the Event of Armed Conflict, The Hague, 29 March 1999.

4   *Sydney Morning Herald*, 29 October 2004.

5   *Le Monde Diplomatique*, February 2003, and *Sydney Morning Herald*, 20 March 2004.

6   UNESCO press statement, 22 March 2004.

7   Treaty of Versailles, Part VIII, Section 2, Special Provisions.

8   Lambourne, *War Damage in Western Europe*, pp. 24–7.

9   International Military Tribunal Nuremberg, Transcripts and Documents in Evidence, Trials of Major War Criminals, Transcripts of days 54 and 64.

10   Ibid.

11   Article 3 of the Statutes: available at: www.un.org/icty/legaldoc/index.

12   Struger case (IT-01-42), ITCY.

13   Milošević (IT-02-54), ITCY, counts 19–22.

14   Ibid., trial transcript for 8 July 2003.

15   Partial dissenting opinion of Judge Mohamed Shahabuddeen, Appeals Chamber
     hearing in the trial of General Radislav Krstić, ITCY, 19 April 2004.

16   Cited in Avi Shlaim, *The Iron Wall* (New York, 2000), p. 585.

17   Alain Destexhe, *Rwanda and Genocide in the Twentieth Century* (New York,
     1995), p. 4.

18   Raphael Lemkin, *Axis Rule in Occupied Europe* (Washington, DC, 1944), p. 79.

19   Raphael Lemkin, *The Evolution of the Genocide Convention*, Lemkin Papers,
     New York Public Library.

20   Ibid., cited in Samantha Power, *A Problem from Hell: America and the Age of
     Genocide* (London, 2003), p. 43.

21   Ibid.

22   Martin Coward, 'Community as Heterogeneous Ensemble: Mostar and
     Multiculturalism', paper prepared for the ISA Annual Convention, Chicago,
     February 2001.

23   George Orwell, *1984* (London, 1949, repr. 1954), p. 82.

Acknowledgements

There are so many people who need to be thanked for their assistance during the preparation of this book – too many to list here, unfortunately. A simple Thank You to you all. I must, though, mention a few people whose contribution went above and beyond the call of duty, helpfulness, advice or friendship: Alison Cunningham, Samuel Gruber, Orly Halpern, Felice Kiel, George Knott, Tajma Kurt, András Riedlmayer, Cristina Ruiz, Teresa Smith, Aisa Telalovic and Helen Walasek.

I also wish to thank the Australian Academy of the Humanities for its assistance in defraying the cost of the images reproduced in this book.

Photographic Acknowledgements

The author and publishers wish to express their thanks to the following sources of illustrative material and/or permission to reproduce it.

Photo AP/Kostadin Kamenov: p. 204; photos Archiwum Dokumentacji Mechanicznej, Warsaw: pp. 182, 183; photo courtesy of Avotaynu Inc.: p. 108; photos courtesy of the Bosnian Institute, London: pp. 41, 44, 45, 46, 47; photo *Exeter Express & Echo*: p. 76; photos Dinu C. Giurescu: pp. 128, 129, 130; photo © Reha Gunay/Aga Khan Trust for Culture: p. 10 (top); photo Kemal Hadzic: p. 14; photos Imperial War Museum, London: pp. 68 (Q107742), 74 (C2387), 77 (HU646), 81 (photo Herbert Mason/Imperial War Museum, HU36220A), 197 top (HU3318); photo Israel Ministry of Tourism: p. 109; photo Ahmed Jadallah, Reuters/Picture Media: p. 142; photos courtesy David King Collection, London: p. 185; photo Landesarchiv, Berlin: p. 159; photo © Sunil Malhotra, Reuters/Picture Media: p. 135; photo Josef Mueller (courtesy Tibetan Heritage Fund): p. 100; photos National Library of Ireland: pp. 70 (photo Elinor Wiltshire/National Library of Ireland, WIL 18 [8]), 71 (photo W. D. Hogan/National Library of Ireland, HOG57); photos from private collections (including that of the author): pp. 51, 58, 59; photo Ciril Ciro Rajic, Mostar Institute for the Protection of Monuments: p. 177; photos courtesy of the Republic of Cyprus Press and Information Office: pp. 165, 166; photos Rex Features: pp 63 (Rex Features/SMM, 389739E), 87 (Rex Features/Sipa Press, 455056C), 91 (Rex Features/Sipa Press, 413101M), 124 (Rex Features/Sipa Press, 333871C), 125 (Rex Features/Sipa Press, 334355A), 157 (Rex Features/Sipa Press, 442131D), 161 (Rex Features/Sipa Press, 165228D), 167 (Rex Features/Sipa Press, 287827B), 171 (Rex Features/Brendan Beirne, 208643A), 184 (Rex Features/Sipa Press, 239865D), 197 foot (photo Rex Features/Action Press, 458189L); photos Roger-Viollet, courtesy Rex Features: pp. 123 (© Collection Roger-Viollet, RVB-04763: in the Musée du Louvre, Paris), 196 (photo © LL/Roger-Viollet, 13058-5); photos András Riedlmayer: pp. 18, 19, 178; photos courtesy of Shaml Palestinian Diaspora and Refugee Centre: pp. 149, 150; photo Tibet Information Network: p. 99; photo from the Tourist Association of the City of Sarajevo: p. 179 (pre-war photograph); photo http://www.vakuf-gazi.ba : p. 180.

Index

232